"The difficult but very important thought material d. this book has had and will continue to have a profound effect on the understanding and reception of the gospel of Christ today. Intellectual life is strongly influenced by it—and that includes the thought life of Christians as well as non-Christians. I especially encourage those in positions of Christian leadership to study it carefully, and above all those who expect to be helpful to young people now entering higher education or the professions. You are not likely to find a better guide than Benson."

DALLAS WILLARD, PROFESSOR OF PHILOSOPHY,
UNIVERSITY OF SOUTHERN CALIFORNIA

"Graven Ideologies is a clear and coherent exposition of the importance of Nietzsche, Marion and Derrida to Christian consciousness. It will go a long way toward not only correcting the reductive misreadings of these works by many theologians but strengthening Christian intellectual life in its ongoing dialogue with philosophy."

CLEO KEARNS, VISITING FELLOW AT THE CENTER FOR THE STUDY OF
RELIGION, PRINCETON UNIVERSITY

"Rooted in a deep biblical faith that is as reflective as it is committed, informed by a thorough study of the authors discussed, and written with an inviting and accessible lucidity, this volume gives us a splendid guide to the thought of three major postmodern thinkers."

MEROLD WESTPHAL, DISTINGUISHED PROFESSOR OF PHILOSOPHY,
FORDHAM UNIVERSITY

"This succinct little book gives us an excellent critique of recent discussions of idolatry. Benson is both fair to Levinas and Marion, and astutely perceptive concerning the questions which they fail to raise."

JOHN MILBANK, FRANCES MYERS BALL PROFESSOR OF PHILOSOPHICAL
THEOLOGY, UNIVERSITY OF VIRGINIA

"Graven Ideologies *meets a long-standing demand for a presentation of the theological significance of the work of Nietzsche, Derrida, Levinas and Marion in American English, that is, in a language we can all understand. It raises the level of discussion of these provocative continental thinkers by showing the positive import of their critique of metaphysics—which is mistakenly assumed to be something destructive—as a critique of idolatry, an essential ingredient in any biblical view. By doing all this in lively, readable and illuminating comparisons and contrasts, Benson has made a significant contribution to the growing American discussion of theology from a continental perspective."*

JOHN D. CAPUTO, DAVID R. COOK PROFESSOR OF PHILOSOPHY, VILLANOVA UNIVERSITY

GRAVEN
IDEOLOGIES

NIETZSCHE, DERRIDA & MARION
ON MODERN IDOLATRY

BRUCE ELLIS BENSON

InterVarsity Press
Downers Grove, Illinois

InterVarsity Press
P.O. Box 1400, Downers Grove, IL 60515-1426
World Wide Web: www.ivpress.com
E-mail: mail@ivpress.com

InterVarsity Press® is the book-publishing division of InterVarsity Christian Fellowship/USA®, a student movement active on campus at hundreds of universities, colleges and schools of nursing in the United States of America, and a member movement of the International Fellowship of Evangelical Students. For information about local and regional activities, write Public Relations Dept., InterVarsity Christian Fellowship/USA, 6400 Schroeder Rd., P.O. Box 7895, Madison, WI 53707-7895, or visit the IVCF website at <www.ivcf.org>.

Scripture is taken from the New Revised Standard Version of the Bible, *copyright 1989 by the Division of Christian Education of the National Council of the Churches of Christ in the USA. Used by permission.*

Cover illustration: © Mimmo Jodice/CORBIS

ISBN 0-8308-2679-3

Printed in the United States of America ∞

Library of Congress Cataloging-in-Publication Data

Benson, Bruce Ellis, 1960-
    Graven ideologies: Nietzsche, Derrida & Marion on modern idolatry/
Bruce Ellis Benson.
        p. cm.
Includes bibliographical references.
    ISBN 0-8308-2679-3 (pbk.: alk. paper)
    1. Christianity—Philosophy. 2. Phenomenology. 3. Idolatry. I.
Title.
    BR100.B423 2002
    261.5'1—dc21

                                                                                    2002004050

| **P** | 18 | 17 | 16 | 15 | 14 | 13 | 12 | 11 | 10 | 9 | 8 | 7 | 6 | 5 | 4 | 3 | 2 | 1 |
| **Y** | 16 | 15 | 14 | 13 | 12 | 11 | 10 | 09 | 08 | 07 | 06 | 05 | 04 | 03 | 02 | | | |

To my father,

WARREN S. BENSON
(1929-2002),

who taught me far more
than he realized

CONTENTS

PREFACE

Nietzsche and Derrida on *idolatry?* Might this be a how-to manual—
something like *Idolatry for Dummies?* Actually, if anything, this is a how-
not-to manual in which Nietzsche turns out to be one of the instructors
not because of his own idolatry (though he is guilty of that too) but
because of his substantial abilities as idol detector. It may be difficult to
imagine thinkers such as Nietzsche acting as spiritual mentors, but—at
least in regard to idols—they have much to teach us. As the reader will
soon discover, the philosophers considered in this book are particularly
helpful in both detecting idolatry and showing us how idolatry functions.

Before we proceed, though, I need to provide an explanation, sketch
an outline, give an apology and add a disclaimer.

Explaining

What do Friedrich Nietzsche (1844-1900), Jacques Derrida (1930-) and
Jean-Luc Marion (1946-) not only have to do with one another but also
with Edmund Husserl (1859-1938), Martin Heidegger (1889-1976) and
Emmanuel Levinas (1906-1995)? The answer is wrapped up with what
has been termed the religious or theological turn in phenomenology. In
1991 Dominique Janicaud published a text titled *The Theological Turn of
French Philosophy.*[1] Unlike the phenomenology practiced in the early

---

[1]Dominique Janicaud, *Le tournant théologique de la phénoménologie française* (Paris:
Éditions de l'Éclat, 1991), translated as "The Theological Turn of French Phenomenol-
ogy," pt. 1 of *Phenomenology and the "Theological Turn": The French Debate* (New York:
Fordham University Press, 2000), hereafter *PTT.* As Janicaud tells us, his text was written
as a *constat,* a report on the French philosophical landscape between 1975 and 1990
(*PTT* 16). For Janicaud, the most remarkable feature of philosophizing in that period was
its concern for the transcendent (or, as he puts it, "the opening to the invisible, to the
Other, to a pure givenness, or to an 'archi-revelation'"—*PTT* 17). All of that may sound
incomprehensible at this point, but it should become considerably clearer as we proceed.
Also see Janicaud's "sequel" to *Tournant théologique* titled *La phénoménologie éclatée*
(Paris: Éditions de l'Éclat, 1998).

stages of its reception in France, say with Jean-Paul Sartre (1905-1980), the "new phenomenologists" such as Jean-Louis Chrétien, Michel Henry and Jean-Luc Marion use phenomenology to focus on religion. That turn in phenomenology is made possible by two transition figures, Levinas and the later Heidegger. Even though Levinas can be counted among the first French phenomenologists (in one sense), he makes the theological turn possible by turning phenomenology's gaze toward "otherness" (that which is "different" from ourselves), particularly that of ultimate Other.

Heidegger is likewise a pivotal figure due to the increasing interest in religious themes in his later philosophy. And although already deeply influenced by Levinas in the 1960s, in the last two decades of the twentieth century Jacques Derrida himself became increasingly concerned with transcendence as worked out in ethics and religion, no doubt in part due to the influence of his former student Marion. While it may be too simple to say (as does Janicaud) that there has been a move from "atheist phenomenology" to "spiritualist phenomenology," such has been the trend not just in France but also in the rest of European philosophy.[2]

But this trend represents a significant reorienting of the focus of phenomenology.[3] Whereas the founder of phenomenology, Edmund Husserl, stressed the essential "immanence" to consciousness of the phenomena, Levinas and Marion argue that phenomena remain transcendent (or "other" to us) and thus outside of our control. Although such transcendence is particularly true for God, it is also true of human beings and perhaps even for events or certain objects. This emphasis on transcendence is double-sided: the questioning of the immanence of phenomenology is done in order to "save" the transcendence of the phenomena. Both Levinas and Marion see any claims of having "grasped" not only God but even our neighbor or "the world as it really is" as idolatrous, for we in effect claim to take the place that can be filled only by One.

While one can interpret Levinas and Marion as simply rebelling against the foundational principles of phenomenology (as does Janicaud), one can also read them as stressing aspects that have always been part of phenom-

---

[2]Of course that move is at least partially understandable, given Sartre's lack of religiosity, Levinas's Judaism and Marion's Roman Catholicism.

[3]This is not to say that religion has not been treated phenomenologically. But the relation between religion and phenomenology has always been complicated, to say the least.

enology and so revealing a fundamental tension within phenomenology. The latter is the path I will follow here. However much Levinas and Marion rock the foundations of phenomenology, they remain deeply indebted to Husserl and Heidegger, so that the debate is internecine. When Derrida accused Marion of being a phenomenological heretic at the first Religion and Postmodernism Conference at Villanova University in 1997 (see *God the Gift and Postmodernism*, p. 66), the question was clearly a matter of who has stayed most true to phenomenological orthodoxy.

Yet the argument used by Levinas and Marion was foreshadowed in Nietzsche, who denounces almost the entire Western philosophical tradition as idolatrous. On Nietzsche's read, philosophers at least as far back as Plato have attempted to usurp the place of God and "take control" of the world. So phenomenologists have hardly been alone in such a project, and they have not been necessarily more adept at idolatry than their predecessors. Even the very concept known as "the God of the Philosophers" was simply an idol, created because it was useful to philosophers. Thus "the death of God" for Nietzsche is only the death of an idol that couldn't actually die because it was never alive. For Heidegger, the death of "the God of the Philosophers" spells the end of the project known as "metaphysics" (i.e., the attempt to *comprehend* being) and opens up the possibility that theology can be finally freed from philosophy in order to be true to faith.

Applauding both Nietzsche and Heidegger for helping release theology from its Athenian captivity, Marion argues for the possibility of a revelation that is truly transcendent, a *Logos* freed from any philosophical *logoi*. But in response to Marion, a somewhat less sanguine Derrida questions whether Jerusalem can so quickly rid itself of Athens, or even the degree to which it might wish to do so. Can there be a "phenomenology" of that which by nature escapes our grasp? Can we meaningfully speak (use a *logos*) of the transcendent—that which defies human *logos?* And would we really *want* such a revelation?

Outlining

Linking the Johannine warning against idolatry (1 Jn 5:21) with the Pauline warning against vain philosophy (Col 2:8), the introduction explains the notion of "conceptual idolatry" and examines how both Nietzsche and Jesus "sound out" idols. In chapter one we follow Nietzsche's idol detection as it turns toward such philosophical idols as

"System" and see how Christ as *Logos* differs from philosophical *logoi*. Chapter two examines the meaning of "the death of God" and its implications for the future of philosophy. Nietzsche's surprising moral conventionality (as inheritor of the Greek conception of *agōn*) is contrasted to Christ's fundamental break with "Morality" in chapter three. Chapter four provides a brief sketch of Levinas, with particular attention to the difficulties his thought raises, as background for Derrida and Marion.

Chapter five traces the basic notions of Derrida's early thought and notes how they become central to his thinking on ethics and religion. The problems of "speaking" about God as worked out by Derrida, and the internal problems in Derrida's thought, are the focus of chapter six. In chapter seven the basic account of phenomenology given in the introduction is expanded by a more detailed analysis of the problem of otherness in Husserl and Heidegger. Chapter eight puts that theory to work as we consider the ways Marion attempts to overcome idolatry. The possibility of Marion's project, as well as the internal limitations of phenomenology, is the topic of chapter nine. Finally, the epilogue attempts to consider our position as knowers and witness bearers, in light of both the dangers and the value of philosophy for maintaining orthodoxy.

Apologizing in Advance

Writing about idols is an audacious thing to do. Who am *I* to pronounce on idolatry—or even just to raise a few uncomfortable questions? As the old saying goes, pointing a finger at someone else means there are three pointing back at oneself. The more one considers the ways idols are created and maintained, the more one sees one's own idols for what they are—and the more one humbly realizes that there must be other idols that still go undetected. Marion observes that "one must obtain forgiveness for every essay in theology" (*God Without Being,* p. 2). Theology always attempts the impossible: finite, sinful human beings speaking about the glorious, holy and infinite God. How can we adequately speak of God? Yet how can we do anything else? Such is theology's fundamental *aporia*. We are *called* to speak of God and on his behalf, but we are always inadequate to do so. If theology requires repentance, then deconstructing idols requires even more. For one attempts not merely to speak of God but to show why other efforts in so speaking have gone awry, all the while knowing (or, more accurately, not *really* knowing) one's own inadequacy.

The Fine Print

Finally, a small disclaimer. Any reader who expects that this text will serve as the infallible guide to deconstructing and overcoming idolatry should stop reading *now*. Idolatry is not the sort of thing that one simply overcomes. At best, one becomes aware of its presence and works very hard to root it out, ever aware that it can always return and that even our attempts to overcome idolatry can themselves turn into new forms of idolatry. For an idol is like a clever virus—its presence is often subtle, and it can take on new and shifting forms. But even if there is no effective vaccine against idolatry, it certainly can and must be fought.

*   *   *

This text grew out of a senior seminar on postmodernity that I have taught at Wheaton College for a number of years. The seminar was initially motivated by a summer seminar led by Merold Westphal, hosted by Calvin College and sponsored by the Pew Foundation. My thanks to Merold (who has always been a source of great encouragement and wisdom), the participants in that original seminar and its sponsors.[4] But I am most grateful to my students at Wheaton, from whom I have learned so much. Many thanks to Jonathan Ellsworth for editing a very early version of this text and commenting on the present version. Although the feedback of all of my students has helped in ways too numerous to mention, I am grateful to Drew Dalton for commenting on the manuscript. I am particularly indebted to the careful reading by Daniel Hoisington, who has championed and challenged my thought along the way. James K. A. Smith's extensive comments likewise proved invaluable. John Koenig kept me from committing some errors of New Testament exegesis in the introduction. Of course, the usual disclaimer goes without saying. If there is anything of value in this text, then the wisdom of others undoubtedly helped make it possible. For errors, lack of insight and sheer stupidity I happily take responsibility.

I wish to thank Wheaton College for the release time made possible by the Junior Faculty Achievement Award and a much-appreciated sabbatical.

Finally, no words are adequate to express my gratitude to my wife, Jacqueline Cameron, for putting up with me during this lengthy process.

---

[4]Unfortunately Merold Westphal's book *Overcoming Onto-Theology: Toward a Postmodern Christian Faith* (New York: Fordham University Press, 2001) appeared too late for me to take it into account in this text.

Abbreviations

The following texts are cited parenthetically with page numbers. Although I have attempted to stay as close to the English translations as possible, at points I have provided my own translations. Numbers following abbreviations of Nietzsche texts refer to sections, not pages.

A   Nietzsche, Friedrich. *The Antichrist* (with *Twilight of the Idols*). Trans. R. J. Hollingdale. Harmondsworth, U.K.: Penguin, 1968.

BGE   Nietzsche, Friedrich. *Beyond Good and Evil*. Trans. R. J. Hollingdale. Harmondsworth, U.K.: Penguin, 1972.

BPW   Levinas, Emmanuel. *Basic Philosophical Writings*. Ed. Adriaan T. Peperzak et al. Bloomington: Indiana University Press, 1996.

BT   Heidegger, Martin. *Being and Time*. Trans. John Macquarrie and Edward Robinson. New York: Harper & Row, 1962.

ED   Marion, Jean-Luc. *Etant donné: Essai d'une phénoménologie de la donation*. Paris: Presses Universitaires de France, 1997.

EH   Nietzsche, Friedrich. *Ecco Homo* (with *On the Genealogy of Morals*). Trans. Walter Kaufmann. New York: Random House, 1967.

FL   Derrida, Jacques. "Force of Law: The 'Mystical Foundation of Authority.'" In Jacques Derrida, *Acts of Religion,* ed. Gil Anidjar, pp. 230-98. New York: Routledge, 2002. Also found in *Deconstruction and the Possibility of Justice*. Ed. Drucilla Cornell. New York: Routledge, 1992.

GD   Derrida, Jacques. *The Gift of Death*. Trans. David Wills. Chicago: University of Chicago Press, 1995.

GGP   Caputo, John D., and Michael J. Scanlon, eds. *God, the Gift and Postmodernism*. New York: Fordham University Press, 1999.

GM   Nietzsche, Friedrich. *On the Genealogy of Morals*. Trans. Maudemarie Clark and Alan J. Swensen. Indianapolis: Hackett, 1998.

GS   Nietzsche, Friedrich. *The Gay Science: With a Prelude in German Rhymes and an Appendix of Songs*. Ed. Bernard Williams; trans. Josefine Nauckhoff. Cambridge: Cambridge University Press, 2001.

GT   Derrida, Jacques. *Given Time I: Counterfeit Money*. Trans. Peggy Kamuf. Chicago: University of Chicago Press, 1992.

GWB   Marion, Jean-Luc. *God Without Being*. Trans. Thomas A. Carlson. Chicago: University of Chicago Press, 1991.

HAS   Derrida, Jacques. "How to Avoid Speaking: Denials." Trans. Ken Frieden. In *Derrida and Negative Theology,* ed. Harold Coward and Toby Foshay, pp. 73-142. Albany: State University of New York Press, 1992.

IAD   Marion, Jean-Luc. *The Idol and Distance.* Trans. Thomas A. Carlson. New York: Fordham University Press, 2001.

ID   Husserl, Edmund. *Ideas Pertaining to a Pure Phenomenology and a Phenomenological Philosophy,* bk. 1, *General Introduction to a Pure Phenomenology.* Trans. Fred Kersten. The Hague: Martinus Nijhoff, 1982.

L   Derrida, Jacques. *Limited Inc.* Trans. Samuel Weber and Jeffrey Mehlman. Evanston: Northwestern University Press, 1988.

LI   Husserl, Edmund. *Logical Investigations.* Trans. J. N. Findlay. London: Routledge & Kegan Paul, 1970.

MP   Marion, Jean-Luc. "Metaphysics and Phenomenology: A Summary for Theologians." In *The Postmodern God: A Theological Reader,* ed. Graham Ward, pp. 279-96. Oxford: Blackwell, 1997.

OCM   Heidegger, Martin. "The Onto-theological Constitution of Metaphysics." In *Identity and Difference,* trans. Joan Stambaugh. New York: Harper & Row, 1969.

OG   Derrida, Jacques. *Of Grammatology,* Cor. Ed. Trans. Gayatri Spivak. Baltimore: Johns Hopkins University Press, 1977.

ON   Derrida, Jacques. *On the Name.* Ed. Thomas Dutoit. Stanford, Calif.: Stanford University Press, 1995.

OTB   Levinas, Emmanuel. *Otherwise Than Being or Beyond Essence.* Trans. Alphonso Lingis. Dordrecht, Netherlands: Kluwer, 1991.

P   Heidegger, Martin. *Pathmarks.* Ed. William McNeill. Cambridge: Cambridge University Press, 1998.

PTT   Janicaud, Dominique, et al. *Phenomenology and the "Theological Turn": The French Debate.* New York: Fordham University Press, 2000.

RG   Marion, Jean-Luc. *Reduction and Givenness: Investigations of Husserl, Heidegger and Phenomenology.* Trans. Thomas A. Carlson. Evanston: Northwestern University Press, 1998.

TAI   Levinas, Emmanuel. *Totality and Infinity: An Essay on Exteriority.* Trans. Alphonso Lingis. The Hague: Martinus Nijhoff, 1979.

TI   Nietzsche, Friedrich. *Twilight of the Idols.* Trans. Richard Polt. Indianapolis: Hackett, 1997.

WD   Derrida, Jacques. *Writing and Difference.* Trans. Alan Bass. Chicago: University of Chicago Press, 1978.

WN   Heidegger, Martin. "The Word of Nietzsche: God Is Dead." In *The*

        Question Concerning Technology, trans. William Lovitt. New York: Harper & Row, 1977.

WP   Nietzsche, Friedrich. *The Will to Power.* Ed. Walter Kaufmann, trans. Walter Kaufmann and R. J. Hollingdale. New York: Random House, 1967.

Z   Nietzsche, Friedrich. *Thus Spoke Zarathustra.* Trans. R. J. Hollingdale. Harmondsworth, U.K.: Penguin, 1972.

INTRODUCTION

A History of Idolatry

"Little children, keep yourselves from idols" (1 Jn 5:21). So John the elder concludes his first epistle, one written to no church in particular. Why does John make this sudden reference to idols at the end of a text in which idols have so far not even been mentioned? Moreover, what exactly does he mean by *idols?* Is he talking merely of graven images, things carved out of wood and stone?

Graven Ideologies

The principal theme of John's first epistle is the danger of believers' becoming disconnected from the true faith. Thus he warns them against the danger of accommodation, of being stained by the world and of infection by the spirit of antichrist. As a spiritual compass, John notes characteristics of true believers, particularly stressing love and obedience.

If we look back to the beginning of the epistle, the context for its ending becomes even more clear. John exhorts his readers to hold firm to the received faith (to which he testifies in the opening verses of the book, 1:1-3), in light of deception by various antichrists (who preach a different gospel, 2:18, 22-24). But those "who believe in the name of the Son of God" are connected to the true God (5:13, 20). Given the general context of John's letter, idols would seem to be anything that (1) takes God's place and (2) separates us from God and the true faith.

We shall return shortly to the first aspect, substitution, but here we need to consider the second, separation, in some detail. Separation can take place in at least two senses. We can be separated by failing to *know* the truth. But we can also be separated in the sense of failing to *do* the truth. These two sorts of separation seem to be closely linked in John's thought, for he says, "Little children, let us love, not in word or speech, but in truth and action. And by this we will know that we are from the truth" (1 Jn 3:18-19). Our knowledge of the truth is attested by our actions.

It is John who gives us the vivid metaphor of *walking* in the truth (3 Jn 3). The truth of the gospel in effect provides the space in which we live and the motivation behind the deepest desires of our hearts. Obviously, if we are separated from the truth because we lack knowledge, we cannot walk in the truth. Yet we can know the truth and still fail to walk in that the truth. In such a case we are separated from the truth in the most important sense. Indeed we are in a particularly unenviable position: our failure to walk in the truth is not due to lack of knowledge, and so we are particularly culpable for our shortcoming.

These two senses of separation come together in a third sense: our relation to God. John makes it clear that a proper relation to the truth requires a proper relation to God himself. Since God and his truth are closely connected, when God's truth is in us so is God in us. Thus these three senses of separation and connection—knowing, doing and being related—are interlinked. John says that the purpose of his epistle is that the reader would have "fellowship" *(koinōnia)* not only with other believers but "with the Father and with his Son Jesus Christ" (1 Jn 1:3). Conversely, idols separate us from God, for they effectively act as a screen between God and us.

So the theoretical and practical implications of idolatry are very closely connected. If one goes awry in either, the other is affected. As A. W. Tozer perceptively notes, "A right conception of God is basic not only to systematic theology but to practical Christian living as well. . . . I believe there is scarcely an error in doctrine or a failure in applying Christian ethics that cannot be traced finally to imperfect and ignoble thoughts about God."[1] Tozer is not hyperbolic when he says that "scarcely an error" in either our thinking about God or our actions is not ultimately based on idolatry. One reason the commandment against idolatry is the *first* of the Ten Commandments is that the others are rooted in it. As we shall discover time and again in this book, even instances of error that seem to have nothing to do with idolatry often prove to have idolatry as their principal source.

But what are idols, and how can they be detected? Since the category "anything that separates us from the true faith" is rather broad, the

---

[1]A. W. Tozer, *The Knowledge of the Holy* (New York: Harper & Row, 1961), p. 10.

potential for the creation of idols would seem almost unlimited. Scripture speaks repeatedly about the dangers of idolatry and devotes more space to it than to any other single theme. Reflecting on our potential for idol creation can be an overwhelming and even frightening exercise. Not only are we capable of creating idols and worshiping them, we are likewise capable of being almost or completely blind to their existence. Worse yet, we are often quite capable of providing a defense (and sometimes a remarkably respectable defense) for why our particular idols are worthy and even orthodox. Our recognition of idols for what they are is often selective. Most of us have reasonably well developed idol-detectors when it comes to the idols of others. Yet it is probably safe to say that all of us have our own particular repertoire of idols.

We tend to think of idols as material (either images or materials that can be worshiped as God), but *eidōlon*—the term John uses—can also denote images and concepts. The apostle Paul talks about those who "exchanged the glory of the immortal God for images resembling a mortal human being or birds or four-footed animals or reptiles" (Rom 1:23). Yet John's concern seems to be less for material representations than *intellectual* representations of God.[2] Thus my focus in this book will be on idols of an intellectual or, more specifically, *conceptual* nature. Conceptual idolatry is either the creation or the adoption of a concept or idea that we take to be equivalent *to* God and thus worship *as* God.[3] Although it might seem that so-called intellectuals such as philosophers and theologians would be most likely to fall into such idolatry, it should become clear that in conceptual idolatry there is equal opportunity for all. Creating conceptual idols requires no formal training and no theological sophistication.

But how does conceptual idolatry happen? Moreover, what do I mean by "graven ideologies"? To answer these questions, we first need to consider the relation between the Greek terms **eidō*, *eidos*, *eidōlon* and *eikōn*. From there we will move to the meaning of "ideology" and "vain philosophy."

The Greek root **eidō* has to do with sight, and thus *eidos* can be

---

[2]F. F. Bruce observes, "The 'idols' or false appearances . . . against which John warns his readers to be on their guard are not material images; they are false conceptions of God. Any conception of Him that is at variance with His self-revelation in Christ is an idol" (*The Epistles of John* [Grand Rapids, Mich.: Eerdmans, 1979], p. 128).

[3]Of course anything we put in God's place is always *less* than God.

translated as "outward appearance" or "form." Of course "outward appearance" should not be read as contrasting with an internal or invisible reality. For the ancient Greeks, an *eidos*—the true reality of something or what it *is*—can be *seen*. Plato uses the term *eidos* for his Forms or Ideas. An *eidos* is an outward manifestation of that which is essential. But the term *eidos* is not used merely by ancient Greek philosophers. While *eidos* appears infrequently in the New Testament, there are at least two important passages in which it occurs. Speaking of the Father, John makes the statement (in Jn 5:37) that "you have never heard his voice or seen his form *[eidos]*." Both "hearing God's voice" and "seeing God's form" are roughly equivalent to "knowing God as he truly is."[4] John simply assumes that those to whom he is writing have not experienced God in this way (and could not do so, being human), though he likewise implies that they could still have experienced God in some important sense. Our experience of God is never equivalent to God as he truly is. In technical philosophical terms, there is a lack of equivalence or "adequation" between the two.

Paul implies that this lack of adequation (in Latin *adaequatio*) is a central part of a relationship to God based on faith when he says that "we walk by faith, not by sight" (2 Cor 5:7). The contrast here between *pistis* (faith) and *eidos* (sight) is ultimately one between faith *(pistis)* and knowledge *(epistēmē)*. Whereas *pistis* is unable to provide its own ground, *epistēmē* (particularly as construed by Plato) is self-grounding. And the difference has to do with *eidos*. When I have *epistēmē*, I have insight into the nature of something. Thus according to Plato (and much subsequent Greek thought, with which Paul would have been acquainted), when I know the *eidos* of something, I am certain concerning its existence and essence and so have *epistēmē*. But if I do not know its *eidos* (that is, my sight is imperfect or incomplete), then all I have is belief or faith *(pistis)*. As believers, we walk not by knowledge but by faith.

The writer of Hebrews, though, makes clear that faith is not a shot in the dark based on nothing at all. "Faith is the *assurance* of things hoped for" (Heb 11:1) and involves a deep conviction. But these things are not "seen" (here *blepomenōn*). In Hebrews 11:8 we read, "By faith Abraham

---

[4]We shall return to the significance of hearing God's voice and seeing his form in the epilogue.

obeyed when he was called to set out for a place that he was to receive as an inheritance; and he set out, not knowing *[epistamenos]* where he was going." So Abraham did not possess *epistēmē*.

Scripture does affirm, however, that we can "know" God in some sense. Whereas in secular Greek the verb *ginōskō* implies a complete grasp of the nature *(eidos)* of what is known in theoretical or detached way, *ginōskō* in Scripture is significantly different. First, knowledge of God is always a gift, given to us by revelation. Second, knowledge of this sort goes with a personal relationship. We know *because* we are in relationship to God. As the good Shepherd, Jesus says, "I know *[ginōskō]* my own and my own know *[ginōskousi]* me" (Jn 10:14). Similarly, when John in the last chapter of his first epistle says "we know" three times, he refers to a knowledge based on personal experience. "We know *[oida]* that the Son of God has come and has given us understanding [or insight] so that we may know him who is true; and we are in him who is true, in his Son Jesus Christ" (1 Jn 5:20). We know the truth because we know the Son. *Oida* likewise has to do with sight, yet our knowledge of God is not a theoretical grasping of his *eidos* but an experience of God through Jesus Christ.

But how is God made visible to us through Jesus Christ? Although the Old Testament prohibits any images of God, Paul describes Christ as the "image" *(eikōn)* of God (2 Cor 4:4; Col 1:15). Here we need to turn to the contrast between the idol and the icon—*eidōlon* and *eikōn*. Connected to **eidō* and *eidos,* the word *eidōlon* (idol) denotes something that can be seen. Homer uses the term to denote shadows or phantoms in Hades.[5] But although these things can be seen, they lack substance. Thus the image in a mirror is an *eidōlon,* and so are all "images" and "ideas" that are unsubstantial. In the Septuagint version of the Old Testament, the term is always used for pagan gods. Indeed in the Ten Commandments the clause "you shall have no other gods before me" is immediately followed by "you shall not make for yourself an idol" (Ex 20:3-4). Here we already have the connection between separation and substitution in idolatry. When we put an idol in God's place, there is something separating us from God.

The Old Testament prophets continually emphasize the vanity and lack of power of idols. Isaiah contrasts the almighty power of "the LORD,

---

[5]See *Iliad* 5.451 and *Odyssey* 4.796.

who created the heavens (he is God!)" (Is 45:18) with an idol made from gold and silver as follows:

> Those who lavish gold from the purse,
>   and weigh out silver in the scales—
> they hire a goldsmith, who makes it into a god;
>   then they fall down and worship!
> They lift it to their shoulders, they carry it,
>   they set it in its place, and it stands there;
>   it cannot move from its place.
> If one cries out to it, it does not answer
>   or save anyone from trouble. (Is 46:6-7)

So idols are images we create. Moreover, they are always mirror images of us. Even though we may think they represent God, they actually represent *God as we have created him*. Thus Marion is not quite right when he says, "The idol reflects back to us, in the face of a god, our own experience of the divine. The idol does not resemble us, but it resembles the divinity that we experience, and it gathers it in a god in order that we might see it" (*IAD* 6). In reflecting back to us what we take to be God, it reflects ourselves. Thus idol is characterized by *immanence,* always held captive by our imagination. In the same way that Plato considered that knowing the *eidos* of something gave the philosopher a kind of control, so having an image of a false god gives the possessor mastery of that god.

Eikōn can also be translated as "image," but it denotes something strikingly different. An *eidōlon* is a reflection of us; an *eikōn* is an image that represents something other than ourselves. The icon transcends our thought and is not held hostage by human imagination. Moreover, the iconic image is strongly connected to the thing (or person) that it represents. Colossians 1:15 says that Christ is the *eikōn tou theou tou aoratou*—literally, "icon of the invisible God" (though *eikōn* is usually translated "image" in this passage; see also 2 Corinthians 3:18). With the advent of Jesus Christ, we truly have "God with us" (Mt 1:23). Understandably, John says that the one who has seen Jesus "has seen the Father" (Jn 14:9). But Jesus as the image of God is unlike idolatrous images precisely in that Jesus has been *sent* to us. He is *not* of our creation, nor under our control. That Jesus could not be mastered—by the religious leaders of Israel, his disciples or even his own mother—is constantly demonstrated in the Gospels (this will be examined further in the chapters on Nietzsche). Even his closest followers could not co-opt his agenda.

What, then, is a "graven ideology"? The King James Version's rendering of the first commandment—"Thou shalt not make unto thee any graven image" (Ex 20:4)—is familiar to most of us. The now obsolete verb *to grave* (going back to the Old English *grafan,* to dig or engrave) means "to carve or sculpt," but it is easily extended figuratively. The term *ideology* is of much more recent vintage.[6] While *ideology* has been used in a variety of ways, in its most benign form it refers to an attempt to provide a coherent set of ideas or else to the study of such ideas. Interestingly enough, the term *idea* also has its roots in *eidos* and so implies a kind of insight. Not only are Plato's Forms also called "Ideas," but the original meaning of *idea* implies insight into something's nature. Thus "to have an idea concerning a particular object" can mean to understand its essence. The suffix *-ology* (which comes from the Greek *logos,* meaning "structure" or "reason" or "order") denotes not merely an attempt to make sense of something but the putting of that thing into a kind of logical order. While the French *idéologie* was originally proposed as a new term for "epistemology," the term in both French and English has come to mean a conception (or, to use a more Hegelian and Marxist term, "consciousness") of society—that is, the conception that society has both about itself and the world. Even though the term is of recent vintage, it is safe to say that there have always been ideologies.[7] To whatever extent people have had a consciousness of themselves and their world, they have had an ideology.

However, from its coining *ideology* has generally had negative connotations. Three aspects of "ideologies" are particularly significant for our consideration.

First, when ideologies are denounced, it is often because they are taken to be *contradictory.* On the one hand, that contradiction can be between the ideology and the world. The charge here is that one's ideology fails to reflect the world as it is.[8] On the other hand, the contra-

---

[6] *Ideology* appeared first in French (as *idéologie*) at the end of the eighteenth century.

[7] Note that the term *ideology* was in use *before* it became associated with Karl Marx and Frederick Engels (in their *The German Ideology,* ed. and trans. S. Ryazanskaya [London: Lawrence & Wishart, 1965]).

[8] This is one of the charges in *German Ideology.*

diction can be within the ideology itself. That is, one holds to incompatible theses.

Second, ideologies are often held dogmatically, with little or no reason given. Thus ideologies are difficult to discredit, for there is no real evidence to dispute.

Third, despite that lack of justification, ideologies are usually claimed to be the final word. Considering the etymology of the term, such is easy to understand. *Ideology* implies essential insights that are put together into a reasoned structure—what else could one add?

It is not difficult to see, then, that ideology and idolatry are remarkably similar. In the same way that *eidōlon* "always carries with it the suggestion of unreality,"[9] so ideology suggests a skewed conception of reality. There is likewise an inherent contradiction in idolatry, particularly of a Christian sort. While orthodox Christians maintain that God is above all material or intellectual representations, the moment they claim their particular picture of God or theological belief to be "the final word" is the moment they step into idolatry. And if ideologies are held dogmatically, idols are often held even more so. Since they are our creations (and since we like the look of ourselves), we are hard pressed to give them up. Criticism usually results in our holding them all the more dogmatically. Understandably, Denys Turner claims that "for the Christian, *ideology* and *idolatry* are synonyms."[10] This connection can be seen in Paul's thought, to which we now turn.

The Danger of Vain Philosophy

The characteristics of ideology and idolatry considered here are precisely what Paul seems to have in mind in his warning against "philosophy and empty deceit" in Colossians 2:8. Although his admonition is sometimes read as directed against philosophy in general, Paul is talking about a particular sort of thinking that can be philosophical or even theological in nature. It is what we might call "vain philosophy."

Christian philosophers are apt to get defensive when someone mentions Colossians 2:8—"See to it that no one takes you captive through philosophy and empty deceit, according to human tradition, according to the elemental spirits of the universe, and not according to Christ." As

---

[9]C. H. Dodd, *The Johannine Epistles* (London: Hodder & Stoughton, 1946), p. 141.

[10]Denys Turner, *Marxism and Christianity* (Totowa, N.J.: Barnes & Noble, 1983), p. 227.

they rightly point out, the emphasis here is not on philosophy per se.

The first aspect of the danger Paul describes is that one is taken captive by a particular philosophy. More literally translated, Paul warns against philosophy that "makes a prey of you." Being "captive" to a philosophy is the state of being so in its grip that one is unable to question it, or perhaps even to see that it holds a grip on one's life and thought. "Falling prey" usually takes place when one believes something without adequate scrutiny. Such is precisely the dogmatic character of ideology.

Second, Paul connects "philosophy" with "empty deceit." Since he has just been describing Christ as the one who holds "all the treasures of wisdom and knowledge" (Col 2:2-3), it would be difficult to argue that Paul has something against philosophy in the abstract. After all, philosophy is "the love of wisdom," even if philosophers have sometimes been unwise and sought what only appeared to be wisdom. The writer of Proverbs again and again exhorts us to love wisdom, and there is no reason to think that Paul would disagree. Instead Paul objects to *false* philosophy or wisdom. Such philosophy appears to be wisdom, but is in reality the sort of sham wisdom that is served up with what Paul terms (in Col 2:4) "plausible arguments." Of course, philosophers themselves have often railed against just such false philosophy. Both Plato and Aristotle, for example, criticized the group of philosophers known as the Sophists, not merely because they were dispensing falsity but because they used specious arguments to convince their hearers of its truth.

The kind of philosophy Paul has in mind becomes more clear when we consider the two terms he pairs with it: *kenēs apatēs* (Col 2:8). The adjective *kenos* can be variously translated as "impotent," "false," "empty" or "baseless." *Apatē* means deception, seduction or trickery. Put together, then, "empty deceit" comes down to a nothing that passes itself off as something and seduces one into belief. Again, one is reminded of ideology.

There is strong connection between *kenēs apatēs* and the term *eidōlon*. An *eidōlon* is a kind of likeness—whether material or immaterial—that is ultimately empty, since there is really nothing there. It is seductive in that it shifts our focus away from God.

Both *kenēs apatēs* and the *eidōlon* are characterized by "vanity." Indeed *kenos* is rendered as "vain" in the King James Version. But while the term *vain* and its cognate *vanity* well capture all of the senses listed above, they also add an important sense that is helpful for understanding the nature and origin of "vain philosophy" and idolatry: pride or conceit. A vain person has an inappropriate preoccupation with self that arises from overemphasizing his or her importance. Just as in English *vain* is related to *vainglorious,* so in Greek *kenos* is related to *kenodoxos.* Although something that is vain isn't necessarily vainglorious, the two often go together. Such seems to be the case here, for Paul goes on to describe this philosophy as being "according to human tradition, according to the elemental spirits of the universe, and not according to Christ." Whether Paul is referring to any particular tradition is not clear. Likely he has various pagan philosophies in mind. In any case, in Colossians 2:20 Paul in effect equates "the elemental spirits" with "the world."

The idea of being "according to human tradition" is of particular concern here. "Vain philosophy" is aptly named not merely because it is empty but because it has its roots in vanity. Is not the source of vain thought almost always vaingloriousness? Paul rightly says that this vain philosophy is "according to *human* tradition." While human tradition is not necessarily suspect, here the problem is that it *passes itself off as something divine.* Thus the move is self-exaltation: we attempt to take God's place by devising ideas and theories (idols) that we put in the place of God. By creating our own conceptions of God, we effectively *become* God (for we are the source of these conceptions).

But the problem is even more complicated. One might be tempted to think, *Yes, those philosophers are the problem. They're idolaters because they import pagan conceptions of God.* And, of course, such has not been infrequently the case. Yet theologians—even Christian ones—are not necessarily immune to the idolatry of ideology. Not only do they borrow concepts from pagans (just as philosophers do), but even their "Christian" conceptions of God can become idolatrous. It won't do to say, "OK, I'll avoid idolatry by avoiding philosophy and theology altogether." For even *biblical* notions of God can become idolatrous. If, for instance, I think of Jesus Christ as "my good shepherd" whose principal purpose for existing is to meet my needs, then I have seriously distorted a biblical conception for my own purposes. There is every reason to think that Paul also has religious thinkers in mind when he speaks of "vain philosophy."

The problem of idolatry is not simply *which* concepts and images we employ (though it is that also) but *how* we employ them. Friedrich Gogarten claims that "whenever we claim to have found God in *this* world, we have found nothing but an idol; this happens more often than we think, since it is rarely noticed."[11] But that is only partly true. It is not that we cannot encounter God in this world. Scripture and our own experience bear witness to the fact that we can. Yet if we claim that we have encountered God *as he is,* we are sorely deceived. Orthodox Christian theology continually treads this difficult line.

Phenomenology and Idolatry

But how do conceptual idols arise? Do they come out of nowhere? A helpful perspective from which to discuss the origin and status of conceptual idols is that of phenomenology. Although the philosophical theory of phenomenology ends up being quite complex, its basic structures are relatively simple and provide a useful framework for discussion. Phenomenological theory will be considered in greater depth at later points in this book. For now, a brief discussion of the goal and method of phenomenology may give us a better idea of what conceptual idols are and how they arise.

An appropriate starting point in explaining phenomenology is the term itself. There are two parts to *phenomenology—phenomenon* and *-ology.* A phenomenon is simply "that which appears." If I look out the window and see a tree, there is the "phenomenon" of a tree appearing before me. The world is in effect a collection of phenomena. Given what I have already noted about *logos,* it should be no surprise that phenomenology is "the study of phenomena."

Although phenomenologists disagree concerning the precise parameters of phenomenology, there is a general agreement concerning the goal of phenomenology: to allow the phenomena to be seen for what they are.[12] According to Husserl, too often philosophers construct their own pet theories and then try to bend the world to fit their theories. Husserl thinks philosophy should begin with the actual phenomena of the world and then theorize on the basis of those phenomena. In other words, theory should reflect the actual reality of the world in which we live.

Yet there is an important complication here, one that has a great deal to do with the problem of conceptual idolatry. Husserl's ultimate goal was to arrive at a *logos* that arises *from the phenomena them-*

---

[11]Friedrich Gogarten, "The Crisis of Our Culture," in *The Beginnings of Dialectic Theology,* ed. James M. Robinson (Richmond, Va.: John Knox, 1968), p. 290.

[12]Of course even Husserl realized that there are some significant complications to this goal, as we shall see in chapter seven.

selves, rather than one that was merely superimposed on them. His motto for phenomenology was "to the things themselves" *(zu den Sachen selbst).* While such a goal is highly commendable, the extent to which it is possible—and has actually ever been achieved—remains a problem that has haunted phenomenology ever since. What Husserl terms the "the principle of all principles" is the idea that *"everything originally . . . offered* to us *in 'intuition' is to be accepted simply as what it is presented as being, but also only within the limits in which it is presented there"* (*ID* 44, Husserl's italics). In other words, we ought to take phenomena at face value, without embellishing or "interpreting" them. Even Martin Heidegger, who had significant disagreements with Husserl as to the possibility of "uninterpreted" phenomena, speaks of the phenomenon as "the showing-itself-in-itself" and insists that "the function of the *logos* lies in merely letting something be seen" (*BT* 54, 58). But is the *logos* ever so "mere" as that? Does it always stay within the limits of what is presented? Or might it instead be imposed from outside of those limits, *from us?*

Perhaps we should frame the question as follows: to what extent is any given "ology" really a kind of idolatry (which is to say, a *logos* formed in our own image) that in turn corrupts the phenomenon? As commendable as is phenomenology's emphasis on allowing phenomena to show themselves just as they are, note that a basic assumption of phenomenology is that phenomena can be fully "immanent" to our minds. As we will see later, it is this assumption that causes Levinas and Marion to argue for a kind of manifestation that is not (at least strictly speaking) a "phenomenon."

At this point, though, it should be clear that at least one danger in philosophizing is that our theories reflect more of ourselves than of the phenomena we are attempting to explain. That such a situation has been not merely a possibility but often the reality becomes apparent when we consider the way the goal of Western philosophy has been worked out in practice.

The Idolatry of *Adaequatio*

Even though Paul's cautionary word should not be taken as being necessarily against philosophy in general, I think it is not too much to say that Western philosophy has at least tended toward idolatry from its very beginning. Indeed Nietzsche thinks that the whole history of philosophy has been more or less one idol after the next. That reading is undoubtedly too severe, but Nietzsche is far more right than I—a philosopher by profession—would care to admit. On Nietzsche's read, traditional philosophical concepts have been idols in the sense that they are images of our own creation which we hold up (and sometimes venerate) as "true" reality. In other words, philosophy has tended to assume the possibility of an unmediated immanence in which "all that is" can be known directly and completely.

The result is that philosophy ends up being all too often a rather "big story" of human origin. Jean-François Lyotard defines postmodernism as "incredulity toward *grand reçits*."[13] While the term *grand reçits* is often translated as "metanarrative" or "grand narrative," more literally it just means "big story." One might be tempted to interchange *grand reçits* with "ideologies." Though all ideologies are *grand reçits*, however, not all *grand reçits* are necessarily ideologies. One characteristic of all *grand reçits* is that they are encompassing enough to explain everything. Of all *grand reçits*, the big story of philosophy, as first told to us by the ancient Greeks and then retold by philosophers ever since, is about as big as one could imagine. Briefly put, that story says that something like "ultimate reality" exists *and* that human beings are capable (or somehow could be capable, given proper methodology or the right *logos*) of knowing it *directly* and *completely.*

Husserl describes the birth of philosophy as the advent of a "fantastic dream." There arises, he says, "a *new sort of attitude* of individuals toward their surrounding world."[14] By "surrounding world" Husserl means not merely our physical environment but also the ideas, beliefs, traditions and practices that our community holds in common. This world is so much a part of our experience that normally we never notice its existence. Philosophy begins when we both take notice of this world and call it into question. While such questioning is characteristic of philosophy in general, it is particularly pronounced in Plato (c. 430-347 B.C.), who likens living in this world to being imprisoned in a dark cave in which mere shadows (appearances) are taken to be

---

[13]Jean-François Lyotard, *The Postmodern Condition,* trans. Geoff Bennington and Brian Massumi (Minneapolis: University of Minnesota Press, 1984), p. xxiv.
[14]Edmund Husserl, *The Crisis of European Sciences and Transcendental Phenomenology,* trans. David Carr (Evanston, Ill.: Northwestern University Press, 1970), p. 276 (Husserl's italics).

reality.[15] Thus the "love of wisdom" (the literal meaning of *philosophy*) requires that one go beyond the contingent, conditioned "truths" of the surrounding world to arrive at Truth that is universal, necessary and thus utterly dependable.

According to Husserl, the result is a "new man" characterized by a "love of ideas." We become captivated by "ideal objects." Platonism's most significant contribution to the philosophical tradition is the development of the idea (found already in certain pre-Socratic philosophers) that things like Goodness and Beauty really are *things.* As already noted, Plato calls them Forms. Nietzsche clearly has the Forms in mind when, in the foreword to *Twilight of the Idols,* he writes:

> This little book is a *great declaration of war,* and as for sounding out idols, this time they are not just idols of the age, but *eternal* idols that are touched here with the hammer as with a tuning fork—there aren't any older idols at all, none more assured, none more inflated. . . . And none more hollow. . . . That doesn't stop them from being the ones that are *believed* in the most—and, especially, in the most prominent case, they aren't called idols at all.

These Forms (which "aren't called idols at all") are for Plato "eternal." They are not things in the sense of physical things; instead they have even *more* reality than physical things. Interestingly enough, Plato explicitly contrasts these Forms with idols (which, for Plato, are mere appearances or illusions).

Ever since Plato, the very idea of Truth has tended to be defined (in varying degrees and sorts of ideality) in terms of ideal objects.[16] For instance, justice for Plato is not merely a *characteristic* of just actions; it is an actually existing *thing* (Justice) by which all particular just actions can be measured. On Plato's account, the extent to which an action embodies Justice is the extent to which it may be pronounced just.

In positing this idea of a universal Truth, Plato in effect sets up a double transcendence. The first aspect of this transcendence is metaphysical. Plato claims that Truth has a particular sort of *being,* beyond any

---

[15]Plato scholars disagree concerning the extent to which the Platonic dialogues give us "Plato's view" versus "Socrates' view." Here I assume that what Socrates says goes for Plato as well, and use the terms *Socratic* and *Platonic* interchangeably.

[16]Even Aristotle, who rejects Plato's account of universals, still thinks there is an ideal "something" (which he calls an "essence") that makes an object what it is.

particular spatiotemporal boundaries and so beyond the realm of changing reality. The second transcendence is epistemological. Human beings can transcend themselves and the world of immediate experience. The radicality of the dream becomes clear when we consider what it entails. The goal of Plato is neither simply a quest for knowledge of his own historical, contingent world nor simply a sort of practical knowledge enabling one to navigate life. Rather he seeks a theoretical knowledge of the way the world "really" is.

But note that this second sense of transcendence negates the first sense. If I am able to transcend the boundaries of my world and my time, then that which I seek to understand is *itself* no longer transcendent. This point is particularly important in regard to idolatry. If I can transcend my finitude to understand God in his fullness, then God is—at least to me—no longer transcendent. One cannot have it both ways. Either *God* is transcendent and so my knowledge of him never fully transcends the limits of my time and place, or *I* become transcendent and God thereby becomes fully immanent to me. There is, of course, a middle ground here: God can both be immanent to me (in certain respects, to certain degrees) and yet still remain transcendent. Such is a properly orthodox Christian conception of God. But to whatever extent God becomes immanent, to that extent he loses transcendence.

Practically, the result of Plato's leap is dramatic, in two respects. First, the vision of Absolute Truth (and its correlate of Absolute Knowledge) brings about a change in the hierarchy of values. Socrates makes it clear that once one discovers (for example) the Form of Beauty, one becomes progressively less interested in beautiful things and increasingly filled with an *eros* for Beauty itself. Thus Husserl claims that the *Urstiftung* (original founding) of philosophy in effect sets up an *Endstiftung* (a kind of *telos* to be realized someday): the ultimate end of human knowing is the eventual knowledge of reality in its totality.

Given this possibility of transcendence, Plato adopts a critical attitude toward traditionally accepted "truths," relegating them to the level of mere *doxa*—opinion. No longer can opinions be accepted without further justification. True, Socrates admits in the dialogue *Meno* that "true opinion is as good a guide as knowledge for the purpose of acting rightly," but opinions need to be properly "tethered"— to use Socrates' metaphor—if they are to count as knowledge (epistēmē).[17] Whereas true opinion tells us *that* something is the case, it does not tell us *why*. In other words, it lacks a proper ground or foundation.

Plato's demotion of opinion is a complex epistemological move. To deny the validity of opinion is in effect to deny the validity of tradition and custom. That one's community takes something to be true is not sufficient reason, thinks Plato, to assume that it *is* true. Thus tradition and custom need to be questioned. Further, Plato sets up a hierarchy of knowledge that clearly privileges philosophical ways of "knowing." Although this move might seem to be simply a case of special pleading on behalf of philosophy (and such a case can, I think, be made), Plato claims there is a very good reason for making it. Simply put, philosophy can lead us directly to the thing itself, whereas other ways of "knowing" are *indirect*. In other words, philosophy provides us with immanence.

Consider, for instance, the difference Plato draws between philosophy and art or rhetoric. According to Plato, an artist or poet can provide only a "picture" of the Truth (either literally or metaphorically). For example, if an artist makes a painting of a tree, that depiction is twice removed from the Form, since the painting is a copy of an actual physical thing (the tree) which is itself a copy of a Form (the Form of "Treeness"). The artist's truth, then, is at best metaphorical—that is, removed from reality—and incomplete. In contrast, Plato thinks that philosophy has the potential to give us the Truth directly and completely. By philosophizing, we can eventually come to know the Truth in its fullness, so it is no longer transcendent.

So what counts as Truth and what does it mean to know it? In Socrates' dialogue with Euthyphro, Socrates makes it clear that a true knowledge of holiness, for example, is not equivalent to being able to provide an example of a holy action; rather it is knowing "the essential form of holiness which makes all holy actions holy."[18] To know holiness is to know its *eidos*—the stuff that makes it what it is (or its "what-isness"). In *Phaedo* and *Republic* Socrates clarifies this goal further. Philosophy, he tells us, is directed toward knowing the Forms of all things

---

[17]Plato *Meno* 97b-e. All quotations from Platonic texts can be found in *The Collected Dialogues of Plato*, ed. Edith Hamilton and Huntington Cairns (Princeton, N.J.: Princeton University Press, 1961).
[18]Plato *Euthyphro* 6d.

(not merely of holiness). To know the forms is not merely to "apprehend" or catch a glimpse of them but to "comprehend" or *grasp* them in their entirety. Moreover, "true knowledge" of the Forms is for Plato complete knowledge, which means that one knows all of the Forms and understands their interconnectedness.

Of course exactly what it would mean to comprehend the Forms is never fully spelled out in Platonic thought, even though Socrates speaks of "the man who pursues the truth by applying his pure and unadulterated thought to the pure and unadulterated object."[19] The result of this quest is, as Socrates puts it, that we "gain direct knowledge of all that is pure and uncontaminated—that is, presumably, of truth *[alētheia]*."[20]

We find this same sort of account in Aristotle, who construes knowledge as the state in which "the thinking part of the soul" is "identical in character with its object."[21] The ideal in both of these conceptions (though particularly clear in Aristotle) is *adequation,* in which the mind's conception of an object is "adequate" to the thing itself. To be adequate in this sense of the term, the two must be "equal in magnitude or extent; commensurate; neither more nor less."[22] It is what medieval philosophers refer to as *adaequatio intellectus ad rei* (adequation of intellect and substance).

Such an ideal is not limited to ancient and medieval philosophy. It is found, for instance, in John Locke. Note how he defines "adequate" versus "inadequate" ideas:

> Of our real *Ideas,* some are Adequate, and some are Inadequate. Those I shall call *Adequate,* which perfectly represent those Archetypes, which the mind supposes them taken from; which it intends them to stand for, and to which it refers them. *Inadequate Ideas* are such, which are but a partial, or incomplete representation of those Archetypes to which they are referred.[23]

Such is the rather tall order of philosophy as set out by Socrates, and it is a vision that has—albeit with significant modifications along the way—

---

[19]Plato *Phaedo* 66a.

[20]Ibid., 67b.

[21]Aristotle *On the Soul* 3.4, in *The Complete Works of Aristotle,* vol. 1, ed. Jonathan Barnes (Princeton, N.J.: Princeton University Press, 1984). Further references to Aristotle will be to this edition.

[22]*The Oxford English Dictionary,* 2nd ed. (Oxford: Clarendon Press, 1989), s.v. "adequate."

[23]John Locke, *An Essay Concerning Human Understanding,* ed. Peter H. Nadditch (Oxford: Clarendon, 1975), p. 375.

more or less characterized philosophy ever since.[24] It is a kind of beatific vision of presence, in which knowledge and truth become fully present to one's mind. But what would such an "immaculate perception," as Nietzsche memorably puts it (*Z*, "Of Immaculate Perception"), look like?

Probably the easiest way to parse out the ideal of adequation is by returning to Husserl, who gives us as clear and detailed a version as anyone. Husserl works out this ideal in terms of intentionality, intuition, evidence and interiority. Considering Husserl's account should give us a much better idea of what the vision of *adaequatio* looks like in actual practice. Although Husserlian terminology may sound intimidating, the basics of Husserl's theory are really not that complicated.

When I look out my window and see a tree, Husserl would say that I "intend" that tree. Perception is, for Husserl, an example of an "intentional act." Here "intentional" does not mean that when I look out my window "I *meant* to see the tree" (which is why I looked out the window). That may be true too, of course: perhaps I looked out my window *in order* to see the tree. In any case, there are two senses of *intention* at work in Husserl's account, and they are easily confused. One is the ordinary sense of *intention,* such as when I say, "My intention is to write a book." The other is Husserl's use of the term in a more general sense—when I perceive an object or think a thought, I am "intending" that object or thought. There are, of course, different ways of "intending" an object in this general sense. I may *perceive* a tree; I may *imagine* a tree; I may *remember* a tree in the backyard of my childhood home; I may *judge* that the tree is beautiful. These are all cases of "intending." *Intentionality* for Husserl refers to the manner that we, as subjects, relate to objects of our consciousness.[25] Through our intending, the world becomes present to us; that is, what stands as transcendent to us becomes immanent in the presence of consciousness. In effect, intending allows the phenomena of the world to come

---

[24]One could argue that other philosophers *might* provide us with a different way of defining truth and knowledge, one that *might* escape the criticism Nietzsche brings to bear against Platonism. I won't attempt such an argument here. Nietzsche's attack on the ideal of *adaequatio* between "truth" and "human knowing" would seem to apply to the Western philosophical project *as such*. That the attack is more effective against certain philosophical visions than others does not mitigate the force of the attack in general.

[25]Husserl first develops his conception of intentionality in the fifth of the *Logical Investigations*. While the notion of intentionality was substantially refined in his later works, those differences do not affect our discussion here.

into our purview. For Husserl, our relation to the world is always as intending subjects directed toward intended objects, since "consciousness is always consciousness of something."[26] Intentionality constitutes our fundamental relatedness to the world.

Not only are there different ways we can intend objects, there are also different degrees to which an intended object can be present to our consciousness. Husserl speaks of intentionality as being empty or filled, vague or distinct.[27] I can intend an object "emptily," such as when I use a word without having that object before my mind. In such a case the object is not really present to me. Conversely, I can intend the object with a strong sense of presence.

An example might help. I can speak of Westminster Abbey on the basis of a visit I made there last year. When I use the term *Westminster Abbey,* I refer to it in a more "empty" way than if it were present to me through direct perception, though not as "emptily" as if I had never been there before. When I stand before Westminster Abbey and say, "That's Westminster Abbey," I refer to the abbey (in Husserlian terms, "intend" it) in a much less empty way. In perception, it is present to my mind. Of course, even standing before it does not make it *fully* present to my mind. If I stand in front of it and follow the visual outline of the building and note its surroundings, it becomes more present to me. I can increase the level of presence by wandering through the cloister or reading the inscriptions on the monuments in Poets' Corner, as well as any number of other perusals. And even a guided tour of the premises of Westminster Abbey results in a less distinct apprehension of it than that afforded by a more complete excursion into its nether regions (say, if I had a friend who worked there and had access to all of the places off limits to tourists). All of this would make the physical entity Westminster Abbey more *fully* and also more *distinctly* present to my consciousness. The stronger this sense of presence, the more justified I would be in saying that I "know" Westminster Abbey.

Having seen what Husserl means by intentionality, we can now understand his idea of "intuitive-givenness." When we "intend" something in a genuine sense, Husserl says that it is intuitively given to con-

---

[26]Edmund Husserl, *The Paris Lectures,* trans. Peter Koestenbaum, 2nd ed. (The Hague: Martinus Nijhoff, 1967), p. 13.

[27]Edmund Husserl, *Formal and Transcendental Logic,* trans. Dorian Cairns (The Hague: Martinus Nijhoff, 1969), pp. 56-62.

sciousness. Although the term *intuition* carries a good deal of connotative baggage, Husserl's use is relatively simple. When I intuit a phenomenon, that phenomenon is "given" to me so that it "fills" my intention. I see a tree; that tree is given is to me; my intending is filled. What Husserl means by "intuitive presence" becomes clearer when we consider the opposing ends of the intuitive spectrum. For Husserl, the lowest level of presence is *signitive* presence.[28] Reading the name *Westminster Abbey* is coming in contact with a sign representing an edifice in England. The sign stands in for the physical entity, as a sort of substitute for the real thing. But in reading the sign one does not have the thing present to one's mind. A step up from signitive intending is pictorial intention: a postcard allows us to intend Westminster Abbey somewhat more directly and also more fully. We cannot point to the words *Westminster Abbey* and say, "It's Westminster Abbey," but we are able to point to an image of it and use this locution. In perception we realize the highest level of intuitive givenness of real objects, since they are immediately (rather than indirectly) given to our mind. That is, our intention of them is *unmediated.*

When objects are given to consciousness directly and fully, they come with what Husserl terms "evidence," or self-evidence, by which he means the "mode of consciousness that consists in the *self-appearance,* the *self-exhibiting,* the *self-giving*" of an object to consciousness. The object is "'itself there,' 'immediately intuited.'"[29] Or, as Husserl puts it in a clarifying preface to the *Logical Investigations,* "I can simply look at that which is *meant as such* and can grasp it absolutely. There is no evidence that could ever be superior to this."[30]

Where does all this happen? For Husserl, true presence is inner presence, taking place within the subject. To perceive an object is to have it given in such a manner that it is immanent to (rather than "exterior to") one's consciousness. The more present that object is to consciousness,

---

[28]As Husserl puts it, signitive acts "possess no fullness whatever" (*LI* 761).

[29]Edmund Husserl, *Cartesian Meditations,* trans. Dorian Cairns (The Hague: Martinus Nijhoff, 1960), p. 57. Evidence represents an achievement for Husserl in that it comes about through a process of synthesis of intentional acts. We experience evidence of something when an intentional act, such as an act of perception, is accompanied by a confirming act in such a way that the two are joined together. This synthesis has the character of a fulfillment. That is, the second of the two acts fulfills or substantiates the first.

[30]Edmund Husserl, *Introduction to the Logical Investigations,* trans. Philip J. Bossert and Curtis H. Peters (The Hague: Martinus Nijhoff, 1975), p. 27.

the more perfectly one's *noesis* (act of knowing) corresponds to the *noema* (object known). Thus adequation is made possible by way of presence. Husserl puts it as follows:

> Where a presentative intention has achieved its last fulfillment, the genuine *adaequatio rei et intellectus* has been brought about. *The object is actually "present" or "given," and present as just what we have intended it;* no partial intention remains implicit and still lacking fulfillment. (*LI* 2:762)

Just as Locke points out that adequate ideas are those that are not "partial," so true *adaequatio* for Husserl is "fulfillment" of that which was once partial.

Yet—and here we come to a crucial qualification—there is a limit to the possibility that a "real" object (one located in space and time) like Westminster Abbey can be present to my mind. None of the explorations of the abbey that I mentioned above—nor even all of them combined—could ever serve to enable me to reach an optimal level of presence of Westminster Abbey to my mind. I may see all the various aspects of Westminster Abbey in my tour of it; I cannot, though, see them simultaneously, nor can I ever really exhaust them. There will always be at least certain perspectives and aspects not fully present to consciousness (whether side chapels or the myriad gargoyles placed so high that they cannot be seen). In other words, a real entity like Westminster Abbey can never be fully present to consciousness.

Husserl explains it as follows: "The perception of a physical thing involves a certain *inadequacy*. Of necessity a physical thing can be given only 'one-sidedly'; and that signifies, not just incompletely or imperfectly in some sense or other, but precisely what presentation by adumbrations prescribes" (*ID* 94). Real objects are always present to us incompletely, and thus imperfectly, because they are always perceived in a particular way, from a certain perspective. Husserl points out that it is possible to multiply these perspectives and thus gain an increasingly "adequate" knowledge of the object being perceived. However, the goal of a perfect adequation is for Husserl an "idea in the Kantian sense"—a kind of ideal toward which we strive but which we never realize (*ID* 342-43).

In terms of intentionality, intuition, evidence and interiority, there is nothing more exemplary than an ideal object—one *not* located in space and time. Whereas real objects can never be fully intended by consciousness, Husserl thinks that ideal objects *can* be intended fully. In other words, with ideal objects there is the possibility of an absolute presence—a purely intuited givenness to consciousness with one hundred percent evidence. In fact, the evidence we have of them can, claims Husserl, be of the absolute sort Husserl thinks we have of our own selves. Thus, from a Husserlian standpoint, a knowledge of (say) the essence of Justice could be absolute, at least in principle (though not in practice).

Could there be anything like an "absolute" *adaequatio?* The philosopher G. W. F. Hegel (1770-1831) argues that one day "truth" and our knowledge of it will finally be absolutely "at one." Yet Hegel's explanation of that state undermines the very ideal of *adaequatio*. According to Hegel, at some as yet unknown point in the future there will arise a state of "absolute knowing" in which the mind's idea will perfectly correspond to its object (or, as Hegel puts it, "Notion corresponds to object and object to Notion").[31] But in order for there to be a perfect one-to-one correspondence, *noesis* (the act of knowing) cannot merely "correspond" to *noema* (the object known). Instead *noesis* must be identical with *noema*.

So the epistemological claim turns out to be a metaphysical claim. For Hegel, perfect knowing requires being at one with the object known. In order to have a perfect understanding of God, I would need to *be* God. We would not merely "see" face to face, but the two faces would have to merge. As long as there is *any* difference between the knower and object known, there cannot be "absolute" knowing (for there is still a "potential" knowing that has yet to be "actualized"). Yet if Hegel is right in the way he describes what absolute knowing would look like, then the goal of absolute *adaequatio*—or "full presence to consciousness"— turns out to be not merely a false dream but one that makes little sense.[32] If I were to know God truly "adequately," God would no longer be God and I would no longer be me.

Now that I have sketched out the philosophical ideal of *adaequatio,*

---

[31]Georg Wilhelm Friedrich Hegel, *Phenomenology of Spirit*, trans. A. V. Miller (Oxford: Oxford University Press, 1977), §80.

[32]Of course, given that Hegel spends a scant fifteen pages on absolute knowing in his massive *Phenomenology*, this vision proves to be merely a distant ideal. Knowing in the here and now is quite different. "Truth" for Hegel may *ultimately* prove to be static, but at the moment it is in flux. Such is likewise the case for knowledge.

it is not inappropriate to ask, just how much have philosophers *really* claimed a kind of adequation between their knowledge and the world? That depends on the philosopher or particular school of philosophy. Certainly not all philosophers have made claims of an absolute *adaequatio*. In the following chapter we shall turn to Socrates' own disclaimers concerning the success of his project.

Yet the history of Western philosophy is undoubtedly the history of relatively extravagant claims. Philosophers have often claimed to have given us an "adequate" picture of "the way things truly are." From what we have seen, though, such cannot possibly be the case. At best, they are able to give us a view of the world that is only partially "adequate." At worst, they have sometimes given us a picture of reality that is significantly skewed by their own interpretation and perspective. If philosophers were to add the disclaimer "Here is just a picture of the world as I see it, from my limited perspective," then there would be no problem. The claims become idolatrous when philosophers set themselves up as the ultimate adjudicators of what counts as true reality. This is a position that only God rightly has.

Of course Christian theologians have often been only a *little* less arrogant in their claims about God and who he is. A particularly poignant example is the project of theodicy, in which some theologians (and philosophers) have attempted to provide detailed reasons why God allows evil. But the extent to which we can "know" the mind of God is—to say the least—limited.[33]

Yet how do we come to see idols for what they truly are? Nietzsche suggests that they need to be "sounded out."

The Hammer of the Postmoderns

In the foreword to *Twilight of the Idols,* Nietzsche tells us that his personal motto is *"increscunt animi, virescit volnere virtus,"* which can be translated as "The spirit increases and strength is made whole through wounding" (*TI,* foreword). The "wounds" are ones that we receive, and their "curative power" (as Nietzsche describes it) is that they force us to become stronger. We shall shortly return to the curative power of wounding. For the moment, though, note what Nietzsche goes on to say:

---

[33]That God himself (in Job 38) seems to feel no compunction to reveal his mind to Job must be kept in mind.

Another way to recover, which under certain circumstances I like even better, is *sounding out idols*. . . . There are more idols than realities in the world. . . . To pose questions here with a *hammer* for once, and maybe to hear in reply that well-known hollow tone which tells of bloated innards—how delightful for one who has ears even behind his ears . . . in whose presence precisely what would like to stay quiet *has to speak up*. (*TI*, foreword)

One must read this passage in light of Nietzsche's subtitle for *Twilight of the Idols—How to Philosophize with a Hammer*. Given Nietzsche's penchant for trenchant criticism, it might be thought that the hammer here is a literal hammer for smashing idols to bits. Admittedly, there are times when such seems to be the effect of Nietzsche's acerbic prose. Yet his "hammer" is much more subtle. It is a tuning hammer, used to check whether our so-called realities ring true, or whether they have a "hollow sound" demonstrating that they are mere idols.

Musical metaphors are not uncommon in Nietzsche's writings, though it is not always clear how one should take them. If idols have a hollow "ringing" tone, then true realities must "ring" with a kind of solid thud. It seems that both a consonance and a dissonance are at work here. Between us and our idols is a consonance, since they are formed in our image. By nature, our idols do not create a sense of dissonance in us but simply reinforce our feelings of harmony. Of course, it is a false and misleading sort of harmony. In contrast, when the tuning fork sounds out an idol, it creates disharmony of two sorts: between itself and the idol and between the idol and ourselves. The perceived consonance between our selves and our idols is disturbed.

One might assume that Nietzsche's goal is an ultimate sense of harmony, but I take it that Nietzsche is attempting to put into question the very ideal of harmony. From his perspective, virtually all of the history of Western philosophy has been an attempt to arrive at harmony. But that harmony has generally been—thinks Nietzsche—at the expense of distortion of the phenomena that philosophy claims to explain. Our relation to phenomena that are genuinely "other" is *not* simply "harmonious," unless we distort them in order to arrive at some kind of false consonance.

What exactly does Nietzsche mean by a deceptive conceptual consonance? On Nietzsche's account, philosophers have been able to arrive at a sense of harmony by conceptualizing the world in their own image. Nietzsche takes the world to be complicated and somewhat inexplicable. Despite this (or, rather, precisely because of it) philosophers recast the world with concepts or ideas that make it seem controllable. Thus they think that they have mastered the world (or at least that mastery is possible).

Nietzsche thinks there are two "ways to recover" from this idolatry—(1) being wounded and (2) having the tuning fork sound out hollowness. While these might seem disconnected, they are actually very closely related. For Nietzsche, many of our cherished theories about the world are really just reflections of ourselves, rather than actually telling us how the world really is. Since these theories are actually idols, to have them shown to be false is to have oneself wounded. We *hurt* when our idols are found out, for criticism of our idols is implicit criticism of ourselves. Since idols reflect us, when they are shown to be frauds, *we* are shown to be frauds. Once we realize that our idols are a sham, we are forced to own up to our self-deception. But such admissions are painful.

Nietzsche's hammer both "wounds" and "sounds out." It calls both philosophical and religious beliefs into question. And that calling into question is one of the principal reasons why Nietzsche's thought is often termed "postmodern." Yet in what sense is Nietzsche—as well as the other figures discussed in this book—"postmodern"?

Over the past couple of decades a great deal has been written on "postmodernism" by both its proponents and its detractors. As far as I can see, there really isn't anything that can be properly labeled "postmodern-*ism*." Jean-Paul Sartre's complaint over a half-century ago that the term *existentialism* had been applied so liberally that it was no longer meaningful could equally be said of the label *postmodernism* today. Moreover, any kind of "ism" would seem to require at least some basic tenets to which its adherents subscribe. Yet postmodern thought—by nature and by design—tends to reject clear tenets and resists categories.

At best, there is a multitude of postmodernisms linked by family resemblances. Thus we are better off speaking of "postmodernity" or the "post" condition. Of course even those terms assume a kind of discontinuity between "modern" and "postmodern" thought that is sometimes exaggerated. Most "reactionary" movements take the form of a simultaneous continuation and rejection of the past, and postmodernity is no exception. It both continues the modern project—at least in certain ways—and calls it into question. Thus it is difficult to draw a clear line between postmodern and modern philosophy, or between postmodern philosophy and the very project of philosophy itself. "Moderns" often have "postmodern" aspects to their thought—and "postmoderns" never *simply* repudiate modernity, however much they may question it. Moreover, neither the history of Western philosophy in general nor that of modern philosophy in particular represents a clearly unified body of thought. For instance, there are significant differences among such "modern" philosophers as Descartes, Locke, Hume, Spinoza and Kant. So the shape of any given postmodern philosophy is strongly dependent on the particular modern philosopher or concepts to which it reacts.

All of this should caution us against thinking of modernity and postmodernity as simple and discrete categories. But in the same way that historians make distinctions between medieval and renaissance periods (all the while knowing that—to the average peasant—the distinction probably didn't make a great deal of difference), so philosophers can indeed make some broad generalizations regarding the different outlooks of modernity and postmodernity. If there is anything that unites postmodern thinkers, it is their reaction to the story of modernity, which is to say the story of the Enlightenment. As we will see in the following chapter, for Nietzsche the Enlightenment story is really just a continuation of the story of Western philosophy in general, but there are some particularly pronounced tendencies of modern thinking.

We might characterize the "standard" history of modernity roughly as follows:

1. Modern thinkers place a great emphasis on the autonomy of the individual. They assume that human beings both are and ought to be free to define themselves. A general result of this emphasis is that modernity is often characterized by a repudiation (or at least a suspicion) of tradition and authority.

2. Modern thought is usually characterized by a strong confidence in the powers of human reason in general and the rationality of the individual. Moderns tend to assume that reason is capable—at least in time—of solving most significant problems.

3. Reason is usually taken to be pure and objective. One might not always reason in an objective way, but objective reason is taken as an achievable goal. Thus moderns assume that what we call "reason" has been (and will continue to be) the same for all eras, places and cultures.

To see how these tendencies get worked out practically, let us briefly consider two examples, René Descartes (1596-1650) and Immanuel Kant (1724-1804). Each of them displays distinctly "modern" traits, yet each exhibits certain aspects that might be termed postmodern.

As the so-called father of modern philosophy, René Descartes seems distinctly modern. As a young man, Descartes came to wonder about the certainty of all that he had been taught. Descartes begins the first of his *Meditations* by saying, "Some years ago I was struck by the large number of falsehoods that I had accepted as true in my childhood, and by the highly doubtful nature of the whole edifice that I had subsequently based on them."[34] We have all had the painful experience of discovering that certain ideas we held as children turn out not to be true. Understandably, Descartes decides that it is high time to be clear as to what he can and cannot believe. He decides to put everything to into question, "to demolish everything completely and start again right from the foundations."[35] As admirable as that move is (at least in some respects), there is a catch. Not only is he no longer content to take things on faith, demanding that his beliefs should instead be turned into knowledge, he wants to get rid of "everything" that he currently believes. But can he really do that? In any case, during the course of his thoughts (specifically the second meditation), Descartes comes to realize that at least one thing is certain: he is doubting. Reasoning that doubting equals thinking and thinking requires a thinker, he becomes convinced that he (defined as "a thing that thinks")[36] exists. Thus he comes up with the famous formula *cogito ergo sum*. In effect, his own self becomes the foundation of his "proof."

Despite the fact that this interpretation of Descartes's *Meditations* has been highly influential in the history of Western philosophy (and not without some warrant), it is complicated by at least two aspects (which one might be tempted to term *postmodern*) found in the third meditation. First, having been convinced of his proof in meditation two, Descartes now recognizes that his proof was possible only because of what he calls "the natural light"—reason. So his proof is not ultimately based on himself but on something outside him. Thus Descartes's certainty depends on the reliability of reason. But there is no way for Descartes to

---

[34]René Descartes, *The Philosophical Writings of Descartes*, trans. John Cottingham et al. (Cambridge: Cambridge University Press, 1984), 2:12.
[35]Ibid.
[36]Ibid, p. 19.

prove that his reason is reliable—no way to "ground" his reason. Reason may tell him that he should assent only to what is "completely certain and indubitable," but there is no way that that principle *itself* can be shown to be "completely certain and indubitable."[37] It is simply something that he has been given by the natural light. And that lack of grounds sounds remarkably postmodern.

Second, Descartes gives us an argument for God's existence that calls also into question the idea that he himself is the foundation of his system. Descartes notes that he conceives of God as One that is "infinite, external, immutable, independent, supremely intelligent, supremely powerful, and which created both myself and everything else."[38] Since he himself is characterized by none of those qualities, then he could not have created this idea. Reasoning that the cause must be proportional to the effect, Descartes concludes that there really must be an infinite being. Although it is true that this idea of God is found *within* Descartes's consciousness, it is an idea that *exceeds* his consciousness. Descartes admits that "my perception of the infinite, that is God, is in some way prior to my perception of the finite, that is myself."[39] So both reason and God end up being beyond Descartes's mastery.

Immanuel Kant's story is somewhat similar. Making the self the ultimate adjudicator of truth is central in what might be termed the "modernist manifesto"—Kant's essay "What Is Enlightenment?" It too is a story about growing up. In saying that the motto of the Enlightenment is *Sapere aude,* a quotation from Horace that could be loosely translated into English as "Be bold enough to think for yourself," Kant makes it clear that the mature person is the one who stands on one's own. Kant defines immaturity as "the inability to use one's own understanding without the guidance of another."[40] Sounding somewhat like Descartes, Kant says that one ought to be a rational agent who defines oneself and decides for oneself. Although one might get advice from others (and Kant gives examples of advice from one's doctor and one's pastor), one should not simply follow their advice but instead make one's own decision.

---

[37]Ibid., p. 12.

[38]Ibid., p. 31. "Eternal" and "immutable" do not appear in the original Latin text.

[39]Ibid.

[40]Immanuel Kant, "An Answer to the Question: 'What Is Enlightenment?'" in *Kant's Political Writings,* ed. Hans Reiss, trans. H. B. Nisbet, 2nd ed. (Cambridge: Cambridge University Press, 1970), p. 54.

Kant emphasizes the freedom of the individual in the Second Critique *(Critique of Practical Reason)*. On Kant's reading, human beings are truly free to make spontaneous choices. But being "free" for Kant does not mean simply doing anything we wish; rather we are free when our rational will is the sole source of our action. Thus Kant speaks of having a pure or *autonomous* will, as opposed to an impure or *heteronomous* will.[41] In *The Metaphysics of Morals* Kant defines this freedom of the will as self-determination, in which the moral guideline is "the law of *your* own will and not of will in general, which could be the will of others."[42] Similarly, Kant's conception of the artistic genius (as opposed to the mere "imitator") in the Third Critique *(Critique of Judgment)* likewise emphasizes freedom of the individual.[43] However, Kant introduces a complication in this text that is surprising—the communal notion of taste. True, Kant once again reminds us of the maxim "think for oneself." But he also points out that if genius and taste are at odds, then genius needs to give way. So even the genius cannot be an unfettered individual.[44]

Yet, despite Kant's high expectations for reason and what it can accomplish, the *Critique of Pure Reason* (the First Critique) places *limits* on reason. Kant argues that if reason attempts to say much about metaphysics, it ends up postulating contradictory positions. Thus Kant thinks that reason can equally lead to the view that the world is limited or the world is infinite, that freedom exists or that no freedom exists, that God exists or that God does not exist. Reason can go only so far, at least in regard to metaphysical judgments. The only solution here, according to Kant, is to limit what reason attempts to answer. Interestingly enough, the result of Kant's rather severe limitations on metaphysical knowledge is the creation of a different sort of space. As he puts it, "I have therefore found it necessary to deny *knowledge,* in order to make room for *faith.*"[45]

There is a further way in which Kant significantly alters the status of

---

[41]Immanuel Kant, *Critique of Practical Reason,* trans. Mary Gregor (Cambridge: Cambridge University Press, 1997), p. 38.

[42]Immanuel Kant, *The Metaphysics of Morals,* trans. Mary Gregor (Cambridge: Cambridge University Press, 1991), p. 152.

[43]See the sections on the genius in Immanuel Kant, *Critique of Judgment,* trans. Werner S. Pluhar (Indianapolis: Hackett, 1987), §§46-49.

[44]Ibid., §§40, 50.

[45]Immanuel Kant, *Critique of Pure Reason,* trans. Norman Kemp Smith (London: Macmillan, 1929), B XXX (Kant's emphasis). Of course Kant's conception of Christian faith would not be recognized by most Christian believers.

reason. He is firmly committed to the idea that reason is "objective": while Kant thinks that each of us ought to depend on our *own* reason, he assumes that reason itself is universal. Thus thinking for oneself should yield not merely similar but identical results among rational beings. But Kant thinks that the objectivity of reason actually is dependent not on the world but rather on *us* as rational beings. We might say that objectivity for Kant is grounded in subjectivity: because all of us see the world in a particular way, knowledge is objective. Yet it is not hard to see that guaranteeing objectivity by way of the subject clearly opens the door to postmodern thinking. For what if we *don't* all see the world in exactly the same way? For Kant—who never traveled much beyond the boundaries of his hometown—such a possibility was unthinkable.

Postmoderns agree that the first characteristic of modernity—the ideal of "thinking for oneself" or insisting on "grounding" one's beliefs—is problematic. While the ideal of examining one's beliefs and owning them personally is still recognized by most postmoderns as a good and valuable goal, the extent to which one can think fully on one's own is open to question. Whereas Descartes thought discarding all previous knowledge could be accomplished, postmoderns generally recognize that thought can never function without *presuppositions*. And Descartes himself realizes his dependence on the natural light. If thinking can never simply begin afresh, then even the goal of examining one's presuppositions can be realized to only a limited extent. Although Descartes claims to question everything taught him by tradition, he never seriously questions either the power or the purity of his own reasoning. Descartes simply takes it as given that reason is trustworthy. From the perspective of most postmodern thinkers, such a move is complicated. While it may be legitimate for Descartes to trust his reason, postmoderns would point out that such an assumption can at the very least be questioned. Indeed a basic postmodern problem is precisely *how* one can determine that a particular way of thinking truly counts as "rational" (and that others are "irrational" or inferior). Ultimately one must begin with certain presuppositions, and these can only be accepted on something like faith (or whatever one chooses to call it).

Thus Descartes's "proof" is actually based on faith. Whether he is right in making this move is beside the point. What is important is that he *assumes* the reliability of reason, despite the fact that he claims to have no assumptions.

Despite these complications, Descartes's project is usually considered to be an example of "foundationalism." In its strongest sense, foundationalism is the ideal of achieving complete epistemological certainty by providing a ground or "foundation" for one's thought. Interestingly enough, although Descartes's grounding at first seems to be himself, it actually ends up being reason—which he cannot ground. There are, of course, a variety of weaker senses of foundationalism, in which one attempts to provide *some* sort of basis for one's belief.

A second aspect that postmoderns question is the modern confidence in reason. There is no reason—logically—to think that reason will be successful at every junction, that no answers will elude its grasp. Moreover, whereas it once seemed possible that the world could be fully explained by science, that prospect seems highly unlikely today. Certainly the last three centuries have not produced a "rational" answer to all questions, so there is good empirical evidence for questioning reason's prospects. Postmoderns are generally agreed that reason has limitations, though they vary widely regarding how significant those limitations are.

Finally, the modern idea of the objectivity of reason has come under increasing criticism from various quarters. As a kind of example, although Kant thought it was possible to arrive at a moral theory that would be "purely" rational (based solely on rational principles), the ideal of a morality that has no religious basis and to which all rational people can agree seems increasingly questionable. Perhaps there are still moral ideals that many people do or should share, but it seems unlikely that these can be defended on a strictly "rational" basis.

For postmoderns, there is no conception of rationality that automatically wins the day. Even natural science—which would seem to be about as "objective" as anything—works with certain presuppositions that cannot be fully justified. More important for our concern here, postmoderns question whether the modern conception of "reason" can be justified. Under the modern paradigm, certain things counted as reason—basically, whatever could be justified by the modern scientific method. That meant that everything else was dismissed as "feeling" or "faith" or "superstition." But these categories are no longer so clear, nor is it obvious that reason is necessarily superior to faith. Of course, just how much reason is lacking in "objectivity" is a question that is answered quite differently by postmodern thinkers.

The ideal of rational autonomy and purity—whether worked out by Descartes or by Kant—can be linked to the problem of idolatry. At the very least, the attempt to keep one's reason untainted by any outside influence is a *possible* recipe for idolatry. For is not idolatry likely to result when we lean to our own understanding? Indeed how can we help but construct ideas and concepts made in our image in such a case? And if we are unwilling to hear the voice of something outside of us, are we not likely to continue on in our idolatrous ways?

There is a further problem: to what extent is foundationalism *itself* a kind of idolatry? Assuming that Descartes's foundationalism (or rather the usual interpretation of Descartes), in which the self becomes the foundation, is paradigmatic for the project of foundationalism in general, it would seem that foundationalism tends toward idolatry. Why so? To place oneself in the role of "foundation" is in effect to make oneself out to be God. If *I* am the end of the chain of reason, then there is no room left for God. As we shall see, Nietzsche argues against foundationalism in a very similar way. In fact, Nietzsche goes so far as to say that all attempts at foundationalism turn out to be "nihilistic." Both Derrida and Marion will echo these sorts of criticisms.

Jesus the Deconstructor

While it is true that the postmoderns themselves succumb to idolatry (as shall become clear), they are often particularly adept at identifying—and scathingly criticizing—idols created by both philosophers and theologians. Since Christians are likewise concerned about idolatry, the postmoderns' critique can be helpful in sorting out the true from the false. In fact I think the postmoderns often follow a pattern of idol detection that can be found in Jesus' own teaching.

Perhaps the central charge that Jesus lays against the Pharisees and scribes in Matthew 15 is that they are guilty of idolatry. While for many of us *Pharisee* has become a word of opprobrium, we must not forget that Pharisees were exemplary moral followers of Jewish laws, what we are likely to term "good people."[46] Thus Jesus should not be read as giving

---

[46]The question "Just how bad really were the Pharisees and scribes?" has been a subject of much recent debate. See, for instance, Bruce Chilton and Jacob Neusner, *Judaism in the New Testament: Practices and Beliefs* (London: Routledge, 1995). Whatever one decides on the matter, however, Jesus clearly thinks that they are—at least in this instance—guilty of idolatry.

anything like a blanket condemnation of them. Yet Jesus does take particular doctrines of theirs and shows how they end up being idolatrous. A good example of what I call Jesus the Deconstructor is the following:

> Then Pharisees and scribes came to Jesus from Jerusalem and said, "Why do your disciples break the tradition of the elders? For they do not wash their hands before they eat." He answered them, "And why do you break the commandment of God for the sake of your tradition? For God said, 'Honor your father and your mother,' and, 'Whoever speaks evil of father or mother must surely die.' But you say that whoever tells father or mother, 'Whatever support you might have had from me is given to God,' then that person need not honor the father. So, for the sake of your tradition, you make void the word of God. You hypocrites! Isaiah prophesied rightly about you when he said:
>
> 'This people honors me with their lips,
>   but their hearts are far from me;
> in vain do they worship me,
>   teaching human precepts as doctrines.' " (Mt 15:1-9)

Like deconstruction, Jesus' criticism takes apart and destroys. Deconstruction will be considered further in the chapter on Derrida, but for now Jesus' deconstruction can be characterized as follows. Deconstruction involves taking something apart very carefully in order to investigate its components. The reason for the careful examination is both that (1) we are apt to pass over that which is familiar precisely because of its familiarity[47] and (2) many times important aspects of a given idea of belief—aspects that may be foundational for the thinking contained therein—are not obvious and may even be suppressed (not infrequently for underhanded reasons). The very careful taking apart of deconstruction can have (though it does not always have) the effect of exposing something as a sham and, in so doing, destroying it. A natural effect of showing something to be questionable is that people will be less likely to believe it. This is what Jesus does here. He pries apart the system of doctrine that the Pharisees and scribes have set up, showing their error and their true motivation.

There are at least two steps in Jesus' criticism that the Pharisees and scribes have nullified God's commands. Step one: the Pharisees and

---

[47]Martin Heidegger points out that what is most familiar is often most easily overlooked. See *BT*, chap. 1.

scribes put forth the claim "If one gives to God whatever one would normally owe to one's parents, then one owes nothing to one's parents." Step two: they make the further claim (either implicitly or explicitly) that this claim comes not from them but from God (they put forth "human precepts as doctrines"). The problem is that the Pharisees and scribes are in effect claiming more than they are entitled to claim. Not only do they make a rule for which they have no support, they teach that rule as "doctrine." Jesus makes the sharp distinction between their "tradition" and God's Word, accusing them of claiming the status of the latter for the former. Their sin is both metaphysical and epistemological in nature: they invent an untruth (which they claim is really from God) and then claim to "know" it.

Jesus describes them by the term *hypokritēs,* which translates into English as "hypocrite." The two most obvious ways they are guilty of hypocrisy is by their placing a heavy burden of laws on others (even though they themselves do not follow those laws) and by claiming to honor God in their speech but not doing so in their hearts. In both cases, they say one thing and act differently. But at the root of these hypocrisies is a third sort, one far less obvious yet far more dangerous. *hypokrisis* was the verb used by the Greeks to denote acting on the stage. Normally the actor—the *hypokritēs*—spoke using a device to enhance his voice and wore a mask large enough to obscure his face. Thus a *hypokritēs* was someone pretending to be someone else. Although the Pharisees and scribes do not claim to be God in so many words, they do so by inventing a tradition and then ascribing it to God. It is a tradition that reflects *their* minds more than the mind of God. They are—indirectly—guilty of idolatry, for they speak as if they had taken on the persona of God. Thus their idolatry is not merely the act of placing a "something" in God's place: since that something is actually a reflection of themselves, they effectively put *themselves* in place of God. We might say that the Pharisees too are guilty of "vain philosophy." Their way of thinking is the product of their own human traditions.

Not only does Jesus point out that the Pharisees and scribes have fallen into the error of idolatry, he also reveals their selfish motives. Rather than having a pure concern for truth, Jesus claims that they act "for the sake of [their] tradition." There is nothing inherently wrong, of course, with human tradition. What is wrong here is that (1) it is at odds with God's Word, (2) the Pharisees have chosen to suppress God's clear command in favor of their own tradition and (3) they are claiming their tradition to be that of God. In other words, according to them it is not a "tradition"; it is "the Word of God." This is not surprising: a typical characteristic of idolatry is denial of the "situatedness" of moral claims. One postulates a particular moral prohibition and then claims that it has come from God. Just as the Pharisees seem almost unaware of that fact, so we too often think that our moral ideas are those of God.

Finally, the reason the Pharisees have done this is relatively simple (and often repeated): by promoting their own tradition, they further their own ends. It is in their best interests for them to claim the honor due mother and father, in the same way that it sometimes behooves Christian institutions to claim the devotion normally given to one's family.

The call implicit in Jesus' deconstruction is that "anyone with ears to hear" (Lk 8:8)—or as Nietzsche puts it, "one who has ears even behind his ears" (*TI*, foreword)—should take heed. As we shall see in the following chapters, there is much to heed.

1

THE IDOL
OF PHILOSOPHY

Nietzsche's text in which he most clearly targets idols—*Twilight of the Idols (Götzendämmerung)*—is obviously meant as a play on Richard Wagner's opera *Twilight of the Gods (Götterdämmerung)*. Ostensibly their topics differ, since Wagner's opera is about the demise of pagan gods and Nietzsche's book is about the demise of idols. But if we take pagan gods to be idols created in our image, then their topics seem remarkably similar. Both are concerned with what we worship, though Nietzsche wishes to point out that our worship is in vain, in all of the senses of "vain" discussed in the introduction.

While it will hardly come as a surprise that Nietzsche attacks Christianity, it may be somewhat surprising that he attacks philosophy and Platonism even more vehemently. Of course on Nietzsche's read, Christianity is merely a variation on Platonism, and so all the charges that he lays against Platonism are likewise charges against Christianity. That leaves Christians in an interesting position. They can accept Nietzsche's equation of the two and thus be forced to rebut both Nietzsche's criticism of Platonism and his criticism of Christianity. Or they can argue that Christianity is not simply a subspecies of Platonism and thus does not necessarily fall victim to Nietzsche's charges against Platonism. I will take the latter course. Later sections of this chapter will look at Nietzsche's charges against Christianity. In these first sections, though, we consider his quarrel with philosophy in general and Platonism in particular.

Lying About "Truth"

One of the most important sections in *Twilight of the Idols* (perhaps the most important) is titled "How the 'True World' Finally Became a Fiction." Nietzsche gives us six stages of the rise and fall of the "true world," with the first two stages—Platonism and Christianity—clearly the most significant for him. Why is Nietzsche so adamantly against the notion of the "true world"? Further, why does he attack such philosophical values as truth, knowledge, rationality and systematizing—all of which he thinks the notion of the "true world" exemplifies? Briefly put, Nietzsche thinks that the real reasons for the postulation of the "true world" are hubris, lack of integrity and decadence.

Let's start with hubris. From Nietzsche's point of view, Plato is the quintessential pretentious philosopher who makes claims that are clearly impossible for human beings to substantiate. In the preface to *Beyond Good and Evil* Nietzsche criticizes Plato for being the ultimate *dogmatic* philosopher. What makes Plato's thought "dogmatic"? On Nietzsche's read, Plato claims something (the Forms) for which he has inadequate support—more accurately, simply *no* support. Nietzsche thinks that Plato cannot provide any real argument for their existence; rather he simply assumes their existence. So Plato is claiming to know something that he does not and could not in principle ever know. Although Socrates would seem to be a determined opponent of dogmatism of any kind, Nietzsche thinks that Plato (along with Socrates) sneaks it in the back door.

It would not be too much to say that Nietzsche sees Plato's postulation of the Forms as idolatrous much as Jesus takes the move of the Pharisees and scribes to be idolatrous. Each case involves a move to exalt a human perspective and make it into God's perspective. Nietzsche thinks that the very claim of "knowledge"—and here he is clearly referring to the ancient Greek notion of *epistēmē*—is motivated by hubris. One might say that knowledge claims for Nietzsche are inherently ideological. As he says, "In some remote corner of the universe, poured out and glittering in innumerable solar systems, there once was a star on which clever animals invented knowledge. That was the haughtiest and most mendacious minute of 'world history'— yet only a minute."[1]

On Nietzsche's read, philosophers have "invented" such notions as "knowledge," "truth" and the "true world" not out of a pure love of wisdom and truth but out of a love of themselves. They exalt themselves by making claims to possess wisdom and truth, and thus they are able to assert themselves over everyone else by way of their ideologies. From Nietzsche's perspective, these turn out to be idols of Plato's making. What philosophers call "truth" is simply (on Nietzsche's account) "a mobile army of metaphors, metonyms, and anthropomorphisms."[2] Elsewhere Nietzsche says, "You want to create the world before which you can kneel: that is your ultimate hope and intoxication" (*Z,* "Of Self-Overcoming"). Yet if these idols reflect us, then we are actually worshiping ourselves.

As it turns out, Nietzsche thinks Plato did not actually *believe* in the Forms but only invented them to foist on others. Thus Plato was a liar who told lies to make himself (and philosophers in general) look good and gain a superior place in society. As Nietzsche puts it, "The 'true world' is just *added to it* [the apparent world] *by a lie"* (*TI,* " 'Reason' in Philosophy," Nietzsche's emphasis).

Nietzsche has little textual evidence to support this claim, so it is hard to say whether Nietzsche is right. Nietzsche's view on this point is, to say the least, unusual. On the other hand, were it actually true that Plato was simply burdening others with his philosophy and didn't believe it himself, one could hardly expect to find evidence in Plato. And it is true that Plato advocated lying in certain cases. In *Republic* Plato claims that the only way to make society run is to tell those of the lower classes that fate has destined them for this position. This is very clearly a lie, and Plato admits it, referring to it as a "noble lie."[3] It is justified for the good of society—so the end justifies the means.

While Plato never admits that the story of the Forms is a lie, Nietzsche still thinks it is. Of course on Nietzsche's view one often lies *to oneself,*

---

[1]Friedrich Nietzsche, "On Truth and Lie in an Extra-moral Sense," in *The Portable Nietzsche,* ed. Walter Kaufmann (New York: Viking, 1954), p. 42.

[2]Ibid., p. 46.

[3]Plato *Republic* 414b-c.

so Nietzsche may think that Plato himself didn't know he was lying. Note how Nietzsche defines a "lie":

> I call a lie: wanting *not* to see something one does see, wanting not to see something *as* one sees it; whether the lie takes place before witnesses or without witnesses is of no consequence. The most common lie is the lie one tells to oneself; lying to others is relatively the exception. (*A* 55)

So Plato may have deceived even himself. But even if Plato thought he was telling the truth, there can be no question that the invention of the Forms was clearly in his best interest. Plato claims that the problem with poets is that they lie and thus cannot be trusted. Philosophers, on the other hand, are those who know the truth (because they know the Forms) and tell it honestly. Thus Plato claims that the king of the republic should be chosen from the ranks of philosophers. And it just so happens that Plato himself is a philosopher. It's hard to imagine a more self-serving argument. No wonder that Plato also refers to the "noble lie" used to justify the social hierarchy as an "opportune falsehood." Of course one does not have to believe an ideology in order to propagate it.

Just how guilty of self-aggrandizing Plato is, though, is open to question. Perhaps Plato should not be taken to be quite the dogmatist that Nietzsche claims him to be. One can argue that at least Socrates is somewhat modest. He clearly has a robust sense of human ability to know; but he seems to see *himself* as ever on the way and never in possession of true knowledge. While Socrates is convinced *that* there is a "true world" (a metaphysical claim), he is considerably less certain of his knowledge *of* that world (an epistemological claim). In the introduction I noted that Socrates thinks the goal of philosophizing is that we "gain direct knowledge of all that is pure and uncontaminated—that is, presumably, of truth *[alētheia]*."[4] Note that Socrates adds the qualifier *presumably* when he speaks of attaining the truth. It is even more instructive that Socrates (a bit earlier in the dialogue) speaks of "the person who is *likely to succeed* in this attempt most perfectly." Obviously Socrates thinks that there are going to be varying degrees of success in this enterprise. And the fact that he labels it an "attempt" would seem to lower expectations.

At stake here is exactly what Socrates claims for philosophy. The ideal Socrates gives us is pure *adaequatio;* that is clearly the dream. But

---

[4]Plato *Phaedo* 67b.

just how far does Socrates think philosophy can (adequately) go in reaching such a dream? That depends on the degree to which he takes philosophy to be, properly speaking, a *technē*. For the Greeks, a *technē* is a craft (or art) that has a specified set of procedures and produces a defined product. If philosophy truly counts as a *technē* for Socrates, then we have to read his dialectical reasoning as being put forth as the "way" *(poros)* to Truth. While Plato scholars today debate whether Socrates claims that philosophy has the status of a *technē,* their discussion is largely over *how* short of the ideal philosophy falls.[5] As it turns out, the Socratic dialectic seems to be less like a true *technē* and more what the Greeks termed an *elenchus*—that is, a questioning, inquiring or examining that clarifies and enlightens but does not necessarily provide a final answer.

Even if Socrates *does* envision philosophy as at least promising full knowledge, one thing is clear: Socrates never actually delivers the goods. In fact it is in Socrates' own attempts at attaining the truth that the limits of philosophy emerge most pointedly, for he often ends up in *aporia*. Literally, *aporia* is *a-poros,* the loss of one's way or the lack of transport. Metaphorically, *aporia* is a state of confusion or perplexity.[6] Socrates often finds himself in this state. At one point, for instance, he admits that he simply does not know: "The fact is that I am inquiring with you into the truth of that which is advanced from time to time, just because I do not know, and when I have inquired, I will say whether I agree with you or not."[7] Further, in some dialogues not only are his interlocutors perplexed, but he seems perplexed himself. At the end of one dialogue, immediately after his interlocutor has said that he is unable to bring himself to agree with Socrates, he says, "Nor can I agree with myself, Hippias, and yet that seems to be the conclusion which, as far as we can see at present, must follow from our argument. As I was saying before, I am all abroad, and being in perplexity am always changing my opinion."[8] Similarly, Socrates responds to Meno's charge

---

[5]Although the accounts of Martha Nussbaum and Gregory Vlastos are the best known, probably the most nuanced and complete study of Plato's conception of *technē* is David Roochnik's *Of Art and Wisdom: Plato's Understanding of Techne* (University Park: Pennsylvania Sate University Press, 1996).

[6]The Evangelist Luke speaks of people in the end times as being in *aporia* (perplexed) by cataclysmic changes. Cf. Luke 21:25.

[7]Plato *Charmides* 165b.

[8]Plato *Lesser Hippias* 376b-c.

that Socrates is like a stingray that confuses its prey by saying, "It isn't that, knowing the answers myself, I perplex other people. The truth is rather that I infect them also with the perplexity I feel myself. So with virtue now. I don't know what it is."[9]

These admissions of lack of knowledge cannot very well be explained away simply by arguing that Socrates employs a "method" of feigning ignorance in order to help his hearers come to the truth. Rather Socrates seems to be stating what truly is the case: he does *not* know. As Socrates puts it, "Of myself I have no sort of wisdom."[10]

But even if this more moderate interpretation is true, there is still the problem of the postulation of the Forms. Maybe Socrates is humble enough to admit that he does not actually possess anything like full knowledge of the Forms, but he clearly thinks he has enough knowledge to know that they exist. He also seems to claim that through philosophical dialectic the philosopher is capable of coming into contact with the Forms and even knowing them completely. Yet does he really *know* this to be the case? What evidence does he really have? Would it not be more accurate for Socrates to say he *believes* that the Forms exist? If such were Socrates' claim, then it would be a claim of faith, not of knowledge.

Note that there is nothing wrong—at least in principle—with holding to dogma. If one holds a particular belief and admits that one has inadequate support, then one is being honest about the belief. We can say that such a person is not really being "dogmatic" at all. For dogmatism—at least in its pejorative sense—is the inability to recognize one's view as "dogmatic." If we can rightly characterize "dogmatism" as "positiveness of assertion of opinion especially when based on insufficiently examined premises,"[11] then the problem is the lack of adequation between the force with which the view is held and the force of underpinning.

What bothers Nietzsche is that Plato puts forth the theory of the Forms as a knowledge *(epistēmē)* claim, not as a belief *(doxa)* or faith *(pistis)* claim. Though Plato seems confident that he knows the Forms exist, he never really provides a justification for them. Interestingly enough, Nietzsche likewise doesn't really give us any real evidence

[9]Plato *Meno* 80c.
[10]Plato *Thaetetus* 150d.
[11]*Merriam Webster's Collegiate Dictionary*, 10th ed. (Springfield, Mass.: Merriam-Webster, 1994), s.v. "dogmatism."

against the Forms. So in one sense, Nietzsche and Plato aren't really that different after all. However, I take it that Nietzsche would justify his lack of argumentation for his denial of the Forms simply by appealing to Plato's lack of justification for the Forms (of course Nietzsche doesn't provide any such justification for his lack of justification). Moreover, Nietzsche is not dogmatic in the sense that Plato is, for Plato does not seem to realize that his claims concerning the Forms cannot be given a true foundation. In contrast, Nietzsche is well aware that his claims are in this situation. Thus Nietzsche may be read as against dogmatism but in favor of faith *(pistis)*. His claims are truly "faith-based"—and he is well aware of that.

Nietzsche's criticism of Plato raises a basic question about the entire philosophical enterprise. Historically, philosophers have not been among the most modest of people. The problem with searching for wisdom is that though one may indeed find it, one may not always be wise enough to see where that wisdom ends and one's own inventiveness begins. What one takes to be pure, unadulterated wisdom may instead be an adulterated mixture of true wisdom and sham wisdom. This sham wisdom can properly be termed "vain philosophy."

As Aristotle tells us at the beginning of his *Metaphysics,* "All men by nature desire to know."[12] On a Christian account, that desire to know is God-given and in itself is good and noble. Yet this desire can tempt us to make claims in vain in at least two ways. First, they may be vain in the sense of being empty—that is, they correspond to nothing. Second, they may be vain in that their real source is the desire to exalt ourselves and our own abilities. Such claims are rooted in nothing other than our vanity, for they are ultimately attempts to make ourselves out to be better than we are. We make claims to know that which we do not and perhaps even cannot know, because we have an inaccurate picture of our abilities to know.

It may be too much to say, as does Nietzsche, that philosophy "always creates the world in its own image" (*BGE* 9), but the enterprise of philosophy is clearly prone to idolatry. In the case of Plato, Nietzsche thinks he is in effect a *hypokritēs:* he pretends to speak from a point of view that is above and beyond—what we might call a God's-eye view—but his view is very much his own.

---

[12]Aristotle *Metaphysics* 980.

To assume that we know when we in reality do not is foolishness. Lack of knowledge with an accompanying *awareness* of that lack is what we might call "simple ignorance." Although we can sometimes be held culpable for such ignorance—in that we *ought* to know—ignorance is often just part of the human condition. The best way of dealing with ignorance may be simply recognizing it for what it is. But when we *think* we know and do not, then our ignorance is a "complex ignorance." That is, we are not merely ignorant but ignorant of our ignorance. Such is a pitiable state, particularly since our inability to recognize our ignorance means that it will likely persist.

More often than not, Socrates' questioning in the dialogues is designed to show his listeners that they lack knowledge, with the ultimate goal of supplying that lack. Socrates realizes that recognition of ignorance is the first step toward knowledge. As Hans-Georg Gadamer puts it: "In order to be able to ask, one must want to know, and that means knowing that one does not know."[13] Jesus affirms this truth when he says to the Pharisees, "But now that you say, 'We see,'" your sin remains" (Jn 9:41). And Paul speaks in Romans of those who profess to be wise and thereby become fools (Rom 1:22).

Idols of Simplicity, Systemism and the True World

It should be amply clear at this point why Nietzsche thinks Plato—and philosophy in general—is guilty of hubris, but what about lack of integrity? Two of Nietzsche's early aphorisms in *Twilight of the Idols* are "'All truth is simple.'—Isn't that doubly a lie?" and "I distrust all systematizers and stay out of their way. The will to a system is a lack of integrity" (both in the section "Epigrams and Arrows," 4, 6). Nietzsche is criticizing two basic philosophical assumptions. The first is the principle of simplicity, which says that (all things being equal) the simplest theory is to be preferred because it is more likely to be true. So simplicity in effect equals truth—or at least it "signals" truth. The second is the idea (quite common in German philosophy of Nietzsche's day, though less common today) that coherent systems are (again, all things being equal) more likely to be true. So coherence in effect equals truth.

What is wrong with the ideals of "simplicity" and "coherence"? Does

---

[13]Hans-Georg Gadamer, *Truth and Method,* 2nd rev. ed., trans. Joel Weinsheimer and Donald G. Marshall (New York: Crossroad, 1989), p. 363.

Nietzsche mean to suggest that we hold up complexity and incoherence as alternative ideals? Such, I think, is not Nietzsche's position.

Gilles Deleuze reads Nietzsche's comments on "systematizing" as an implicit criticism of Hegelianism and even Nietzsche's own early "Hegelian" work *The Birth of Tragedy*.[14] There is much to commend in Deleuze's reading of Nietzsche. Reflecting on *Birth of Tragedy*, Nietzsche says that it "smells offensively Hegelian" because it describes the entire history of metaphysics in terms of "a few formulas" and a basic "antithesis" (*EH*, "The Birth of Tragedy," p. 1). While Nietzsche doesn't altogether repudiate that reading, he comes to see it as quite simplistic, as something to be overcome. Indeed one can argue that Nietzsche devotes the rest of his writing career to doing just that. The problem with both simplicity and coherence, thinks Nietzsche, is that they tend to be idols created in our image, rather than some overarching characteristics of "Truth."

Why we would value simplicity shouldn't be difficult to see. A theory that is simple has a kind of beauty and elegance. Even more important, it is easy to grasp. However attractive the aspects of beauty, elegance and "graspability" may make a theory, they still don't necessarily make it *true*. If anything, as Nietzsche seems to suspect, something that we can easily grasp is *unlikely* to be true. Nietzsche's charge is that since we like these characteristics, we tend to "make" Truth in that image. In Platonism and philosophy in general, ultimate reality is postulated (on Nietzsche's account) as consisting of "the most universal, the emptiest concepts" (*TI*, "'Reason' in Philosophy," p. 4). To ensure simplicity, philosophers "mummify" those concepts. Otherwise they would be subject to change and development (and were that the case, they would inevitably become complicated rather than simple). As Nietzsche puts it, "Everything that philosophers have handled, for thousands of years now, has been conceptual mummies; nothing real escaped their hands alive. They kill and stuff whatever they worship, these gentlemen who idolize concepts—they endanger the life of whatever they worship" (*TI*, "'Reason' in Philosophy," p. 1). Nietzsche's charge is as follows: whereas real life is characterized by complexity and variability, philosophers have attempted to tame reality by reducing it to simple, unchanging essences.

---

[14]Deleuze sees Nietzsche as attempting to overcome the very movement of *Aufhebung* which characterizes all of Hegel's philosophy. See Gilles Deleuze, *Nietzsche and Philosophy*, trans. Hugh Tomlinson (New York: Columbia University Press, 1983).

Although philosophers claim to do justice to true reality by way of their theories, they ultimately dishonor it through distortion.

Thus for Nietzsche, simplicity and what we might call "systemism" tend to distort truth and reality. It is important to be clear as to Nietzsche's position on this point, in at least two respects. First, it is not clear that Nietzsche is against either the aim of simplicity or the attempt to make sense of the world by placing it into some conceptual system per se. If such *is* Nietzsche's position, then I think it cannot be taken very seriously. Human beings simply *are* characterized by a desire to figure out the world—and simplifying and systematizing are means we use (and have always used).[15] From a Christian perspective, that drive to understand—what we might call "the will to understand"—is God-given and fundamentally good. It is meet and right for us to take pains to understand God, our neighbors, the world around us and ourselves. If we fail to understand, we are likely to treat one or more of these improperly. One might argue that there is a kind of double dialectic here. First, if we fail to respond to any one of these elements correctly, we are all the more likely to respond to the others incorrectly. For example, failure to love the Lord our God properly will likely result in failing to love others and ourselves properly (and vice versa). Second, our action is strongly correlated with our thinking. If our thinking about others is wrong, then our action is likely to be as well (and to a roughly equal degree). But acting aright is also key to thinking aright. If we act improperly toward our neighbors, we are likely to misunderstand them.

Yet one can agree to some extent with Nietzsche's criticism of "systemism" without denying the possibility that there is some sort of "system" to the world or to God's thought.[16] Note that simplicity and

---

[15]Heidegger points out that "understanding" or interpreting the world is a basic feature of human existence. See *Being and Time* ¶41.

[16]It is understandable that Douglas Groothuis would cite Nietzsche's invective against systematizing and then go on to say, "But Nietzsche was wrong. As Arthur Holmes put it, 'In a universe subject to the rule of one creator-God . . . truth is seen as an interrelated and coherent whole.'" Yet Groothuis fails to make a crucial distinction. A Christian can easily (and quite rightly) agree that *God's truth* is coherent and still have significant questions about the ability of human thought to apprehend and systematize that truth *without distortion*. Or perhaps I should put it as follows: Holmes is right that "all truth is *God's* truth," rather than "all truth is *our* truth." It is when we claim the latter that we get into trouble. See Douglas Groothuis, *Truth Decay: Defending Christianity Against the Challenges of Postmodernism* (Downers Grove: InterVarsity Press, 2000), p. 80, and Arthur F. Holmes, *All Truth Is God's Truth* (Grand Rapids, Mich.: Eerdmans, 1977), p. 7.

systemism embody what Nietzsche calls the "will to truth." The problem with the will to truth for Nietzsche is not that the desire to know is wrong but that it often takes a particular form. In the introduction I discussed the tension between the phenomena and the *logos* of phenomenology. Even though the *logos* of phenomenology is supposed to arise from "the things themselves," the danger is that it is instead superimposed from outside. Such, thinks Nietzsche, is what happens in Platonism. Plato's simple and coherent conception of ultimate reality and Truth fails to do justice to the phenomenon of the world. But Plato's system of philosophy also shows a lack of integrity in that it fails to do justice to his senses. Instead of recognizing the reality of what he perceives, he dismisses it as just "shadows." So Nietzsche sees Plato as setting up idols (the Forms) to satisfy his need for systems.

The problem with "understanding" is that our tendency is to reshape the phenomena in our own image and create ideologies. In one sense, of course, we cannot help but do so. If I encounter something that is new to me, then I can make sense of it only in terms of what I already know. There is nothing wrong with this move of recasting the phenomena in order to understand. Scripture acknowledges this human tendency by describing God as "Father" and Jesus as "Shepherd." But either of these descriptions can go horribly wrong. If, for instance, when I think of God as Father, I think of the father down the street who is an alcoholic and beats his children, then I do not understand God aright. And even if I think of my own father (who beautifully characterized such fruit of the Spirit as love, kindness, faithfulness and gentleness—though I'm a bit biased on the subject), I still have to be careful of recasting God too much in that image. To simplify God to my own human father would be to *mis*understand God. And to build a system in which that image is central would demonstrate a lack of integrity, for it would fail to do justice to God. So while attempts to simplify and systematize are not in themselves "bad," both run the risk of distorting the phenomena. When they do so, they become "simplicity" and "systemism."

Far from merely criticizing philosophy, Nietzsche should be taken as criticizing systems in general. Since systems tend to become ideologies, one can easily read Nietzsche as criticizing ideologies. But one can also read Nietzsche in light of current debates on the nature and possibility of systematic theology. Again, while systems help us in making sense of the world and so can serve a very useful function, they almost always (and my guess is that an *unqualified* "always" here would probably be more accurate) do so at the expense of at least *some* distortion. Systematic theology is not inherently idolatrous, but it runs a risk of veering in that direction.[17] For any "system" of theology must—by its very nature—build on fundamental assumptions about God and his character. But those assumptions cannot but help be simplified versions of who God is and thus only partial truths.[18] If one recognizes the assumptions for what they are—simplifications that help us better understand God—then one *may* avoid idolatry. Of course, there isn't any guarantee here either. The construction of systems tends to *reinforce* rather than cause us to be more cautious about our conceptions of God. And so theological systems have at least a tendency to promote idolatry. As always, the question here is less about the *what* than the *how*.

What then of the "true world" and the very idea of "truth"? Nietzsche predicts that the last stage of the "true world" (stage six) will be the time when it is long forgotten. In place of the true world will simply be this world (and no more talk about any other worlds). In place of "truth" that is simple and ahistorical, there will be truth that is complex and changing.

Various commentators have attempted to make sense of Nietzsche's view of truth, the most exhaustive of such work being that of Maudemarie Clark, who argues that Nietzsche's view of truth changed substantially from his early to later writings.[19] Nietzsche's thought on truth probably did mature in the intervening years. But I take the attempts to "systematize" Nietzsche's thought on truth to be exemplary of precisely what he denounces—the idea that truth is "simple" and the expectation that it be "coherent." Nietzsche doesn't give us a systematic view of truth, and that omission is probably intentional. Note how Nietzsche describes truth in one of his texts:

> Just suppose that truth is a woman—what then? is not the suspicion well
> founded that all philosophers, to the extent they have been dogmatists,

---

[17]For instance, William C. Placher argues that although theologians such as Aquinas and Calvin were well aware of the difficulties of speaking adequately of God, their modern heirs lost some of that nuance. See *The Domestication of Transcendence: How Modern Thinking About God Went Wrong* (Louisville, Ky.: Westminster John Knox, 1996).

[18]A partial truth is still a *truth*. But when it is held to be "the whole truth," it becomes in effect an untruth.

[19]Maudemarie Clark, *Nietzsche on Truth and Philosophy* (Cambridge: Cambridge University Press, 1990).

have had little understanding of women? that the ghastly seriousness, the clumsy obtrusiveness by which they have until now approached truth have been inept and improper ways of winning a wench? Certainly she has not let herself be won—and every sort of dogmatism stands sad and discouraged. If it continues to stand at all! (*BGE,* preface)

It would be easy to dismiss Nietzsche's characterization of truth as "woman" as simply male chauvinist nonsense (or just plain nonsense).[20] As usual, Nietzsche is here quite politically incorrect. Yet I take him as trying to say something important about truth. While his stereotypes of men and women are questionable, the contrast that he uses them to draw is clear in at least one respect. On the account he seems to assume here, women are far more complex and unpredictable than supposedly reliable, logical and straightforward men.[21] Thus if truth is like a woman, then it is subtle and elusive. There is always something about truth that escapes our grasp, something we cannot categorize or arrange neatly in a system. And precisely because it escapes our grasp, we cannot draw a sharp line between what we do know and what we do not know.

Nietzsche is attacking something as old as philosophy itself: the idea that truth can be mastered and delimited. Philosophers have often attempted to master the truth by way of systems that put everything in their place and are presented to us with what Nietzsche terms "the solemn air of finality" (*BGE,* preface). True, not all philosophers have argued that *they* have reached such a point (though some of them certainly do *sound* as if they think they have), but Nietzsche thinks that such an ideal has been held up by philosophers as their goal—and is often assumed to be in principle attainable.

---

[20]Nietzsche has often been dismissed as simply misogynistic. Without question there is considerable reason for doing so. It is hard to go far in most of Nietzsche's texts without encountering a slander against women. Yet apart from the fact that Nietzsche personally fared rather poorly with women, his thinking about the feminine is much more ambivalent than it might at first seem. As just one example, note that in the same work in which we find perhaps Nietzsche's most infamous quote about women—"Are you visiting women? Do not forget your whip!" (*Z,* "Of Old and Young Women")—he depicts life as a woman (*Z,* "The Second Dance Song"). One must not forget that Nietzsche reveres life more than anything else. Recent Nietzschean scholarship is much more aware of the complexity of Nietzsche's views on women. See, for example, Peter J. Burgard, ed., *Nietzsche and the Feminine* (Charlottesville: University of Virginia Press, 1994).

[21]Of course Nietzsche gives a very different picture of women in §411 of *Human, All Too Human,* trans. Gary Handwerk (Stanford, Calif.: Stanford University Press, 1995). There Nietzsche says that "the intellect of women manifests itself as perfect self-control." I'll resist the temptation to explain this contrast here.

But there is something very paradoxical about Nietzsche's claim. In rejecting the ideal of giving us the things as they are, of course, Nietzsche seems to be appealing to this very notion, for he seems to be telling us how things are. So is Nietzsche claiming that there is nothing like "truth" (a metaphysical claim) or that we cannot know this "truth" (an epistemological claim)? If it is the former, then his claim would seem to end up being "The 'truth' about the 'truth' is that there is no 'truth.'" If it is the latter, then it would be "There is (or may be) 'truth' but we cannot know it." The first possibility immediately raises the question of the status of such a claim: if there is no truth, can the statement "There is no truth" be true? On my account, Nietzsche is not giving us anything like a theory of truth. His denial of the true world is in effect a denial of "truth" as defined by Plato. If such truth doesn't exist, then we cannot "know" it. Yet however strongly or weakly one construes the claims Nietzsche seems to be making, they turn out to be problematic. There is an obvious self-referential problem with the claim that "there is no truth." Nietzsche appears to be well aware of this problem, but he does nothing to solve it. On his view, all human claims to define truth run into the problem of getting outside of truth precisely in order to define it. Put in other words: the point of a philosophical definition of truth is to arrive at a *true* definition; but to arrive at such a definition presupposes that one already has an idea of truth (or else it couldn't be recognized when found).[22]

Having shown (at least to his satisfaction) that the notion of "truth" is complicated and cannot ultimately be worked out, Nietzsche continues to use the term. However, given Nietzsche's denial of the existence of the "true world," now "truth" merely means *adaequatio* between our knowledge and *this* world. Note that we cannot really call this world "the world of appearances," because Nietzsche rejects such a distinction.

Philosophy's *logos* and Christ the *Logos*

How ought Christians to respond to Nietzsche regarding the "true world" and the idea that there is "truth"? On Nietzsche's view, Christianity is merely a version of Platonism, in which the "true world" becomes "more refined, more devious, more mystifying" (*TI*, "How the 'True

---

[22]This problem is as old as philosophy itself. Meno raises it in talking with Socrates, who responds by saying that we must have some previous knowledge of what we are looking for in order to find it. See Plato *Meno* 80d.

World' Finally Became a Fiction"). Yet despite the fact that Christianity maintains that a "true world" and "truth" exist, are there not important differences between Platonism and Christianity?

It seems to me that the two differ—significantly—in both their respective *logoi* and their conceptions of knowledge and belief. First, in terms of *logos,* Nietzsche claims that what was "simple" in Platonism becomes complex in Christianity. I think Nietzsche is right. The reason is that whereas the *logos* of Platonism is ultimately a human creation, Jesus Christ the *Logos* (Jn 1:1) is divine and so does not submit to human reason *(logos).*

Nietzsche claims that with Christianity the "true world" becomes "unattainable for now, but promised to the wise, the devout, the virtuous" (*TI,* "How the 'True World' Became a Fiction"). But is that really the exact promise made to Christians? True, the apostle Paul says, for example, that God "has made known to us the mystery of his will" (Eph 1:9). Yet is that to be construed as a general claim that Christians now possess all of God's knowledge and wisdom—that our knowledge is "adequate" to that of God—or even that they shall one day know all that God knows? Whereas Plato held out the possibility of knowing truth in all its fullness, Jesus Christ nowhere makes such a promise to his followers. It is not just that such knowledge is "unattainable for now"; it is that however much has already been revealed and however more will one day be revealed to us, we will still never have God's knowledge. And certainly our knowledge in the present is even more limited. This claim in no way denies that Christians can have some degree—and a very significant degree—of knowledge of the truth. Indeed the advent of Christ is the revelation of God's plan of salvation. But that claim needs to be carefully tempered with a healthy sense of human limitations.

While there are different ways of working out the criticism that Western philosophy has tended to be "logocentric," clearly a very important aspect of this claim is that philosophy is an attempt to *master* the world by way of reason. Christians ought to agree with Nietzsche that human beings' claims to "truth" are often rooted in pride. We ought also to acknowledge that all human claims of truth are incomplete: that is, none of them can claim to have (or, more accurately, *be*) the truth in an absolute sense—the sense in which Plato was claiming. Of course that in no way means that human claims cannot get closer to the truth or that they cannot be genuinely true to some extent. The *euangelion* is not just "good" but *true* news. Christians claim that God's truth is Absolute. Yet the truth *as we know it now* is certainly not absolute. The truth—as we understand it—is partial and shaped by our own understanding. There is nothing necessarily wrong with that fact, but it is important that we recognize it.

There is a further complication with the Christian conception of the *Logos*. While the notion of Absolute Truth defined in terms of static essences may be an appropriate pagan philosophical notion, it is considerably less clearly an appropriate Christian notion. Scripture speaks of Christ as being the truth (Jn 14:6) and instructs us to walk in the truth (2 Jn 4). Is Christ, then, the essence of truth? Perhaps, but that way of thinking may not be the best way of understanding who Christ truly is. In any case, if Christ *is* truth, then truth from a Christian perspective must be quite different from that of a classical Greek perspective: not impersonal and objective (in the sense of being defined by an "object") but personal and subjective (in the sense of being defined by a "subject"—God and his character). Truth from the Christian perspective must be closely related to the person of Christ. As such, it would appear to be both unchanging and historical. To have an understanding other than this would be to take a position dangerously close to various heresies that arose early and that the church has been battling ever since. Theological orthodoxy, of course, is the course that steers between these two aspects without derailing into one or the other.

While Plato claimed to have (or at least be able to obtain) *epistēmē* of the Forms, Christians claim to have faith *(pistis)* in God and his truth. For Christians, faith in God is characterized by an "assurance of things hoped for, the conviction of things not seen" (Heb 11:1); but that assurance and conviction is based on God's trustworthiness, not on our own rational abilities. Since God and his word are trustworthy *(pistos)*, we are confident to trust in them. A properly Christian viewpoint recognizes—from the beginning—that Christian claims are ultimately based on faith, not on human reason. Or perhaps it should be put it as follows: the truth of the claims of Christianity depends not on us and our reason but on God.

In this respect Platonism and Christianity are quite strikingly different. Whereas Plato wrongly claimed that his theory of the Forms was based on *epistēmē* (and so is appropriately criticized by Nietzsche as being "dogmatic"), Christians freely admit that their belief is "dogmatic" in the sense that it cannot (as well as ought not) be grounded in human reason. The *Logos* in whom we believe escapes our rational control and human mastery. Indeed that *Logos* masters and controls us. Christ the *Logos* is neither of our own making nor under our control. Just when we think we have finally categorized, systematized and simplified the *euangelion* of the *Logos,* our human thought *(logos)* is disrupted and confounded. The *Logos* is the ultimate ideology buster.

Oddly enough, Nietzsche's image of truth as a woman is actually remarkably compatible with a properly Christian conception of truth, in at least two ways. We do not "suppose that truth is a woman": we *believe* that "truth is a man"—the Son of God, who is fully God but also fully man. Further, since Christ the *Logos* is the definition of truth, then on both the Nietzschean and Christian conceptions, truth is complex, elusive and even surprising. Even though sometimes Christians have mistakenly assumed that Jesus' teaching is simple and easily system-atized, even a cursory study of the Gospels makes it clear that such is not the case.

Of course Nietzsche believes in neither Plato's *logos* nor Christ the *Logos.* Yet Nietzsche does realize that his own beliefs are dogmatic—that they are *belief* claims—and that he cannot possibility provide a ground-ing for them. Still, why does Nietzsche hold the views he does? Whereas Nietzsche's reasons for rejecting Platonism should be amply clear at this point, what are his reasons for rejecting Christianity? That is the question taken up in the next chapter.

2

"GOD HAD TO DIE"

G od is dead'—Nietzsche. 'Nietzsche is dead'—God." So reads a popular "Christian" T-shirt. While I know of no recorded revelation in which Nietzsche's death is pronounced by God, Nietzsche does indeed speak of God's death. The question, though, is exactly how we should take this claim. An obvious possibility is put by Heidegger as follows:

> One could suppose that the pronouncement "God is dead" expresses an opinion of Nietzsche the atheist and is accordingly only a personal attitude, and therefore one-sided, and for that reason also easily refutable through the observation that today everywhere many men seek out the houses of God and endure hardships out of a trust in God as defined by Christianity. (*WN* 57)

Heidegger dismisses this reading, partly because it misses Nietzsche's point that metaphysics is at an end. While Heidegger's read of Nietzsche as metaphysician (to which we shall return at the end of the chapter) has much to commend it, the death of God really does have a specifically *religious* impact. Moreover, Nietzsche's pronouncement must be understood from the viewpoint of his own life and that of the culture at large.

Who Died?

There is every reason to think that Nietzsche was a devout and true Christian believer in his childhood. Since his father and grandfather were Lutheran ministers and he was raised in a Christian home, Christian belief came to him naturally. At age thirteen Nietzsche wrote the following:

> I have firmly resolved within me to dedicate myself for ever to His service. May the dear Lord give me strength and power to carry out my intention and protect me on my life's way. Like a child I trust in His grace: He will preserve us all, that no misfortune may befall us. But His holy will be done! All He gives I will joyfully accept.[1]

It is hard to imagine a stronger expression of genuine piety. Yet by the time he was eighteen, he no longer had any faith left. What happened?

Given Nietzsche's later attitude toward Christianity, one might expect that some traumatic event was responsible for his loss of faith. Such does not seem to have been the case. Moreover, although one might be tempted to speculate that Nietzsche rebelled against an overly strict upbringing, there is no evidence to that effect. When Nietzsche finally told his mother about his turn from faith, his demeanor seems to have been marked more by reluctance than by rebellion. His explanation to her was that he now thought Christianity to be simply superstition. Much later in life he described the change as "a skepticism that first appeared so early in my life, so spontaneously, so irrepressibly, so much in contradiction to my environment, age, models, origins" (*GM,* preface, p. 3). In his last text, Nietzsche claimed that his aversion to Christianity came about "from instinct."[2]

But what exactly was Nietzsche skeptical about? While I shall venture an answer to that question, it seems to me the answer is far from clear. Jörg Salaquarda notes that

> Nietzsche was familiar, above all, with two types of religious faith: on the one hand, the practical faith of his mother, which lacked theological reflection and sophistication entirely; and, on the other, the more rationalistic tradition of his aunt Rosalie, who was the dominating theological figure in the family after the death of his father.[3]

---

[1]From Nietzsche's *Aus meinem Leben (From My Life),* quoted in R. J. Hollingdale, *Nietzsche: The Man and His Philosophy* (London: Ark, 1985), p. 19.

[2]*EH,* "Why I Am So Clever," p. 1.

[3]Jörg Salaquarda, "Nietzsche and the Judeo-Christian Tradition," in *The Cambridge Companion to Nietzsche,* ed. Bernd Magnus and Kathleen M. Higgins (Cambridge: Cambridge University Press, 1996), p. 92.

One might argue that Nietzsche's mother was the dominant influence on his faith in his early years. Certainly the kind of piety he expressed at thirteen seems more reflective of her faith than of Rosalie's rationalistic faith (what we might term today "classic liberal theology"). But as Nietzsche's thought matured, understandably Rosalie's influence became more prominent. Much of Nietzsche's adult criticism of Christianity is probably read most accurately as attacking the rationalistic strand of Christianity, in which Christianity is reduced to something purely "rational." Put bluntly: while Nietzsche as an adult cannot take his mother's pietistic sort of faith seriously, he is reluctant to criticize it. Conversely, while he takes the rationalistic expression of Christianity seriously, he finds that it rings hollow. In effect, Nietzsche applies his tuning hammer to this particular brand of "Christianity" and finds it to be simply an idol.

However questionable counterfactual speculation—asking "what if" questions—may be, it is interesting to wonder what Nietzsche might have made of a serious pietism that was coupled with robust theological reflection. Note that his mother and Aunt Rosalie provided him with examples of each taken separately. How might Nietzsche have responded to a faith that he would have been forced to take seriously that did not succumb to the criticism of being soulless? Perhaps his opinion of Christianity would have been somewhat different.

In any case, despite the fact that Nietzsche's skepticism was a personal phenomenon, it clearly reflected the culture of the time. Whereas belief in God had once been a dominant part of European culture, it was on the wane in Nietzsche's day. Thus Nietzsche's loss of faith seems to be the result of a realization that educated people of his day were finding religious belief decreasingly acceptable. His own move from devout faith to disbelief, then, parallels what he sees as the wider cultural shift. Note that the so-called death of God is proclaimed as a cultural phenomenon.

> Haven't you heard of that madman who in the bright morning lit a lantern and ran to the marketplace crying incessantly, "I'm looking for God! I'm looking for God!" Since many of those who did not believe in God were standing around together just then, he caused great laughter. Has he been lost, then? asked one. Did he lose his way like a child? asked another. . . . "Where is God" he cried. "I'll tell you where. *We have killed him*—you and I. We are all his murderers." (*GS* 3:125)

The madman—who can be reasonably interpreted as representing

Nietzsche—considers himself an accomplice in the crime but not its architect or even executor. The role of the madman is instead prophetic in nature: he proclaims what has taken place and predicts what is to come. God's death places us in "an infinite nothing," in which there is only "empty space" (*GS* 125). Interestingly enough, the madman's hearers are described as "those who do not believe in God." While there may be others who do not already know the news, the people in the public square certainly do. Indeed they are comfortable enough with the news to heckle the messenger. Yet later in the same passage they are depicted as responding with "astonishment." Why so? One way of explaining their reaction is that while they already "know," they are surprised to hear anybody actually say it aloud and in public. It is a social outcast who is bold enough to say what many people think but are uncomfortable saying. It is likewise appropriate for a madman to *see* that to which some people are blind. As far back as the medieval period, it was thought that the insane have a special ability to discern what others might miss.[4]

Who were these people "in the know"? Certainly the group would have included radical thinkers of Nietzsche's day. Nietzsche was not the first to write of the death of God. During his time as a university student, he undoubtedly read and was deeply influenced by Max Stirner.[5] Nearly thirty years before Nietzsche's own proclamation, Stirner had written that "man has killed God in order to become now—'*sole* God on high.'"[6] The parallel between this passage and the one above are striking.

But many unbelievers were to be found within the church. Such people attended church and made pretensions to belief. After all, in Nietzsche's day these were culturally expected behaviors. Although Nietzsche descended from a line of Lutheran ministers, it is hard to know how serious their respective Christian commitments were. Hollingdale comments that Nietzsche's grandfather, who was a significant influence on the young Friedrich, "strikes one as being about as

---

[4]It might also be tempting to say that without God one goes mad, though that is probably not a point that Nietzsche (who did eventually go mad but hadn't at this point) would have had in mind.

[5]Nietzsche never actually refers to Stirner in any of his texts, but he clearly had read him. See Max Stirner, *The Ego and His Own,* ed. John Carroll, trans. Steven T. Byington (London: Cape, 1971), p. 25, and Irving M. Zeitlin, *Nietzsche: A Re-examination* (Cambridge: Polity, 1994), pp. 113-22.

[6]Stirner, *Ego and His Own,* p. 109.

devout and other-worldly as Laurence Sterne," but there is no indication that Nietzsche's father had been a paragon of piety either.[7] Søren Kierkegaard's complaints about the sickly state of the Lutheran Church in Denmark are well known, and the German Lutheran Church was no better.[8] Both had degenerated into bodies more important for conferring social status than for promoting genuine faith. The "faith" of many members had little to do with what committed Christians would consider real. Christian belief in the Germany of Nietzsche's day was clearly under attack. Although there were many factors at work, three important ones should be mentioned.

First, exactly half a century before Nietzsche's birth, Immanuel Kant published his *Religion Within the Boundaries of Mere Reason* (1794).[9] There he argued that religion—specifically Christianity—needed to be reconfigured to meet the demands of reason. Anything not acceptable to modern science ought to be scrapped. One result of this rationalistic house-cleaning was that anything "miraculous" was no longer to be taken seriously. In effect, Kant gives us a philosophical version of the Jefferson Bible. But far more important, the basic categories of Christianity were subverted. Kant exchanges original sin and Christ's incarnation for, respectively, "the evil principle" and "the good principle." Being "religious" involves following the commands of "the Legislator of all duties." God becomes no more than a moral commander, and Christianity is reduced to an exemplary moral system. There is still a need for God in such a system, but only as a kind of ground for moral responsibility. In turn, Christ's place in Christianity is as moral example. No doubt much of the Christianity that Nietzsche experienced was this rational sort, in which Christ is merely a good man and following him is roughly equivalent to following the Golden Rule.

A second, and even more serious, blow to Christianity came from Ludwig von Feuerbach's *The Essence of Christianity* (1841), in which he argues that the concept of god (specifically, the God of Christianity) is

---

[7]Hollingdale, *Nietzsche,* p. 3.

[8]One might argue that Kierkegaard and Nietzsche represent two very different responses to the Lutheran church of their day. Whereas Kierkegaard embraces a radical faith that requires that the individual choose either Christ or the world, Nietzsche rejects faith in Christ in favor of faith in the world (and we shall see what Nietzsche's "worldly faith" looks like in the following section).

[9]Immanuel Kant, *Religion Within the Boundaries of Mere Reason,* trans. Allen Wood and George di Giovanni (Cambridge: Cambridge University Press, 1998).

the product of human invention. What Christians call "God" is simply a projected composite of their own characteristics taken to the highest level of perfection. Thus Feuerbach contrasts "the true or anthropological essence of religion" (part one of his book) with "the false or theological essence of religion" (part two). Whereas Christians think their religion is theologically based, it actually has an anthropological basis. Religion arises from a desire of human beings to elevate themselves above other animals, to project a kind of vision of what they could become.

> Man—this is the mystery of religion—projects his being into objectivity, and then again makes himself an object to this projected image of himself thus converted into a subject. . . . Thus man, while he is apparently humiliated to the lowest degree, is in truth exalted to the highest. . . . Man has no other aim than himself.[10]

So religion ends up being like truth for Nietzsche: a way in which human beings exalt themselves. Like Nietzsche, Feuerbach thinks he is merely pointing out what actually *is* the case. While the idea that God is merely the result of "projection" has become the almost unquestioned orthodoxy among secular psychologists and many others, we must not forget how startling Feuerbach's thesis must have seemed in Nietzsche's day.

Given the reductionism of Kant and the atheism of Feuerbach, it is understandable why a further shift takes place. If Christ ends up being merely an example and Christianity only a set of moral teachings, why do we really need either? In his *Life of Jesus* (1835) David Strauss argued that Christianity is based not on "the historical Jesus" but on "the ideal Christ"—our moral example. Later, in *The Old Faith and the New* (1872), Strauss—who had read Feuerbach and been deeply influenced by him— took the next logical step and rejected Christianity altogether, even though he retained Christian morality. By the time Nietzsche was writing—the 1870s and 1880s—Strauss's "new faith" had become quite popular, even among many for whom church attendance was still a part of their routine.

It is in this context that the madman makes his announcement. So who died? The death of God involves for Nietzsche at least four deaths. First,

---

[10]Ludwig von Feuerbach, *The Essence of Christianity,* trans. George Eliot (New York: Harper & Row, 1957), pp. 29-30.

there is the loss of "the God of Christian faith"—the God of Abraham, Isaac and Jacob, who sent his Son Jesus Christ. Of course it is not so much that this particular God has "died" as that religious belief in any gods is, on Nietzsche's account, no longer plausible. Nietzsche doesn't argue that their existence is impossible; he just assumes it is very unlikely.

Nietzsche also finds implausible, second, "the God of the philosophers"—the *ens realissimum* (literally, the most real being). This is merely the "highest concept" of philosophy, "the last, the thinnest, the emptiest" (*TI,* " 'Reason' in Philosophy," p. 4). In the same way that Plato's Forms were postulated out of thin air, so this concept of God is simply a philosophical creation. As noted earlier, Nietzsche doesn't really argue against the Forms. Neither does he provide an argument against the God of the philosophers. But with the demise of the true world comes the demise of the god of the philosophers. Even philosophers cannot believe in this god anymore. Of course since the concept has precious little content, the death of the god of the philosophers does not represent much of a loss. Or we might go so far as to say that instead of being a loss, the death of the god of the philosophers represents a significant gain. For that god is merely an idol (what Levinas calls "a certain god inhabiting the world behind the scenes," *OTB* 185), whose hollowness has finally been sounded out by Nietzsche's hammer. "That which dies does not have any right to claim, even when it is alive, to be 'God,'" points out Marion (*IAD* 1). The death of this god, this "nongod" who cannot hear and has no power and simply leads us astray, is cause for rejoicing. In this important respect, even if not in certain others, Christians can find in Nietzsche an ally—someone who proclaims what they themselves should have been more vocal in proclaiming.

Third, Nietzsche decries "the Christ of faith." It is not merely that this figure is mythical but that this figure is the bearer of *bad* news, what Nietzsche calls the *dysangel.* Simply put, Christ's bad news is a denial of life (we will address this charge shortly).

Fourth and finally, the historical figure of Jesus (who for Nietzsche is merely human) is a much more complicated story. Nietzsche makes a sharp distinction between him and Christianity. Speaking of Jesus, he says, "In reality there has been only one Christian, and he died on the Cross. The 'Evangel' *died* on the Cross. What was called 'Evangel' from this moment onwards was already the opposite of what *he* had lived" (*A* 39). Jesus the man—like all of the others—is dead, though at least he actually was once alive, whereas the other three are simply fictions.

Not surprisingly, Christians of Nietzsche's day tended to respond to his announcement of God's death in one of two ways.[11] On the one hand, some saw his writings as simply attacks on Christianity and its message. Nietzsche was on this read a blasphemer, a dangerous madman, an immoral person and an antichrist. Since his "doctrines" were simply negations of the gospel, they were to be avoided. Certainly they were not to be taken seriously. The best antidote against Nietzschean poison was lack of contact. On the other hand, some Christians took Nietzsche and his criticism seriously. They saw Nietzsche as a perceptive critic who had accurately described the state of Christian belief in their time.

Among those who took Nietzsche's criticisms seriously, there were at least two responses. One was to argue that while Nietzsche's ideas were wrong, there was much to be learned from his astute diagnosis. Responding himself to the bankruptcy of liberal theology in the early part of the twentieth century, Karl Barth pointed out that what is called Christianity sometimes stands squarely against the teachings of Jesus.

> The greatest witness against Christianity is the pitiable figure of the everyday Christian, whose complacency—he has no thought of seeking his salvation with fear and trembling—is a clear demonstration that the decisive assertions of Christianity are of no importance. It is the Church, which is the very thing against which Jesus preached and taught His disciples to fight, embodying the triumph of that which is anti-Christian no less than the modern state and modern nationalism.[12]

While Barth certainly does not adopt Nietzsche's ideas, he is convinced that Nietzsche's assessment of Christendom is—at least in some regards—all too true. The other response that took Nietzsche's criticism to heart argued that Nietzsche's ideas were not so far from Christian ideas after all. While I shall later argue that there is something to this claim, the attempt by figures such as theologian Hans Gallwitz to argue that Christianity needed to recover its more "manly" values seems questionable.[13]

---

[11]For an enlightening account of Nietzsche's reception in Germany, see Steven E. Aschheim, *The Nietzsche Legacy in Germany, 1890-1990* (Berkeley: University of California Press, 1992), pp. 201-31.

[12]Karl Barth, *Church Dogmatics*, 3/4, *The Doctrine of Creation*, trans. Harold Knight et al. (Edinburgh: T & T Clark, 1960), p. 238.

[13]Hans Gallwitz, "Friedrich Nietzsche als Erzieher zum Christentum," *Preussische Jahrbücher* 83/84 (1896). I shall take up the topic of "manliness" shortly.

Yet all of these are distinctly Christian responses *against* Nietzsche. How did Nietzsche himself interpret the death of God? One can read it as being simply the next stage in the maturing of humanity. In order for human beings to grow up, God needed to die. Only then could they be (as Stirner had aptly put it) "*sole* God on high." God's existence is problematic because it creates responsibility. Thus, says Nietzsche, "we deny God, and denying God we deny responsibility" (*TI*, "The Four Great Errors," p. 8).[14] If God is dead, we are no longer responsible to anyone other than ourselves. This idea of maturity is a particularly modern one, exemplified by Kant's essay "What Is Enlightenment?" Just how "mature," though, is this idea of God's death? If one considers what Nietzsche says in *Thus Spoke Zarathustra,* there would seem to be a kind of childish aspect to the death of God. "But to reveal my heart entirely to you, friends: *if* there were gods, how could I endure not to be a god! *Therefore* there are no gods. I, indeed, drew that conclusion; but now it draws me" (*Z*, "On the Blissful Islands").

One could possibly read these remarks as Nietzsche's (or Zarathustra's) simply rejecting the God of the philosophers. If one takes this path, then the God being rejected is not the incarnate God. Yet I will not take such a path here. Although it may be dangerous to construe these remarks too autobiographically, I think they may give us an important clue to the real reason Nietzsche rejects God in general and Christianity in particular. True, it is Zarathustra who claims to "reveal [his] heart," but it is hard not to think that such is Nietzsche's heart also. Note the logic of this passage. God's existence is not denied, say, because arguments for his existence fail to be persuasive. It is denied because Zarathustra cannot bear to acknowledge something or someone above him. If someone is going to get to be God, then it is not going to be someone *else.*

This idea that the death of God is not merely a general cultural movement but a direct result of personal will is taken up again later in *Thus Spoke Zarathustra,* where "the ugliest man" says:

He—*had* to die: he looked with eyes that saw *everything*—he saw the depths and abysses of man, all man's hidden disgrace and ugliness. . . .
He always saw *me*: I desired to take revenge on such a witness—or

---

[14]Another possible way of reading Nietzsche here is that he is denying causality. But I won't take that route.

cease to live myself. The god who saw everything *even* man: this god had to die! Man could not *endure* that such a witness should live. (*Z*, "The Ugliest Man")

Note that God "dies" because human beings are unwilling to allow him to live. They may feel that they can no longer believe in him, but the inability may be self-induced. No one forces any of us into that position.

The death of God is, for Nietzsche, both positive and negative. At times Nietzsche depicts God's death as a great loss. After making his announcement, the madman "forced his way into several churches and there started singing his *requiem aeternam deo*" (*GS* 3:125).[15] It must not be forgotten that the madman prefaces his announcement by saying, "I'm looking for God!" There is a sense of resignation to having lost something that one once truly loved, like the child who mourns that she can no longer believe in Santa Claus. There is a further—and much more ominous—possible result. Christianity had provided the backbone of European culture. If it is lost, then does not nihilism loom in the future? Such a possibility worries Nietzsche. But the solution was not shoring up a sinking edifice but taking it down all the way. As he puts it, "That which is falling should also be pushed" (*Z*, "Of Old and New Law Tables," p. 20). One pushes, even if there is a tinge of nostalgia for what once stood. Of course at other times Nietzsche speaks of this transition buoyantly, calling it a "relief" (*GS* 5:343).[16] With God out of the way, it is finally time for something that affirms life.

But where does one go from there? Whereas Kant had reduced Christianity to little more than law with a lawgiver, Strauss takes the further step of removing the lawgiver. But he still retains the moral system of Christianity. So why not follow Strauss's way of dealing with the death of God? Apart from the fact that Nietzsche labels Strauss a philistine (and subjects *The Old Faith and the New* to merciless logical, stylistic and even grammatical criticism), he (rightly) takes Strauss's new "faith" to be baseless. Nietzsche writes that Strauss "announces with admirable candor that he is no longer a Christian, but that he does not want to disturb anyone else's solace. . . . [B]ut we realize with consternation that his ethics are constructed independently of the question: 'How do we conceive

---

[15] *Requiem aeternam deo* translates as "grant God eternal rest."
[16] One could criticize Nietzsche for being inconsistent here. Or one could just recognize that feelings are often conflicting.

the world?"[17] In other words, even though there is now no metaphysical basis for Christian morality, it remains quite undisturbed for Strauss. But how can one still take Christian morality seriously when its source and undergirding are no longer intact? Nietzsche thinks such a move is impossible.

> If you give up Christian faith, you pull the *right* to Christian morality out from under your feet. This morality is simply *not* self-evident: one has to bring this point home again and again, despite the English dimwits. Christianity is a system, a view of things that is conceived as a connected *whole.* If you break off a major concept from it, faith in God, you break up the whole as well: there are no necessities left to hold onto anymore. . . . Christian morality is a commandment; its origin is transcendent; it is beyond all criticism, all right to criticism; it is true only if God is truth—it stands and falls with faith in God. (*TI,* "Raids of an Untimely Man," p. 5)

Although this passage is explicitly directed against George Eliot (one of the "English dimwits"), it can be taken as a general critique.[18] If what we call God is merely an idol, then his "truth" is merely an ideology. One cannot logically renounce the first and retain the second (as "Truth"), for the very conception of moral law requires a lawgiver. Thus to avoid being merely a blind ideologue, Strauss needs to take not just a half-step but a full one.

In *Thus Spoke Zarathustra* Nietzsche refers to people who have lost faith in God but are still looking for something higher than themselves to justify their existence as "the last men" or "the ultimate men." These are—for Nietzsche—the true nihilists. They assume there must be an "otherworldly" (literally, "metaphysical") answer to the question "What is the meaning of life?" But they fail to find it. Some, like Strauss, attempt to erect an idol of morality even though they deny its otherworldly metaphysical foundation. Others erect what Nietzsche calls "the new idol," the ideal of the state. But Nietzsche would consider both of these to be blatant examples of ideology—and also unsuccessful. Even though

---

[17]Friedrich Nietzsche, "David Strauss the Confessor and Writer," in *Unfashionable Observations,* trans. Richard T. Gray (Stanford, Calif.: Stanford University Press, 1995), §2.

[18]Despite the fact that Nietzsche's caricature of Eliot as a "dimwit" is, even for Nietzsche, rather over the top, one must not forget that Eliot had championed and translated both Strauss's *Life of Jesus* and Feuerbach's *Essence of Christianity.* On Nietzsche's read, she just didn't understand the implications of their thought. Having given up Christian theology, she had to make herself "respectable again as a moral fanatic in the most frightening way" (*TI,* "Raids of an Untimely Man," p. 5).

he cannot have Christianity as a whole, Strauss is willing to keep Christian morality because it consoles him. But what he ends up keeping is really just a version (or, more accurately, a *perversion*) of Christian morality that he has created to fit his own needs. For Strauss, following Christ means little more than "being a good person." The kind of radical abandonment of oneself to Jesus Christ—taking up one's cross—is simply nowhere to be found.

Similarly, the promise of the state is that (on Nietzsche's read) "it will give *you* everything if *you* worship it" (Z, "Of the New Idol"). The state is likewise something that we have set up to fulfill our needs. Ultimate Men crave comfort. Zarathustra describes them as follows: "'We have discovered happiness,' say the Ultimate Men and blink. They have left the places where living was hard: for one needs warmth. One still loves one's neighbor and rubs oneself against him: for one still needs warmth" (Z, "Zarathustra's Prologue"). Ultimate Men are still willing to love their neighbor, but their motivation is personal gain. Should neighbor love prove difficult, it would likely be dropped too.

One might be tempted to call these Ultimate Men "the ultimate hypocrites." But how much do they exemplify "genuine" hypocrisy? That depends on the sense of hypocrisy we have in mind. If hypocrisy is claiming to be something that one is not, then they probably qualify as *hypokritai*—actors. After all, they act as if nothing has happened—as if the religious status quo has not been altered (though they "blink"). At least people like Strauss know that such is not the case, for he realizes that his redefined sense of "faith" is not coextensive with Christian orthodoxy.

But Nietzsche makes the seemingly counterintuitive observation that there are relatively few *real* hypocrites. "The few hypocrites I have met were imitating hypocrisy: they, like almost every tenth person today, were actors" (TI, "Raids of an Untimely Man," p. 18). Instead of being hypocrites because they are actors, they are only acting as hypocrites. To have genuine hypocrisy, thinks Nietzsche, there must be real belief. "Hypocrisy belongs to the ages of strong faith, when even if you were *forced* to display a different faith, you didn't let go of the faith you had" (TI, "Raids of an Untimely Man," p. 18). Nietzsche thinks that hypocrisy is hard to find because nobody really believes anything—or at least with strong conviction. The problem of a "lack of hypocrisy," then, is not limited to Christians; rather Nietzsche thinks it is a feature of the intellectual life of the time.

But if Ultimate Men are characterized by a lack of hypocrisy because they are nihilists, can Nietzsche possibly be a nihilist also? Presumably he does not see himself as a hypocrite, at least in regard to beliefs concerning the meaning of life. Would that disqualify him from being a nihilist?

God's Death and the Possibility of Life

For Nietzsche, Christian morality is "*not* self-evident." In fact he thinks that it is at odds with some of our deepest drives and desires. In that observation I think Nietzsche is somewhat correct (as we shall later see). But more important, Nietzsche thinks that Christian morality—not to mention Jewish and Platonic morality, for that matter—is fundamentally opposed to life. Whether he is right in this respect depends on what we mean by "life."

Despite the fact that Nietzsche considers the Ultimate Men to be the nihilists, one of the most widely disseminated ideas about Nietzsche is that he himself is a nihilist. If nihilism is defined as the ideas (1) that human existence (or simply life) is meaningless and (2) that there are no values (moral or otherwise), then we can quite categorically say that Nietzsche is *not* a nihilist. Nietzsche has a very definite set of values and takes these very seriously. Indeed he even has a set of "moral" values.[19] But if nihilism is defined to mean "there are no universal or metaphysically based moral values—values of *true* 'right and wrong'"—then Nietzsche most assuredly *is* a nihilist. Of course since Nietzsche thinks that the very idea of moral values is wrongheaded, he does not consider himself to be a nihilist (and it would be impossible for him to take himself to be a nihilist). But in order to see in what sense Nietzsche qualifies as nihilist, we need to consider what he means by "life." Not only is Christian morality not "self-evident," neither are Nietzsche's conception of life and values.

"The wisest sages of all times have reached the same judgment about life: *it's worthless*" (*TI,* "The Problem of Socrates," p. 1). Such might seem to be Nietzsche's view. But it is actually a view that he attributes to Socrates. Speaking of the "sages," with Socrates particularly in mind, Nietzsche thinks that we "should take a close look at them" before simply accepting their view (*TI,* "The Problem of Socrates," p. 1). On Nietzsche's read, there are at least three problems with the sages' judgment.

First, the very attempt to assess life's value from the perspective of a

---

[19]See the chapter "Nietzsche's Virtues" in the delightful book *What Nietzsche Really Said* by Robert C. Solomon and Kathleen Higgins (New York: Schocken, 2001).

living person is futile. Here Nietzsche seems to be guided by the assumption of modern science that one needs to take an "objective" (outside or removed) position to know something aright. Since we are "parties to the dispute" (*TI*, "The Problem of Socrates," p. 2), there is no way we can step outside, no possibility of making an "objective" judgment on the matter. Of course the claim to be able to step outside is as old as philosophy itself.

Second, the idea that life must have some sort of justification or meaning outside of itself is simply misguided. Already with Socrates there is the perceived need to provide "reasons" that life is valuable and that one's values have a moral force. For Nietzsche, life is simply valuable in itself; it needs no justification or "meaning." He thinks all claims along the lines of "Life is valuable because . . ." are wrongheaded. Life is *intrinsically* valuable, so it needs no further or other justification.

Third, the attempt to judge life places oneself above it. I become superior to life (since I and my reason become its measure), and in effect I take the place of God. It might be thought that Nietzsche advocates precisely this move with his idea of the death of God. But I think Nietzsche suggests (even though he fails to spell it out clearly) exactly the opposite: the death of God means that *no one* can be God. For Nietzsche, Platonic philosophy and Christianity have both been attempts to play God; but neither can be justified. Richard Rorty can be read as an heir of Nietzsche when he calls for the need "to de-divinize the world" in such a way that "we no longer worship *anything*."[20] Of course whether Nietzsche (or for that matter Rorty) ends up attempting to be God (or god) in his own little way is certainly open to question.

Yet why does Socrates feel compelled to provide a justification for life in the first place? On Nietzsche's read, the need is due to an encroaching *décadence* of Athenian culture.[21] Aristocratic Athenians had always assumed that they were noble. They exhibited a remarkable sense of self-certainty, taking it for granted that their particular traits exemplified "goodness."[22] But whereas Athenians had been sure that this conception of virtue *(doxa)* was equivalent to "true" virtue *(epistēmē)*, now they

---

[20]Richard Rorty, *Contingency, Irony and Solidarity* (Cambridge: Cambridge University Press, 1989), pp. 21-22.

[21]Nietzsche always uses the French term, as he does for *ressentiment*.

[22]Elsewhere Nietzsche says that "the 'well-born' simply *felt* themselves to be the 'happy'" (*GM* 1:10).

were not so sure. Already in Socrates' day the Sophists were arguing that Athenian morality was purely provincial and thus could make no claims to universality.

Enter the good doctor Socrates, whose *pharmakon* (literally both "medicine" and "poison") is the art of reasoning or dialectic. Socrates provides an "equation" in which "reason=virtue=happiness" (*TI,* "The Problem of Socrates," p. 10). Because we are by nature "rational" beings, if we act according to reason, we shall be virtuous and thus happy. But since virtue is defined by rationality and since rationality is at least often (even though not always) opposed to our instinctual desires, being virtuous sometimes (often? usually?) requires going against our instincts.

On Nietzsche's account, this formula does not shore up the crumbling foundations of Athenian morality; it instead retools it in a different direction. The old sense of morality was based precisely on instincts. So Socrates' cure for *décadence* proves to be a poison to life. This is why Nietzsche thinks that Socrates gives us only a different sort of *décadence.* For Socrates, life can be given meaning only by way of rational justification; for Nietzsche, rational justification is what kills life, since life needs no justification.

Nietzsche's conception of life *(das Leben)* can be partially explained by his notions of the "will to power" and what he somewhat misleadingly calls "master morality." But one must be clear as to what he means by these terms, for they are often misinterpreted (and complete clarity on them would be, at best, what Husserl terms an "infinite task").

Let's begin with the will to power. The narrower (and most common) interpretation of the will to power goes along the following lines. According to Nietzsche, all of us wish to have power, and indeed our sole motivation for anything we do in life is to have power: whatever would give us power is what we seek.[23] Of course we may not always be correct in determining that something will actually give us power, but such is always our motivation. On this read Nietzsche is a "psychological egoist," someone who insists that however altruistic we may appear at times, our motives are always selfish. Even Jesus Christ is motivated by the will to power.

But there is also a much broader interpretation. David Allison aptly

---

[23]One finds such a read, to varying degrees, in Arthur Danto, *Nietzsche as Philosopher* (New York: Columbia University Press, 1965); Gilles Deleuze, *Nietzsche and Philosophy;* and Walter Kaufmann, *Nietzsche: Philosopher, Psychologist, Antichrist,* 4th ed. (Princeton, N.J.: Princeton University Press, 1974).

characterizes the will to power as "the will to live, the pulsions of instinct and impulse, the continually transforming energy of excess and superabundance that constitutes the whole of organic and inorganic existence."[24] It is the force within us that causes us not merely to strive for high goals but to create ever greater challenges for ourselves. On Nietzsche's account, all that is beautiful, majestic, creative and worthy of praise has the will to power as its source.

Is either of these readings to be preferred at the expense of the other? I think they are both necessary, and even taken together they in no way exhaust the multiple meanings of "will to power." The will to power *is* creative and life-giving—that is, good and beautiful things do indeed spring from the will to power. Yet—at least it seems to me—this creativity is always ultimately directed toward oneself and always involves some degree of appropriation. Robert Solomon and Kathleen Higgins quote the following passage from Nietzsche to show that even love for Nietzsche arises from the will to power; however, Nietzsche's version of love turns out to be highly problematic.[25]

> What distinguishes those good-natured people whose faces radiate good will from the rest? They feel well in the presence of another person and quickly fall in love with him; consequently they wish him well, and their first judgment is: "I like him." In such people there is the following succession: the wish to appropriate (they do not scruple much over the worth of the other person), quick appropriation, delight in possession, and action for the benefit of the person possessed. (*GS* 3:192)

Being well-disposed toward and liking another person are genuine characteristics of love. But appropriating the other, presumably for one's own ends, and treating the other as a possession and conquest are not part of love at all (even if one also takes action on behalf of the other). One does not love by possessing. This passage well shows the intermingling characteristics of the will to power.

---

[24]David B. Allison, *Reading the New Nietzsche* (Lanham, Md.: Rowman & Littlefield, 2001), p. 108.

[25]See Solomon and Higgins, *What Nietzsche Really Said* (in which the Kaufmann translation of *The Gay Science* is cited). Higgins and Solomon are to be commended for helping dispel many long-standing myths about Nietzsche, both in this popular text and in their more scholarly writings. Yet in the attempt to show that Nietzsche's thought is far more plausible than most people assume, they sometimes remove the rough edges of Nietzsche's ideas and make them overly tame. I read Nietzsche as *wanting* to shock the reader with ideas that are not readily systematized or domesticated.

What then of "master morality"? Nietzsche defines it by saying that in the "masters," the good equals noble, proud, exalted; in contrast, bad equals vulgar, plebeian, contemptible. The opposite of these noble people are cowardly and unsure of themselves, people who are followers rather than leaders. Noble people regard themselves as creators of values: they do not adopt the values of others but create them. Aristocrats have historically exemplified master morality, and Nietzsche argues that these people were always originally barbarians whose strength was not primarily physical but of the soul.

Just who are these "masters," though? It is common—though seriously misguided—to assume that Nietzsche has someone like Conan the Barbarian in mind. After all, the film with that name takes as its epigraph a portion of one of Nietzsche's epigrams in *Twilight of the Idols:* "What doesn't kill me makes me stronger" (*TI,* "Epigrams and Arrows," p. 8).[26] Equally misguided is the interpretation of J. P. Stern, who claims that "no man came closer to the full realization of self-created 'values' than A. Hitler."[27] Nietzsche's "overman" is characterized not so much by strength of body (Conan's strong suit) but by strength of character, depth and creativity.[28] Hitler was certainly characterized by determination, but it is hard to imagine Nietzsche considering him creative or particularly "deep." Admittedly, it is true that Nietzsche often speaks of Napoleon in glowing terms, calling him a "master," one of the "great human beings" and even *"ens realissimum"* (*TI,* "Raids of an Untimely Man," pp. 44-45). Yet Napoleon lacks *"noblesse* of character" according to Nietzsche, so there is a deficiency (*WP* 1026).

The poet Johann Wolfgang von Goethe provides a better example for Nietzsche.

> Goethe conceived of a human being who was strong, highly cultivated, skilled in everything bodily, with self-control and self-respect—a human being who is allowed to dare to accept the entire scope and wealth of naturalness, who is strong enough for this freedom; a tolerant human being, not out of weakness but out of strength. (*TI,* "Raids of an Untimely Man," p. 49)

---

[26]Nietzsche also claims that "the free human being is a *warrior"* (*TI,* "Raids of an Untimely Man," p. 38).

[27]J. P. Stern, *A Study of Nietzsche* (Cambridge: Cambridge University Press, 1979), p. 117.

[28]Though sometimes translated as "superman," the term *Übermensch* is more literally rendered as "overman." Kaufmann points out that Nietzsche does not invent this term but finds a precedent in the classical writer Lucian, who speaks of a *hyperanthropos.* See Kaufmann's *Nietzsche,* p. 307.

Although Goethe has a healthy appreciation for all things bodily—such as the passions—he also admires inner control. It is this combination of strengths that Nietzsche so praises. Thus as strange as the juxtaposition might sound, it is understandable for Nietzsche to describe the master or overman as "the Roman Caesar with Christ's soul" (*WP* 983). As we shall see shortly, Jesus is a kind of hero figure for Nietzsche, for he represents a strength of character that Nietzsche finds highly admirable. Coupling the inner strength of Jesus Christ with the Roman emphasis on outer strength would yield a "complete" man—a true "master."

In contrast, "slave morality" arises out of the common herd, the dregs of society, those uncertain of themselves. The slaves attempt to persuade themselves that the aristocrats are not really happy and not truly "good." In place of the master values, the slave exalts precisely "those qualities which serve to make easier the existence of the suffering," such as patience, humility and friendliness (*BGE* 260). Nietzsche goes on to label this a morality of utility. Of course the master also acts according to utility, choosing those values that best enable life to flourish. But adherents of slave morality would not see themselves as practicing it to benefit themselves: they would see themselves as being "good" for "moral" reasons. On Nietzsche's read, however much the slave might wish to protest otherwise, slaves find it useful to adhere to slave morality to better their lot in life.

Nietzsche claims that slave morality arises out of the slaves' resentment *(ressentiment)* of those in power over them. In effect, they are guilty of what retailers call "price switching"—taking an inexpensive price tag and placing it on an expensive item. Except their switch is a complete reversal of all values, in which vices become virtues and virtues are turned into vices. Thus weakness becomes admirable and the strength of the aristocracy is seen as something evil.

Of course the major problem with slave morality is that it denies life, which for Nietzsche is at heart appropriation—taking what we need and making it our own. The very foundation of existence—the will to power—is denied and repressed (even though it still manifests itself in subtle ways). The values of the master, on the other hand, affirm life.

Technically speaking, of course, master morality is no morality at all. Nietzsche considers it "beyond good and evil"—the title of the principal text in which Nietzsche discusses this theme. There are two senses in which this is true. First, a master does not submit to the ruling ideas of what constitutes good and evil. The master has no need of moral affirmation—the recognition by a second party that the "right" thing has been done. Second, such a person recognizes morality for what it is—a human creation that has no real basis. Nietzsche thinks that the concept of "evil" was invented by the ancient Zarathustra (i.e., Zororaster), which is to say, "it did not descend to them as a voice from heaven" (Z, "Of the Thousand and One Goals"). The concept has plagued Western thought ever since. In place of the opposition "good and evil," Nietzsche gives us merely "good and bad," with "good" being whatever promotes life and "bad" whatever impedes it. On Nietzsche's account, there simply is no true moral system that prescribes a moral right and wrong. Morality is not something that has been revealed, nor is it even something we discover by reason. Rather we create it, so it is an idol of our own making. In fact, the very concept of morality is a human creation for Nietzsche. As we have seen, though, Nietzsche stills affirms a set of values.

Heidegger on Nietzschean Idolatry

Does the philosophy of Nietzsche spell the end of transcendence, the end of the possibility that human beings could go beyond themselves (or perhaps just the end of human beings' *thinking* that they could go beyond themselves)? And what becomes of idolatry?

On Heidegger's read:

> The pronouncement "God is dead" means: The suprasensory world is without effective power. It bestows no life. Metaphysics, i.e., for Nietzsche Western philosophy understood as Platonism, is at an end. Nietzsche understands his own philosophy as the countermovement to metaphysics, and that means for him a movement in opposition to Platonism. (WN 61)

For Nietzsche, the *requiem aeternam deo* is likewise the *"requiem aeternam metaphysicae."* Although he seems more than a little unclear as to where thinking ought now to go, certainly it must give up what he takes to be the hallmarks of metaphysics. First, it must avoid nihilism, or at least nihilism of the sort that devalues without revaluing. As we have seen, Nietzsche fears such a nihilism and wishes to keep it at bay. Second, thinking may no longer invoke the suprasensory. If one appeals to that which cannot be verified by the senses, then one makes a move that can be neither supported nor countered. So Nietzsche wishes to avoid getting caught in that game. Third, since for Nietzsche "systemizing" and metaphysics go hand in hand, one must avoid any kind of system that forces reality into an artificial construct. The best way to keep from systemizing is to resist tying up loose ends.

But as Heidegger reminds us, the danger of a countermovement is that it can easily end up being essentially the same as what it opposes. Heidegger gives us what at first glance may seem a rather surprising read of Nietzsche.[29] Even though Nietzsche sees himself as finally having overcome the philosophical failing known as metaphysics, Heidegger argues that Nietzsche gives us yet another instance of metaphysics. In fact, on Heidegger's read, Nietzsche's metaphysics proves to be a particularly spectacular example of metaphysics, one that reduces everything to the basic category of will to power and thus ends up being itself a manifestation of that will to power. Despite all of Nietzsche's talk of moving beyond metaphysics, and thus beyond Western philosophy as usually practiced, he remains at least somewhat entrenched in that tradition.

What are we to make of Heidegger's claim that Nietzsche regards nihilism as "the fundamental event" and "inner logic" of Western history (WN 67)? We have already seen that nihilism can be variously defined, so what does Heidegger mean? Heidegger reads Nietzsche as claiming that the movement of Western metaphysics has been characterized by a simultaneous overturning and repositing of values, making nihilism into "an ongoing historical event" (WN 66). Thus nihilism usually involves a twofold movement—a "devaluing" and a "revaluing" of values.

While such an interpretation of Nietzsche and of the history of Western thought may perhaps be too sweeping,[30] certainly Platonism (not to mention Christianity) can be interpreted as overturning a set of values and setting up another in its place. Similarly, the death of God (the

---

[29]Heidegger's account of Nietzsche has been criticized for (1) being primarily based on *The Will to Power* and (2) overemphasizing the notion of "will to power" in Nietzsche's thought. *Will to Power* is a collection of aphorisms from Nietzsche's notebooks, compiled by his—how might one say this politely?—philosophically challenged sister Elisabeth Förster-Nietzsche. The book (published after Nietzsche's death) was initially acclaimed as the last word on his thinking, but it has now come to be viewed by many as suspect and perhaps even something to be disregarded. My own view places it somewhere in between. While Nietzsche's texts should be taken as the standard for understanding his thought, *Will to Power* is a useful supplement. Moreover, the notion of will to power *does* play a central role in Nietzsche's thought from beginning to end, and often does so without being explicitly named—however much some interpreters might prefer it otherwise.

[30]Heidegger's evidence for this claim is the second aphorism in *Will to Power*: "What does nihilism mean? *That the highest values are devaluing themselves.*"

suprasensory) can be seen as the devaluing of a long-held set of values. Yet this latter movement is only onefold, for it devalues without replacing. Nietzsche calls it "incomplete nihilism," which "attempts to escape nihilism without revaluing our values" (*WP* 28). Such is the solution of the Ultimate Men like Strauss, who undermine the old values but still hold on to them. In contrast, Nietzsche wants to be a "complete nihilist" by taking the further step of revaluation.

There are several ways Nietzsche might be criticized for being merely a partial nihilist. However much he criticizes Strauss, he may perhaps be more like Strauss than he cares to admit. Nietzsche actually does admit to being a *décadent,* but he claims to have "resisted."[31] To whatever extent, though, that Nietzsche exemplifies and thus fails to overcome Christian values—in the sense of not merely renouncing them intellectually but also giving up all traces of them practically—to that extent he is only a partial nihilist.[32] But Heidegger suggests that there is an even more serious problem. On his read, to escape metaphysics altogether (as opposed to becoming merely a countermovement that ends up being swept into what it opposes) requires "the overturning of the nature and manner of valuing" (WN 70), not merely the substitution of one set of values with another. Nietzsche attempts to break with metaphysics and its valuing system by adopting the value of "life," which ostensibly does not appeal to any realm beyond and so would seem to be classifiable as a nonmetaphysical value. Does Nietzsche *really* overturn "the nature and manner of valuing"? Does he not instead just substitute a different sort of value? Is his system really all that different, then?

It seems to me that one can add a third aspect to this charge of not being a "complete" nihilist. Not only does Nietzsche not really break from the valuing game, but his "new" values turn out to be not so new: he is the champion of some very old-fashioned values. Thus for all of Zarathustra's brash talk of being the one "who smashes [the] tables of values, the breaker, the law-breaker" (*Z,* "Zarathustra's Prologue," p. 9), Nietzsche *himself* knows better. He heartily endorses earthly values and sees the move of anarchy as fraught with *aporia.* Instead of being a cre-

---

[31]Friedrich Nietzsche, *The Case of Wagner,* trans. Walter Kaufmann (New York: Random House, 1966), preface.

[32]Of course if "overcoming" requires giving up all traces, then there is simply no overcoming. Yet if Nietzsche exhibits specifically *Christian* values, he is (by his own definition) a *décadent."*

ator, Nietzsche is more a Stoic affirmer of life and its values. Indeed the
ideal of the creator seriously conflicts with Nietzsche's adoption of the
essentially Stoic view that one ought to accept the past, present and
future for what they are rather than attempt to change them. If these
moments are all essentially what they are, there is no real sense in
which one can be a creator. At best, one "creates" by accepting what is
and must be.

Here it is helpful to turn back to the discussion of Colossians 2:8 in
the introduction. In that passage Paul characterizes "philosophy and
empty deceit" as "according to human tradition" and "according to the
elemental spirits of the universe" (Col 2:8). The term "elemental spirits"
or simply "elements of the world" *(stoicheia tou kosmou)* is not completely clear in Paul. Since *stoichea* derives from *stoichos* (row or rank),
one can read Paul as referring to a hierarchy of spiritual powers (as do
many commentators) or even the Old Testament law.[33] But since Paul
links "philosophy" with these "elemental spirits," it seems plausible to
interpret him as talking about philosophy that is concerned with the elements. Of course much of early Greek philosophy is concerned with
understanding the elements of the world, whether material elements like
earth, air, fire and water or more spiritual elements like the *nous* and
logos. But it is hard to imagine a more obvious candidate here than Stoicism, which takes its basis precisely from the *stoicheia* of the cosmos.

Since Paul himself exhibits certain Stoic tendencies and there are striking similarities between Stoic and Christian thinking, he should not be read
as simply denouncing all aspects of Stoic thought. Paul's point is not that
philosophy (or Stoicism in particular) is simply "wrong" but that it has been
surpassed (and thus shown to be inferior) by the advent of the *Logos.* Thus
he says that "while we were minors, we were enslaved to the elemental
spirits of the world" (Gal 4:3) and Christ represents our final overcoming of
that enslavement (whether defined as philosophy or as the law).

An important comparison can be drawn here between Jesus and
Nietzsche. Jesus overcomes the law by fulfilling it (a point to which the
next chapter will return at length). We can argue that he does the same
with the *logos* of philosophy. His is not the simple overturning or negation of either the law or philosophy but a *fulfillment* that both affirms

---

[33]Paul implies that the "weak and beggarly elemental spirits" are the rules and observances
of the law (Gal 4:9-10).

and negates. Likewise, Nietzsche rereads Stoicism. Yet does Nietzsche truly overcome or surpass it? The next chapter will return to this question as well.

Far from being a complete nihilist, then, Nietzsche seems to exemplify precisely what he seeks to overcome. Heidegger accuses Nietzsche of not really understanding the essence of nihilism, which for Heidegger is the very attempt of "valuation." The problem with the valuation game is that in order to value something, one must place oneself above it in the role of judge. But in so doing one *de*values that thing. To be fair to Nietzsche, he seems to understand rather well that this is the problem with all philosophical attempts at valuing life (a point noted earlier). Yet I wonder whether Nietzsche might fall into the trap of valuing life by some conception of life. Does he ultimately place himself under life, or does he allow life merely to value itself?

Further, does Nietzsche fall prey to the charge of systemizing? On the one hand, we have seen that sometimes he goes to great lengths to avoid any reductive philosophizing. This is particularly evident in his discussion of truth. Certainly Nietzsche does not display the usual philosophical discomfort with loose ends and even contradictions. On the other hand, the notion of the will to power can be read as the ultimate unifying idea in Nietzsche's system. It is hard to imagine that anything would escape its grasp. While the will to power may not be the most systematic *logos,* it still seems to qualify as a *logos* of sorts and proves to be a heavy-handed explanation. And following in Plato's footsteps, Nietzsche never really *argues* for the will to power; rather it is merely asserted.

We have seen that for Nietzsche the whole of Western thought can be characterized by a successive overturning of values that is rooted in the will to power. If even valuation itself springs from the will to power, then all valuation must ultimately spring from domination. Heidegger connects the will to power with Nietzsche's emphasis on the creativity of the artist. For Nietzsche, art is the essence of all willing that opens up perspectives and takes possession of them.

Still, Heidegger thinks Nietzsche helps us to see a kind of idolatry that we might easily otherwise miss. Heidegger reads Nietzsche's attack as being directed against a very particular conception of God—as *ens realissimum*—and Heidegger is all for such an attack.

The heaviest blow against God is not that God is held to be unknowable, not that God's existence is demonstrated to be unprovable, but rather that the god held to be real is elevated to the highest value. For this blow comes precisely not from those who are standing about, who do not believe in God, but from the believers and their theologians who discourse on the being that is of all beings most in being, without ever letting it occur to them to think on Being itself, in order thereby to become aware that, seen from out of faith, their thinking and their talking is sheer blasphemy if it meddles in the theology of faith. (WN 105)

Thus Heidegger insists that "the death of God" is best interpreted as the death of Christendom. For Nietzsche, Christendom is the historical, world-political phenomenon of the church and its claim to power within the shaping of Western humanity and its modern culture. Christendom in this sense and the Christianity of New Testament faith are not the same. Even a non-Christian life can affirm Christendom and use it as a means of power, just as, conversely, a Christian life does not necessarily require Christendom. Therefore a confrontation with Christendom is not necessarily an attack on what is Christian, any more than a critique of theology is necessarily a critique of faith, the interpretation of which theology is said to be. So one can view Nietzsche's criticism as against an idol of a particular sort, one that Christians themselves would not wish to affirm.

Of course the true God can never be reduced to *ens realissimum* or the highest being or the greatest value. As Heidegger points out, "Never can man put himself in the place of God, because the essence of man never reaches the essential realm belonging to God" (WN 100). God is always God and resists all of our attempts at idol creation. Yet Heidegger sees these *attempts* as idolatry of the greatest order. Not only are they truly monumental in scale (for what could be a greater idol than, say, "God as highest being"?), but they seem like ways to *honor* God. So they are all the more enticing and deceptive. But they are just further examples of substituting a human *logos* for the divine *Logos*.

This is why Heidegger says that "thinking begins only when we have come to know that reason, glorified for centuries, is the most stiff-necked adversary of thought" (WN 112). Echoing Heidegger, we can say that true worship begins only when we renounce the creations of our own reason and worship God alone.

However much Nietzsche ends up succumbing to an idolatry of his own, he still can prove to be a helpful ally in the fight against idols.

When Nietzsche pronounces the death of God, he pronounces the death of what can be only an idol or an ideology. That death should be the cause for much rejoicing, for the death of an idol means at least the possibility of the life of an icon. As Christians, we should follow Nietzsche in using the hammer to sound out idols, even if they turn out to be idols graven by our own hands or minds. Moreover, Nietzsche is to be commended for his unrelenting attack on the rationalistic forms of Christianity of his day, for they too were idols. There are few more penetrating analyses of the bankruptcy of the "Christianity" of Kant and Strauss than Nietzsche's.

But is Nietzsche right about the meaning of life? How does Nietzsche's conception of life differ from that of Jesus? We turn to those questions in the following chapter.

3

JESUS AND
"MORALITY"

What does Nietzsche think of Jesus? And just how far apart are Nietzsche and Jesus in their views of morality? Surprisingly enough, I think Jesus would agree with Nietzsche that "morality" is an idol that we have created. In general, Jesus' thinking on this topic is considerably more amicable to Nietzsche's than we might expect—at least in some important respects. That claim, though, will take some explaining.

Of course, as we shall see later in this chapter, Jesus and Nietzsche are at fundamental odds as to what being a truly moral person is all about. Ultimately it is hard to imagine two more diametrically opposed views.

Nietzsche and Jesus

Although Nietzsche does make what seem to be negative comments about Jesus (for instance, that he is "a combination of the sublime, the sick and the childish," *A* 31), most of what he says is positive. One might say that Nietzsche is more anti-Christ than anti-Jesus. When he rails against Christianity, he usually does not appear to have Jesus in mind. Indeed it is not too much to say that Jesus is one of his heroes. As Karl

Jaspers aptly puts it, "Nietzsche himself stopped short (an astonishing fact!) before the figure of Jesus. Here he finds the actualization of a way of life in which everything is genuine and without pretense or false-hood."[1] Of course Nietzsche has a rather particular view of Jesus, one with which Christians at points will agree and at other points vehemently disagree.

Nietzsche considers Jesus to be something like a "free spirit" who turns "the whole of Jewish *ecclesiastical* teaching" upside down (*A* 32-33). Whereas the Jewish leaders feel strictly bound by the letter of the law, Jesus "is opposed to any kind of word, formula, law, faith, dogma" (*A* 32). According to Nietzsche, Jesus thinks life cannot be reduced to any formula or dogma. One might say that Jesus is simply trying to be true to the actual phenomena of life. For phenomenologists continually remind us that the phenomena resist reductionism.

Further, whereas the Jewish law embodied a tit-for-tat formula, Jesus does not resist "even the evil man" (*A* 35). Whereas Jewish culture had clear racial and socioeconomic distinctions, Jesus "makes no distinction between foreigner and native, between Jew and non-Jew" in terms of moral obligation (*A* 33). Whereas Jewish religion was strongly tied to notions of sin and forgiveness, Jesus abolishes "the Judaism of the concepts 'sin,' 'forgiveness of sin,' 'faith,' 'redemption by faith'" (*A* 33). There are different ways of reading Nietzsche's qualification "the Judaism of" sin, forgiveness and redemption. Perhaps he is simply renouncing these concepts. But given the context of his criticism in general, "Judaism" here is probably more likely synonymous with "Pharisaical." In any case, it is not immediately clear that Nietzsche denies sin, forgiveness and redemption—even though he clearly denies a particular *version* of these conceptions.

Nietzsche admires Jesus' boldness, exemplified by his unabashed denunciation of hypocrisy and confident teaching in the temple. On Nietzsche's view, "only Christian *practice,* a life such as he who dies on the Cross *lived,* is Christian" (*A* 39).

But exactly what constitutes the practice of Jesus? Nietzsche is right that Jesus is a "free spirit," at least to some degree. He has no place to lay his head and seems unconcerned with typical daily cares. Moreover,

---

[1]Karl Jaspers, *Nietzsche: An Introduction to the Understanding of His Philosophical Activity,* trans. Charles F. Walraff and Frederick J. Schmitz (Tucson: University of Arizona Press, 1965), p. 142.

not infrequently does Jesus use such constructions as "You have heard that it was said. . . . But I say to you" (Mt 5:33-34). For example, "You have heard that it was said, 'You shall not commit adultery.' But I say to that everyone who looks at a woman with lust has already committed adultery with her in his heart" (Mt 5:27-28). Nietzsche is also right that Jesus overturns "Jewish *ecclesiastical* teaching." The introduction noted that Jesus challenged the teaching of the Pharisees and scribes, charging them, at least at points, with having invented their own tradition and put it in place of God's Word. Yet in neither of the two cases cited above does Jesus *contradict* the law of God as found in the Old Testament. Rather Jesus *complicates* it.

Here we come to an important disagreement between Jesus and "morality." Whereas morality is the attempt to codify moral action into a system that can be mastered and controlled, Jesus' teaching resists such attempts. Perhaps we should say that Jesus is not against morality but Morality. It is not that Jesus resists any attempt to calculate moral action, implying that one ought not try to act in a measured way. Instead Jesus shows that such measuring only goes so far. If one commits adultery by simply entertaining the possibility, then the prospects for measuring are rather limited. And Jesus particularly opposes measuring that aims at letting us off the hook. As noted in the introduction, Jesus exposes the attempt of the Pharisees and scribes to reduce the demands entailed by honoring one's parents. The point of Jesus' teaching, then, is not to limit our obligation but to heighten it. A fundamental aspect of the teaching of Jesus Christ the *Logos* is that it resists being mastered or controlled by any human *logos*. One cannot, for instance, reduce the "blesseds" of the Sermon on the Mount to any formula or simple law. Jesus' teaching simply explodes any such attempts. Of course saying that is quite different from saying that Jesus "opposes" the Old Testament law. Jesus' own read of his role is that he comes to "fulfill" the law, so his teaching *supplements* the law. Admittedly, it is a very strange supplement, for it is a radicalization of the law. To say, in effect, that *everyone* is our neighbor is to say that justice cannot be reduced to formula. Further, while "an eye for an eye" represents justice (and given earlier conceptions of justice, it was a significant moral advance), "turning the other cheek" requires a sense of grace that goes beyond the demands of justice. And grace—by its very nature—strongly resists quantification or measuring.

The implications of Jesus' radicalization of moral responsibility will be considered in much greater detail in the chapter on Derrida. For now, they can be summed up as follows. Jesus confounds any formulation of God's law that re-creates it in a human image, any simplification that makes that law easier to master and control—thus turning it into an ideology. As noted earlier, Jesus criticizes the Pharisees for claiming their tradition to be from God (Mt 15:1-9). In so doing they effectively make themselves out to *be* God. So to reformulate God's morality is to claim to be God and thus to make oneself into an idol (and since one's morality is claimed to be from God, it is likewise idolatrous).

If Nietzsche thinks that Jesus "abolishes" the ideas of sin and forgiveness, then Nietzsche is profoundly wrong. But I take it that Jesus instead *recasts* the notions of sin and forgiveness in ways that are paradoxical. Jesus certainly recasts them in ways that make them far less susceptible to human mishandling. But this recasting is to correct deficient formulations of the conceptions, not the conceptions themselves.

It is crucial to note here that *both* the Old Testament law and the Pharisees' recasting of morality are deficient, since they are inadequate as expressions of God's morality. Obviously the laws of the Pharisees are considerably more deficient than those of the Torah. Yet in both cases Jesus gives us a conception of morality with a higher degree of *adaequatio*. The effect of Jesus' move is to make sin and forgiveness more significant, not less so (*pace* Nietzsche). If the bounds of sin cannot simply be circumscribed around "doing the deed" but include "thinking the thought," then sin is much more of a problem than one might at first have thought. Morality is considerably more difficult to master than the idols of Morality we create.

Moreover, Jesus significantly ups the requirement for forgiveness by saying that there is no point at which we can say that forgiveness is no longer appropriate. While Jesus specifically charges the Pharisees and scribes with having invented laws in order to advance their own interests, part of Jesus' message is that any attempt to specify the law in a "once and for all" sense is doomed to failure.

There is a second way in which Jesus opposes Morality. Spelling out the law as a kind of accounting balance is—perhaps not always but often—what the project of formulating Morality ends up being about. Although Nietzsche thinks of Christian morality as merely a continuation of the Socratic formula "reason=virtue=happiness," it seems to me that Jesus and subsequent Christian teaching seriously disturb that formula.

Jesus' teaching simply does not submit to human rationality.

Note that there is a deeply economic character to Socratic morality. Here I use *economic* to indicate any kind of transaction in which the principal motive is the desire to gain something in return. While economic transactions need not involve money, some sort of commodity—which could be power or just a warm feeling of satisfaction—must be involved. For Socrates, virtue makes sense (and is thus economical) because it brings about good results. Thus it is "rational" to be moral. Nietzsche claims that Socrates gives us "the highest form of shrewdness; he calls it virtue" (*WP* 432).

No doubt there are many aspects of Christian morality that make good economic sense, even perhaps of a monetary sort. Honoring one's parents, being faithful to one's spouse and telling the truth are generally going to bring about good personal results. The reward of long life is even promised to those who honor their parents (Ex 20:12; Eph 6:2).

Yet Jesus does not teach that the *principal* motive of moral actions is personal gain. The rewards promised to Jesus' followers appeal to one sort of motivation but not necessarily the highest form of human motivation. Often one first acts in a right way for lower motives—usually some form of avoidance of pain and reward of pleasure. A child may honor her parents because she wishes to avoid punishment, and a college student might do so to guarantee that they continue paying tuition. But if such are their *only* motives, then the parents are not truly being honored at all. In the case of the college student, the parents are simply being used as a means to the student's end.

The Christian emphasis on love as the motivation for action means that moral action ultimately is not about economic calculation. To act out of love for others means that a genuine concern for their welfare motivates my action. True, often the result of acting in a loving way is that love is returned to me (though it may well not have that result), but that gain is not the *only* reason that I act. If it were, then my love for the other would actually be just a disguised form of love for myself. Of course our love for others may often turn out to be just that. That, however, is not what Jesus calls us to do. If we truly love another, then our welfare is not the sole or even primary source of our motivation.

Jesus knowingly and willfully confounds the very notion that morality should make economic sense. It is far beyond the bounds of an economical logic to give one's coat to anyone who demands it (Mt 5:40).

Were someone to offer a good price, that would be one thing. But the idea of also giving them one's cloak—when they have not even asked for it—is to throw all economical sense to the wind. There simply is no "logic" that one can use to make sense of this.

Faith as Anti-*agōn*

If Nietzsche were to characterize Christianity in a nutshell, he would probably say something like the following. A short list of Christian characteristics would include (but certainly not be limited to) self-hatred, a pharisaic attitude and compassion. Nietzsche also depicts Christianity on the basis of what it is against: passion, the body, sensual pleasure, lust for power, selfishness, revenge and life itself.

Many of these aspects—what Christianity exemplifies and what it stands against—are woven together in a section of *Twilight of the Idols* which immediately follows "How the 'True World' Finally Became a Fiction." In "Morality as Anti-nature" Nietzsche claims:

> The Church fights passion by cutting it out, in every sense; its practice, its "therapy" is *castration*. It never asks, "How does one spiritualize, beautify, deify a desire?"—its discipline has always emphasized eradication (eradication of sensuality, pride, the ambition to rule, covetousness, vengefulness).—But ripping out the passions by the root means ripping out life by the root; the practice of the Church is *an enemy to life*. (*TI*, "Morality as Anti-nature," p. 2)

One way of responding to Nietzsche's charges here is to agree, though in two quite different senses.

On the one hand, it can be argued that there have indeed been some of these elements in Christian thought and practice, despite the fact that they ought not to be there. Note that Nietzsche uses the broad term "the Church." His attack is thus not necessarily against the teachings of Jesus, nor against Christian doctrine per se (though at times I think it is against both of these). Does Nietzsche accurately describe actual Christian practice? Well, at least some Christian practice. Frederick Copleston is certainly right when he points out that "it is hopelessly unjust to contrast the best examples of paganism with the worst examples of Christianity."[2] Nietzsche is rather selective with his examples. It would not be hard to

---

[2]Frederick Copleston, *Friedrich Nietzsche: Philosopher of Culture* (New York: Barnes & Noble, 1975), p. 127.

find pagan counterexamples to throw back in his face. Yet one must not dismiss Nietzsche's point too quickly (as I think Copleston tends to do).

Take Christian thought on passion and the body. If one looks back in church history, it is not hard to find (and even hard not to find) instances of a negative attitude toward both. Taking Matthew 19:12 seriously, the early church father Origen provides a rather literal example of the eradication Nietzsche depicts. But castration has usually taken much subtler forms. Christianity has been interpreted by some, both outside and inside the church, as advocating "ripping out the passions." Early in history, Christian orthodoxy declared Gnostic thought—which takes the body and its desires to be inherently evil—to be heretical. But those Gnostic tendencies were clearly present among some early believers and can be found throughout Christian history. It would be difficult to say that the Christian church has not had its share of what Nietzsche calls "the despisers of the body" (*Z*, "Of the Despisers of the Body"). Although Nietzsche can be accused of taking a cheap shot at Trappist monks when he speaks of "those natures who need La Trappe" (*TI*, "Morality as Anti-nature," p. 2),[3] one must agree that there have been some unhealthy manifestations of "despising of the body" in the history of monasticism.[4] And those tendencies are not completely absent from contemporary American evangelicalism. There have been Christians throughout history who have categorically decried sensual pleasure instead of recognizing it as a gift from God that can be used properly or misused.

As to instances of a pharisaic attitude, they are too common and obvious to need citing. Whereas it is far too much to say that Christianity has been characterized by self-hatred, such a claim cannot simply be dismissed. While Christian doctrine does not advocate the hating of oneself in any literal sense (and Jesus clearly affirms a sense of proper self-love in articulating the Golden Rule), throughout church history the Christian idea of subordination of the self has sometimes taken the form of self-hatred. On such a view, love of self is simply wrong. One should be unconcerned about one's own needs and look only to the needs of oth-

---

[3]In French a *trappe* is a flight of stairs or a trapdoor. La Trappe, the first Trappist abbey, provided monks a way to spirituality. But Nietzsche plays on the metaphorical meaning of *trappe,* which is "trap" or "trick."

[4]My own read of monasticism is that, for all its faults, it has been an important agent in promoting genuine Christian commitment and spirituality.

ers. In its most extreme manifestation, this lack of concern for oneself becomes even a hatred of oneself.

What about revenge and "pity"? A Christian might readily admit to the second (though perhaps not so readily once we see what Nietzsche means by "pity"), but what about the first? While Christianity would seem to involve a renunciation of power and selfishness, Nietzsche considers it a particularly sneaky way of gaining power over others.[5] The idea of Christian revenge, then, is that Christians attempt to gain power in order to get back at those who have harmed them.

It is hard to argue that Nietzsche is simply wrong. Perhaps the most obvious and ubiquitous way that Christians attempt to take revenge is by renouncing the world and those who are of it in such a way as to put themselves above it and above "those people." A fundamentalist preacher exhorts us, "My friends, look at those worldly people. They think they're happy, but they're not." Translation: "We're better than those people." Of course there is equal opportunity for smugness and self-aggrandizement in all branches of Christendom. I am often amused to hear so-called liberal, open-minded Christians speak with the same sense of superiority not only about the misguided sinful masses but also about their "close-minded" fundamentalist sisters and brothers. But of course even more amusing (not to mention frightening and humbling) is that I, Bruce Ellis Benson, am writing about the self-aggrandizement of others. Do I really have any room to talk? Marion is right about the need to obtain forgiveness for theological essays. I should be writing this entire book on my knees.

Even more embarrassing to Christians in general, though, is what Nietzsche takes to be the ultimate motivation for being a Christian—the joy of watching unbelievers get what they have coming. All he needs to do to prove his point is to quote a couple of the church's more eminent theologians. Thomas Aquinas, for instance, says that "in order that the happiness of the saints may be more delightful to them and that they may render more copius thanks to God for it, they are allowed to see perfectly the sufferings of the damned."[6] The delights of the heavenly skybox are enhanced by the bliss of human fireworks. The church father

---

[5]I shall return to this charge of Christianity's being *essentially* selfish (as opposed to being merely incidentally selfish) in the section on Derrida.

[6]Thomas Aquinas *Summa Theologica* 3, *Supplementum,* trans. Fathers of the English Dominican Province (New York: Benziger Brothers, 1948), Q94.a1.

Tertullian takes this even further, speaking of the "spectacles" that Christians will one day experience (and at which they will laugh). So many delights to choose from! Former kings "now groaning in the depths of darkness," persecutors "liquefying in fiercer flames than they kindled in their rage against Christians," and (given Tertullian's lack of appreciation of philosophy) "philosophers blushing before their disciples as they blaze together."[7] Were Nietzsche to invent fake quotations it would be difficult for him to improve on these.

Thomas and Tertullian do not accurately reflect the sentiments of all Christians, but such sentiments are likely much more common than Christians are willing to admit. Even though Jesus' message has to do with sinfulness (that everyone is wretched) and grace (that no one deserves forgiveness or eternal life), Christianity can be viewed as a way to take revenge—or even as having revenge at its very core.

Even compassion can be used to exalt ourselves. Shortly we shall consider what would be the consequences were compassion genuine. But Nietzsche is more right about the true motives of Christian "compassion" than we Christians would care to admit. Again, there are numerous ways this charge can be explicated practically.[8] If I visit those in prison, it may be simply an occasion for me to think, *How much better am I than these criminals.* Or I may view the encounter as an opportunity for the inmates to view me as superior—to envy my freedom. The ways that compassion can end up being disguised selfishness are legion. In the end it is *very* difficult (impossible?) to keep compassion from turning into smugness and superiority. Thus even compassion can become an occasion for idolatry, in which I hold up myself as God (*"I* am the good shepherd").

On the other hand, while one can agree with Nietzsche that certain *other* characteristics he cites are indeed to be found in Christian thought and practice, one can (and should) strongly disagree with his judgment of them as undesirable or inimical to life. Here we come to an irresolvable difference between Nietzsche's conception of life and that of Jesus. Central to Jesus' teaching is the affirmation of life. Jesus says that he is

---

[7]Tertullian *De spectaculus,* trans. T. R. Glover (Cambridge, Mass.: Harvard University Press, 1977), §XXX.

[8]"I can think of no more insightful analysis of Nietzsche's charge that compassion is really disguised self-love than that of Merold Westphal in *Suspicion and Faith: The Religious Uses of Modern Atheism* (Grand Rapids, Mich.: Eerdmans, 1993), pp. 219-89.

the "bread of life" (Jn 6:35), that he has come to give not just life but "abundant life" (Jn 10:10) and that he is "the way, the truth, and the life" (Jn 14:6). And this is not Jesus' teaching alone. Paul claims that those whose minds are focused on the Spirit have "life and peace" (Rom 8:6). But life in the Spirit is quite different from Nietzsche's idea of life. To see how, we need to consider what Nietzsche means by "life."

It is interesting that in *Twilight of the Idols* Nietzsche speaks solely of Christianity in the section titled "Morality as Anti-nature." We have already seen that Christianity is not a continuation of the project of "Morality," at least in the economic sense of morality put forth by Socrates. Christian morality is not about learning how to play the system in order to secure the best outcomes for oneself. But it is true that Christ's moral teachings are "against nature," though even this claim needs to be qualified. Nietzsche is right that Christianity "thwarts those instincts bent on preserving and enhancing the value of life" (*A* 7)—if we are using the term *life* to equal "nature" in Nietzsche's sense. The problem with Christianity, at least for Nietzsche, is that it instructs us to go against our nature. In other words, it tells us to do precisely what we are not inclined to do. This is why Nietzsche thinks that Christianity has caused the deterioration of the human race: it has reversed all of the natural human values and put the values of weaklings in their place. On Nietzsche's read, "every form of anti-nature is depraved," and thus "depravity is Christianity."[9] Or: Christianity is depravity. But Nietzsche is right about the cause-effect relationship between Christianity and "deterioration" only if his conception of "life" is right. And that is precisely the issue.

With Nietzsche and Jesus, we have two senses of human flourishing, senses that at points converge but at other points radically diverge. Though Nietzsche rails against Platonic morality, he and Socrates at heart really agree as to what is good. Although Socrates moves away from the earlier Greek ideal of the warrior hero (and so is part of the movement of *décadence* for Nietzsche), I think Nietzsche is profoundly right when he says that Socrates puts in its place "a new kind of *agōn*"

---

[9]These quotations come from "Decree Against Christianity," a short addendum that was originally part of *The Anti-Christ*. An English translation of this section can be found in Gary Shapiro, "The Writing on the Wall: *The Antichrist* and the Semiotics of History," in *Reading Nietzsche,* ed. Robert C. Solomon and Kathleen M. Higgins (New York: Oxford University Press, 1988), pp. 212-13.

(*TI,* "The Problem of Socrates," p. 8). The move is from a bodily strength to a mental one. The good for Socrates are still those who "win," but now the contest is one of dialectics. One might here attempt to exonerate Socrates by claiming that it is the Sophists and not Socrates who are bent on winning. Perhaps so. To be sure, unlike Socrates, the Sophists are bent on winning at any cost—including using specious argumentation and sacrificing truth, if need be. Moreover, the practical effect of the *Apology* was hardly a win for Socrates. Yet however much Socrates seems committed to truth (and I do not question that commitment), the Socratic dialogues certainly seem like a kind of contest in which wits are pitted against wits. Even the *Apology,* while it may have failed to save Socrates' neck, has the goal of presenting a superior argument to that of his accusers. Although Socrates dies, he dies with the knowledge that his argument was superior (and, I would venture to guess, the satisfaction that his interlocutors were fools). So the idea(l) of an *agōn* remains central.

In ancient Greece, an *agōn* was literally an athletic contest, but more generally it denoted the sense of conflict or struggle. Whereas Socrates' display of a personal will to power is much more subtle than that of the warrior hero, there is still a strong sense of his own will prevailing over that of his interlocutors. For both Nietzsche and Socrates, then, those who are admired as strong (most alive) are those who allow their will to power to be central. It is not that Socrates does not exemplify the will to power; rather he is less concerned with political power than with intellectual power. However much of a "political weakling" he might appear to be (and this charge is certainly open to dispute), he is clearly not an intellectual weakling.

While the will to power is often interpreted as political power, it need not be political at all. It can easily be intellectual, religious or simply personal. Moreover, both the acquisition and the demonstration of power can take forms of seemingly deep altruism and love. A shrewd person seeking power is likely to make that move appear as loving and caring as possible, since bald power seeking is often futile.

Whereas Nietzsche depicts those who do not give in to their will to power as weaklings, Jesus demonstrates exactly the opposite. His strength or power lies in taking a position of weakness. Interestingly enough, Nietzsche is able to recognize something similar to (though clearly not identical with) Jesus' "weakness." Speaking of Goethe,

Nietzsche calls him "a tolerant human being, not out of weakness but out of strength" (*TI,* "Raids of an Untimely Man," p. 49). In other words, Goethe is able to show tolerance—which might seem to be a kind of weakness—because of an inner strength.

But Jesus does not merely adopt an attitude or posture. His weakness is demonstrated in action. Jesus voluntarily "emptied himself, taking the form of a slave, being born in human likeness" because he "did not regard equality with God as something to be exploited" (Phil 2:6-7). Jesus' strength is manifested precisely through his voluntary action of taking the position of the weak.

The New Testament gives us a very strange formula for power. "Power is made perfect in weakness" (2 Cor 12:9). We are told, "Humble yourselves before the Lord, and he will exalt you" (Jas 4:10). One way of reading these passages is as presenting a "formula," an economic plan for power. But that would be a serious misunderstanding of true weakness. While we can rightly say that Jesus demonstrates a kind of strength, there is something problematic in talking of Jesus' "strength" here. And that problematic nature must not be resolved but emphasized. Jesus does not exemplify merely a more subtle way of taking power than Socrates exhibits. Jesus' "power" is in renouncing power. Thus it is *truly* weakness that Jesus exemplifies, not a pseudo-weakness designed to get power. To put this another way: Jesus' renunciation of power is a true renunciation.

But in renouncing power, Jesus gains it. So the move is genuinely paradoxical or aporetic. One must *truly* renounce power in order to gain it. But if one truly renounces power, then one cannot even speak of "in order to . . ." The "formula" cannot be "I renounce power in order to gain even more power," for that would end up being simply a kind of economic calculation—a much more clever and subtle one, of course, but one still the same. To renounce is to give up all economic calculations. To receive power, one must give up all attempts to gain it.

The difficulty of trying to articulate the notion of heavenly power is that it confounds all notions of earthly power. If power is in weakness (and if weakness is genuinely weak, as opposed to merely giving the appearance of being weak), then it isn't really power. Or at least it is not power in any way that makes sense to human beings. Of course it does manifest a curious sense of strength, one that confounds Nietzsche's sense. From a Christian point of view, it is easy to give in to the temptation to lord ourselves over others (whether overtly or covertly). In contrast, it is remarkably difficult to make the conscious choice to serve others and submit to them. One can make sense of "serving others" as long as it is designed to promote oneself. If I am kind to others with the objective of making myself look good, that makes sense. But if I do so with no such objective—with no objective that can be termed economic—then it makes no sense at all. That is, it makes no *earthly* sense.

Nietzsche claims that "the best shall rule, the best *wants* to rule" (*Z*, "Of the Old and New Law Tables," p. 21). But Jesus knowingly gives up ruling. Surprisingly, Nietzsche seems in awe of Jesus when he says, "He does not resist, he does not defend his rights, he takes no steps to avert the worst that can happen to him" (*A* 35). How can one act this way—except by some unearthly strength?

So Christians knowingly give up pride and ambition to rule in order to become servants of all. Note that we cannot exactly say "to *be* servants of all," for the process of *becoming* a servant is long, hard and against human nature. Of course putting it that way is not quite right either. Although Nietzsche obviously thinks that his sense of good and bad is not against life and nature, we Christians should be careful not to concede too much. For the proper Christian position is not that Christianity is against nature per se but that it is against *fallen nature*. In other words, the Christian position is the natural position, the one that truly affirms nature and thus life—but nature and life as God intended them to be.

Whereas Nietzsche depicts Christianity as against nature and life, it is Nietzsche himself who is against them. From a fallen perspective, he appears to be right. But the solution is not to merely give in to the will to power of nature as Nietzsche suggests we do; rather we need to see the world from God's perspective—at least as far as such a move is possible.

Jesus Christ overcomes the economic values of both Socrates and Nietzsche and turns us back to a right conception of "human being." However, Jesus does so not by "castration," which is Nietzsche's charge against Christianity, but by a fundamental altering of the will to power.[10] Although it might be thought that Christianity is all about the renuncia-

---

[10]See Jacques Derrida's discussion of Christianity as "feminine" in *Spurs: Nietzsche's Styles*, trans. Barbara Harlow (Chicago: University of Chicago Press, 1978), pp. 89-95.

tion of the will to power, I think it is better understood as its *reorientation*. We have seen Nietzsche claim that Christianity never asks, "How does one spiritualize, beautify, deify a desire?" He accuses it of practicing eradication. But Nietzsche misunderstands the point of Christian sanctification. To stop being motivated by the will to power, one cannot simply pretend it does not exist or just denounce it (since it is a very real force). Christianity does not say no to life in opposition to Nietzsche's clear yes. Instead the will to power as the basic force of life must be transformed. Whereas the will to power is always ultimately directed toward oneself—one's needs and personal advancement—what we might call the "will to love" is a desire for the other. It is no less passionate, but its object is different.

One might be tempted to give in to Nietzsche's gender stereotyping here and say that Christianity moves from a "male" sense of self-exaltation to a more "feminine" sense of caring for the other.[11] But Christ is not the bringer of "castration," nor does he champion "female" over "male" values. If anything, Christ questions the accepted (male) notions of strength as inaccurate and shallow. True strength requires not renouncing one's passions but feeling them even more deeply.

A properly Christian conception of pity or compassion is likewise quite different from what Nietzsche sees it to be. The term Nietzsche uses is *Mitleid,* which denotes "suffering with or alongside," as does the English term *compassion,* the literal equivalent of *Mitleid.* While Nietzsche wonders whether compassion can ever be genuine,[12] were it to turn out to be so, it would be the very epitome of Christianity's anti-agonistic character. Whereas Nietzsche sees his goal as being an individual creator who is free from the demands of his neighbor, compassion ties us to our neighbor in a way that makes freedom (at least as defined in this way) impossible. For if I suffer with my neighbor, making my neighbor's cares *my* cares, then I am in effect chained to my neighbor in a way that would seem to be the very opposite of an agonistic contest. Rather than being in conflict with my neighbor, I am forced to be in sympathy. The New Testament Greek verb *sumpatheō* conveys the idea of having feelings in common because one shares a way of being with

---

[11]In a sense this is what Hélène Cixous does in "The Laugh of the Medusa," trans. Keith Cohen and Paula Cohen, *Signs: Journal of Women in Culture and Society* 1 (summer 1976): 875-93.

[12]I take this in Nietzsche to be truly an open question.

another. How can I then define myself in opposition to my neighbor, which would seem to be the requirement of an agonistic conception of life, nature, reason and morality? While contrived compassion could well serve me in an agonistic relationship (for example, I attempt to seem compassionate in order to get something from another), real compassion can only spell the death of the *agōn*. There is no room for revenge, selfishness or the will to power. Instead of a passion for oneself, life becomes a *com*passion in which the lens of one's self-absorbed focus expands to take the other into view.

We have seen that Nietzsche criticizes the Christian conception of virtue—defined as love—because it does not serve life. And here Nietzsche and Jesus fundamentally part company. For life *is* only to serve love. That is, love exists not for life but life for love. On the one hand, love is the quintessential value, for it is something that one chooses over life. One may give reasons for love, but they all fall short. On the other hand, the believer believes that love is not *just* a value one happens to have chosen, but a "something" (certainly not a "thing") that goes beyond all values, value systems, dogmas and everything else.

So the believer and Nietzsche do agree in one sense. The choice here has to do with faith all the way down (with apologies to Richard Rorty). But it is Nietzsche who ends up being the conservative. Nietzsche wants to preserve the "good old-fashioned" earthly values that are the very opposite of sacrifice and service. In contrast, Jesus calls for *truly disruptive behavior.* When we ask "What would Jesus do?" (WWJD) we do not ask a question with a safe and predictable answer. The potential answer is so frightening that this question can be asked only in holy awe.

If there is any philosopher of the twentieth century who renews not merely a sense of awe in the face of the Other but also makes love central to his thinking, it is Levinas. Although Levinas's read of Western philosophy is strikingly similar to Nietzsche's, Levinas responds to philosophy's legacy in a remarkably different way, one that ends up having a profound influence on Derrida.

4

LEVINAS AND DERRIDA

As the twentieth century drew to an end, Derrida became increasingly concerned with ethical and theological questions. The problem with a morally and religiously attuned Derrida is that it disrupts the caricature beloved by his followers and cursed by his critics. Many—on both sides—took Derrida as opening the door to an infinite textual and intellectual play without rules and responsibility, and certainly without religion.[1] So what happened? Ought we to read Derrida as having undergone a radical conversion or as at least evidencing a transformation in thinking similar to Heidegger's famed *Kehre* (usually translated as "the turn")?

At first glance something along these lines might seem to be the most plausible explanation, simply because Derrida's later thought *appears* to

---

[1]No doubt some may find it difficult to read Derrida's early writings in an ethical and religious light, either because they doubt the genuineness of Derrida's current concern with such issues or because they find Derrida's thought to be unfriendly to religion and morality. While one cannot do much to prove that Derrida's concern is genuine, the discussion here should go a good way toward showing that Derrida's thought can at least be read in a way that is supportive of morality and religion.

be at odds with his earlier thought.[2] His turn to the moral and religious has left his more leftist disciples perplexed (should we say feeling that Derrida is just *too* aporetic for their tastes?) and often unwilling to follow.

But where did this new (and, one would assume, improved) Derrida come from? Was it there all along? And to what extent is it dependent on Emmanuel Levinas?

A New Derrida?

Derrida's move toward moral and religious questions has been long and gradual. John Caputo is right when we he says:

> I do not think there is anything like a "reversal" or massive transformation in Derrida's thought, of the sort one finds in Heidegger, say, anything like Derrida I and Derrida II. But I do think there is a progression in which this originally ethical and political motif in his work, deeply Levinasian in tone, has worked its way more and more to the front of his concerns in the writings of the 1980's and 1990's.[3]

Even in Derrida's early writings there are underlying ethical, political and even religious concerns that have a remarkably Levinasian tone. Of course one may need to have an awareness of Levinas in order to spot them.[4] Given that many readers of Derrida in the 1960s, 1970s and even 1980s were not very aware of Levinas, it is understandable that they were slow to pick up on this connection. But Derrida has clearly been profoundly influenced by Levinas and bears a marked kinship with him. In a 1986 interview Derrida commented that "before a thought like that of Levinas, I never have any objection."[5]

---

[2]There *was* an incident in Derrida's life that, at the very least, heightened his sense of sight and led to his *Memoirs of the Blind: The Self-Portrait and Other Ruins,* trans. Pascale-Anne Brault and Michael Naas (Chicago: University of Chicago Press, 1993). In the summer of 1989 he suffered a facial paralysis that at first left doctors bewildered but eventually was diagnosed as due to Lyme disease. Perhaps that illness particularly heightened his concern for ultimate questions.

[3]John D. Caputo, *Deconstruction in a Nutshell: A Conversation with Jacques Derrida* (New York: Fordham University Press, 1997), p. 127. Note that Derrida's own account of the trajectory of his thought situates his early thinking in relation to moral and religious concerns.

[4]I find this influence already in such an unlikely place as Jacques Derrida, *Edmund Husserl's Origin of Geometry: An Introduction,* trans. John P. Leavey (Stonybrook, N.Y.: Nicolas Hays, 1978), which was first published in 1962, one year after the publication of *Totality and Infinity.* Though most readers have not noted the connection, Jacques Derrida, *Speech and Phenomena,* trans. David B. Allison (Evanston, Ill.: Northwestern University Press, 1973), is clearly indebted to Levinasian concerns.

Caputo does admit that given the climate of the 1960s, Derrida's notion of *différance* tended to sound more Nietzschean than Levinasian. Yet I think one must go further than that. Not only was Derrida interpreted in this more Nietzschean (playful and skeptical) fashion, but I read his early thinking as actually *being* more Nietzschean (at least in tone, if not also substance) than Levinasian. The Levinasian concern was always there, but it wasn't strongly emphasized by Derrida. While Derrida adopts an interest in limits and otherness that can be attributed to Levinas, in his early writing the interest is only tangentially motivated by ethical concerns. Those concerns may be present, but they are submerged.

Beyond this, Derrida's move in an ethical and religious direction is partly due to factors internal to his thought (which is largely Caputo's read).[6] But it is not clear that Derrida moves in this direction simply as a smooth and logical outgrowth. One can argue that Derrida also begins to recognize his own neglect of such matters. That is, moral questions begin to impinge more and more on his thinking. And this impinging is not just internal but also external. Not just his critics but even his disciples and students prodded him to address such questions (notably, Marion). Thus Derrida's mature philosophy evidences a taking of responsibility—moral and religious—that is partly imposed and not just freely adopted. But as we shall see, the idea that moral concerns are imposed on us is central to the thinking of both Derrida and Levinas.

What is this Levinasian tone that becomes continually stronger in Derrida? It will be helpful to survey Levinas's thought as a context for Derrida's thinking, which is both a continuation of and a response to Levinas. On the one hand, Derrida deeply agrees with Levinas's concerns and takes them seriously (and this will become particularly evident in the following chapter); on the other hand, Derrida questions not only the extent to which Levinas is able to solve these problems but also whether a "solution" is even conceivable.

The Other as Radical Transcendence

Emmanuel Levinas and Nietzsche effectively agree on at least one thing: the history of Western philosophy has been the history of an attempt to achieve a sense of totality through a mastery of our experiences. From

---

[5]Jacques Derrida and Pierre-Jean Labarrière, *Altérités* (Paris: Osiris, 1986), p. 74.

[6]John D. Caputo, *The Prayers and Tears of Jacques Derrida* (Bloomington: Indiana University Press, 1997).

its very beginning, philosophy has tended toward ideology. As we saw in the previous chapter, it has the goal of adequation by way of system-izing. Levinas speaks of "the strict coinciding of thought . . . and the idea of reality in which this thought thinks" (*BPW* 130). Yet whereas Nietzsche reads this attempt at adequation and systematizing as episte-mologically and metaphysically problematic, Levinas points out that it is likewise *morally* questionable. It is not just that in philosophizing human beings tend to go beyond their own capabilities; more important, human beings tend to do a kind of *ethical* violence to that which is other—to the phenomena in general, to human "others" and ultimately to God. Whereas philosophers have tended to see what they do as merely an innocent attempt to understand that which is other to them, Levinas sees the desire to systematize as an attempt to control that which is other to me by making it mine. In other words, I wish to recast the other in my own image.

One might read Levinas as saying that idolatry is endemic to the entire philosophical enterprise. For Levinas, the very goal of philosophy (and most particularly metaphysics) is the creation of an image—of the world, of the other, of God—that turns me into God. Levinas is concerned with idolatry in its most obvious sense, the substitution of images for God. But he is likewise (and even more) concerned with idolatry of a much subtler sort. "The ontological event accomplished by philosophy consists in sup-pressing or transmuting the alterity of all that is Other, in universalizing the immanence of the Same *[le Même]* or of Freedom, in effacing the boundaries" (*BPW* 11). When ontology (or metaphysics) "suppresses" the alterity of the other, the other is reformulated in ontology's image. The boundaries that normally separate the other from me are removed, and the other in effect becomes part of me. When either the world or my neighbor is recast in my image, I take the place of God. We have seen that this move is precisely the one that Nietzsche criticizes. Hegel is often taken to be the most extreme example of this systematizing tendency, but his project is more properly viewed as the culmination of this tradition.

All of this needs some unpacking, though. Let us briefly consider some of the basic concepts with which Levinas works: the same and the other, autonomy versus heteronomy, the face, the infinite, desire, and the difference between the human and divine other.

As strange as Levinas's continual talk of "the same" *(le Même)* and "the other" *(l'Autre)* may sound, these terms are simply translations of

Plato's terms (respectively) *tauton* and *to heteron*. Although Plato insists that these two most basic categories of being cannot be reduced to one another,[7] Levinas argues that the history of philosophy has been characterized by a continual attempt to do just that. We have already seen that philosophy tends to impose a *logos* or structure on the world, to put the world into a kind of schema. What Levinas claims is that this schema usually looks like *me,* so that the alterity of the other "is thereby reabsorbed into my own identity as a thinker or a possessor" (*TAI* 33). In other words, the move is usually not making *tauton* into *to heteron* but the other way around. As Levinas puts it, "Autonomy or heteronomy? The choice of Western philosophy has most often been on the side of freedom and the Same."[8] My attempt to make sense of the world usually has the effect of reducing *to heteron* to something with which I am comfortable, and I am always most comfortable with a likeness of myself. Ideology is comfortable because it looks like me.

But there is a further reason for this move. Although it is Kant who stresses the need for autonomy in moral acting, Levinas sees all of Western philosophy as characterized by a deep and fundamental emphasis on autonomy. Literally, autonomy is the state of creating one's own law: in Greek, *auto* (self) + *nomos* (law). I noted in the introduction that Kant thinks that truly responsible action is that which one determines solely by way of one's own reason. Only such autonomous action is for Kant genuinely "free"—both in the sense that it is not coerced by another and in the sense that one has determined it by reason alone. Levinas too sees the move toward autonomy as designed to create a space for personal freedom. But whereas for Kant this freedom is positive, for Levinas it is deeply disturbing. What disturbs Levinas is that my freedom comes at the expense of the other's freedom, my autonomous world at the expense of the other's heteronomy. Thus philosophy is fundamentally characterized by the move to privilege myself—both my reason and my action—over the other, to "proclaim the philosophical birthright of autonomy."[9] Of course such attempts are never really successful. Since the other is *infinitely* other, that otherness can never really be destroyed, though it can be ignored, denied and compromised.

---

[7]Plato *Sophist* 254b-56b.
[8]Emmanuel Levinas, "Philosophy and the Idea of the Infinite," in *Collected Philosophical Papers,* Phenomenologica 100 (Dordrecht, Netherlands: Kluwer, 1987), p. 48.
[9]Ibid., p. 93.

So what (or who) is this other? Answering this question is tricky, for all "answers" risk denying or destroying the very otherness one is attempting to define. Definition would seem to be almost inescapably the reduction of the other to the same, for defining involves setting limits on something, and the limits that I impose are likely to be my own creation. One way of characterizing "otherness" is as that which escapes any totality or what cannot be controlled by a system.

Levinas speaks of *to heteron* as "infinite," because the infinite cannot in principle be enumerated. Such a way of speaking and thinking attempts to be truly phenomenological by allowing the other to supply its own *logos*. But while Levinas in one sense is phenomenological, he goes against Husserl's conception of intuition in which phenomena are "possessed" by consciousness. Whereas intuition for Husserl implies that "we relate directly to the object, we reach it," Levinas makes a distinction between "aiming at something and reaching it."[10] What complicates this attempt is that the otherness or the beyond does not stand completely outside the totality but can be glimpsed from within. It is precisely the possibility of otherness's piercing through the totality that allows for the possibility of encountering the other without its being simply swallowed up (and thus nullified) by the totality.

One of Levinas's metaphors for the otherness of the other is the face. Our faces convey a sense of who we are in our very being—our thoughts, emotions and identity. But what registers on the face is only a kind of mark, a "trace" of who we really are. Even our words convey only a very limited sense of our true being. Thus the face is a manifestation that appears truly but does so in a highly incomplete and partial way. The face is an appearance of other to us, but an appearance that signals an otherness lying behind it. "The face is present in its refusal to be contained," says Levinas (*TAI* 194). "The face resists possession, resists my powers. In its epiphany, in expression, the sensible, still graspable, turns into total resistance to the grasp" (*TAI* 197).

The "spontaneity" celebrated by Kant is put into question by the other. "To approach the Other is to put into question my freedom, my spontaneity" (*TAI* 303).[11] I want to master the other, but the face will not let me do so.

---

[10]Emmanuel Levinas, *The Theory of Intuition in Husserl's Phenomenology,* 2nd ed., trans. André Orianne (Evanston, Ill.: Northwestern University Press, 1995), p. 67.

[11]Of course Levinas also thinks that my encounter with the other actually gives me a new sort of freedom (*TAI* 302-4), since I am freed from the tyranny of myself.

My attempts at mastery of the other are often manifested by way of cognition. Here we come to a complication in Levinas, one difficult to resolve. On the one hand, to recognize the other as truly other is to recognize the other as a subject rather than merely an object of my cognition. On the other hand, in an important sense I do not "recognize" the other at all, according to Levinas. The other is not merely some phenomenon that submits to consciousness and cognition. I want to control the other by defining the other as I wish, but the other simply refuses that control and continually disrupts it. The other comes to me in a direct and unmediated way—not mediated by my categories. Thus the other is truly transcendent.

Levinas describes the face as "the bearer of an order, imposing upon me."[12] Instead of my being able to impose my own order on the other, the other imposes that order on me in a way that I cannot simply ignore. As should be clear, the recognition of the other as infinite means that any idea I have of the infinity of the other is always inadequate. There is an *asymmetry* between me and the other, rather than an *adaequatio*.

Moreover, the order imposed on me is violent in nature, so that it subjects me to a kind of trauma. We will consider the problem of violence in the following chapter, but here I need to point out that for Levinas violence is an essential feature of the other's otherness: "violence is originally justified as the defense of the other."[13] In order for the other to be truly other, the other must break into my world and disturb my ideology. The other intrudes upon my consciousness and wrecks havoc upon my thinking, leaving me traumatized (*OTB* 111). Interestingly enough, Levinas says that "the absolutely defenseless face" actually "opposes my power over it."[14] The face appears to me as naked and destitute, as widow and orphan. But that face actually speaks to me *from on high*. It commands my respect.

Respecting the infinity of the other is accomplished in actual practice by welcoming the other. Although Levinas speaks in terms of giving hospitality, the sort of hospitality he has in mind does not involve a carefully chosen guest list and engraved invitations. Instead we might say that the other just arrives uninvited. It is like the arrival of in-laws who

---

[12]Emmanuel Levinas, *Alterity and Transcendence,* trans. Michael B. Smith (New York: Columbia University Press, 1999), p. 170.

[13]Ibid., p. 172.

[14]Levinas, *Collected Philosophical Papers,* p. 21.

announce that they will be staying for a month. Note that the good Samaritan simply happens upon the traveler in need. So our neighbor is just *there,* given to us without our permission in advance.

The relation that I have to the other is not primarily an epistemological one in which I "know" the other. The other just arrives—and I never really get to "know" the other, who is constantly beyond my conceptual grasp. It is not that Levinas is giving an injunction to "allow the other to be transcendent." The other just *is* transcendent.

Levinas says that "ethics is an 'optics'" (*TAI* 29), but it is a very strange optics. For to allow the other to be transcendent is to allow one's sight to be limited, to resist a kind of practice in which theory dominates. For the other to break my totality, there can be no place from which the relation to the other can be viewed (even by someone outside of that relation) from above, for this would have the effect of destroying the otherness of the other. Of course there is a problem in even articulating this relation: if I speak of a relation of "I" and "other," in one sense I am assuming (or acting as if) this I and this other have definite identities. But not only does the other not have an identity that I can specify (or else could not be other), neither do I. The "I" is not a thing with a stable identity but a being "whose existing consists in identifying itself, in recovering its identity throughout all that happens to it" (*TAI* 36).

Levinas speaks of a right relation with the other as characterized by desire. At the very heart of metaphysics is the desire of that which cannot be seen, that which is unfamiliar, the alien land, the other. The typical expression of this desire for that which is other is the move of absorbing the other into me. But this desire for the other can never—in principle—be satisfied: if it were satisfied, then the other would no longer be other. True, one desires an absolute presence of the other: one wants to know the other without any barrier at all. Yet once this happens, the other is no longer other to me. This is why Levinas is opposed to mysticism, for he reads mystics as seeking an absolute presence of the other.[15] To have an absolute presence of the other (which, as I noted earlier, Husserl speaks of in terms of "absolute givenness" to consciousness) would serve to negate the very otherness that one wishes to experience. The desire for the other is in principle never satisfied; rather it is even deepened by the other. In this sense Levinas con-

---

[15]It is not clear to me that this is the only way to interpret mysticism.

trasts desire with need. Whereas needs can be satisfied, desire "can not be satisfied" (*TAI* 34) and always remains to be fulfilled.

With Socrates, Levinas agrees that something similar to the passionate desire of *eros* is fundamental to philosophy. As Socrates says, the philosopher desires that which is transcendent.[16] But this relation to the transcendent is an odd one, for the other is a something or someone that cannot be adequately grasped or even adequately intended. To put it in technical terms, the noetic act of desire could never be adequate to the noematic object that is desired.

The Ultimate Other

How might all of this be applied to God? If philosophy has done a conceptual injustice to the phenomena of the world and of human others, such has been even more the case with God. Levinas claims that philosophy "compels every other discourse to justify itself before philosophy" and that rather than rebel against this expectation, "rational theology accepts this vassalage" (*BPW* 129). Levinas is utterly unwilling to give philosophy the upper hand, to allow it the privilege of passing judgment on other discourses.

The problem with placing God within the confines of philosophy is that "this God is situated within 'being's move.' He is situated there as the *being* par excellence" (*BPW* 130). Once God becomes part of philosophical discourse, he can be only what philosophy allows him to be. When Levinas speaks of "being" here, he means the realm that philosophy circumscribes, whatever it calls its own and can control by way of its *logos*. This is why Levinas says that "being excludes all alterity" (*BPW* 74), for whatever is included in the realm of being is that which is *tauton*. Placing God in that category removes his transcendence and creates an idol that reflects human rationality. In contrast, "the God of the Bible signifies the beyond being, transcendence" (*BPW* 130). Unlike the human other who is still within being, God is the ultimate other who transcends even that category. As we shall see in chapter seven, Heidegger makes the same sort of criticism, as does Marion, who wishes to move beyond any attempt to hold God "captive" by way of philosophy.

Note that Levinas is not merely opposing "the god of the philosophers" to "the god of faith." He is not saying that whereas "rational" the-

---

[16]Plato *Symposium* 206a.

ology is bad because it has bought into philosophy's *logos*, "biblical" or "experiential" theology is the good alternative. Levinas questions the very dichotomy, for several reasons.

First, to accept it is already to have submitted to philosophy's *logos*. If "for the benefit of religion" one "reserves a domain from the authority of philosophy" (*BPW* 129-30), then one accepts philosophy's conditions and agrees to play by its rules. Levinas is unwilling to allow philosophy to adjudicate theological discourse.

Second, opposing faith to knowledge privileges philosophy or philosophical ways of knowing. One effectively concedes that philosophy holds the keys to knowledge and that anything else is second rate. In a previous chapter we saw that Plato dismisses *doxa* as inferior to *epistēmē*. To opt for faith in place of knowledge is to admit that one has opted for something inferior. Instead Levinas insists that there are other ways of "knowing" and meaning that are not controlled by philosophy.

Third, to say that God is real *because* he has revealed himself to us (either by Scripture or by religious experience) is to reduce God to immanence or presence *to us*. In effect we create an idol. That point in no way undermines God's revelation; but it should remind us that God's existence transcends that revelation and thus is not dependent on it (which is to say that God is not dependent on us and our knowledge for his existence).

Levinas wants to break away so radically from the philosophical *logos* that it will in no way compel or control one's thinking about God. One "knows" God in a way that is (as Levinas memorably, if enigmatically, puts it) "otherwise than according to knowledge" (*BPW* 154). But now we have a new problem. For if defining God takes away from his transcendence and constitutes an idolatry of one sort, a lack of definition threatens confusion and thus an idolatry of at least two other sorts.

First, how does one distinguish the "true God" from all impostors, the God of the Bible from that of rational theology? If God is so protected from human predication and *Sinngebung* (literally, the act of "giving sense," but here the idea is that *we* give the sense *to* God), then can God have an identity for us at all? Can a distinction between such a God and idols be drawn? And if not, is there anything *but* idolatry?

Second, if both human beings and God are "other" in an infinite sense (and thus a sense that cannot be grasped or properly thematized), then can we even make a distinction between human others and the divine Other? Are human beings and God simply other? If so, the possibilities for idolatry would seem literally endless: *everyone* could become a idol for me. For the otherness of any particular other could easily stand in for the otherness of God. Indeed in *Totality and Infinity* Levinas makes no real distinction between human others and God, speaking of "the alterity of the Other and of the Most-High" (*TAI* 34).[17]

But in "God and Philosophy" Levinas gives us a surprising answer to these problems, using Descartes's classic argument for God's existence. I noted in the introduction that in the third of the *Meditations* Descartes gives us an argument for God's existence based on his notion of an infinite, all-powerful God. Since he is finite, Descartes reasons that he could not have just "thought it up." Therefore there must actually be a God who really is infinite, One who put that idea into his mind. And Descartes notes that this infinite being is prior to the conception he has of himself. Whether this really works as a "proof" of God's existence is not Levinas's concern. He points to the fact that this conception of God provides a "breakup of consciousness" (*BPW* 136), a radical challenge to my attempts to make myself into god. Here is an idea that I *cannot* fathom, one that shakes the very foundations of my thought, and so I cannot be the author of it. The mark of the true God is that he cannot be contained or mastered. He is the God who refuses any human limitations or definitions, even identifying himself (when Moses insolently demands an identification) simply as "I AM." Levinas speaks of God as "near but different: Holy" (*BPW* 140) and goes on to say:

> God is not simply the "first other *[autrui]*," the other *[autrui]* par excellence, or the "absolutely other *[autrui]*," but other than the other *[autre qu'autrui]*, other otherwise, other with an alterity prior to the alterity of the other *[autrui]*, prior to the ethical bond with the other and different from every neighbor, transcendent to the point of absence, to a point of a possible confusion with the stirring of the *there is*. (*BPW* 141)

To what extent does Levinas answer the two questions posed above? In one sense he simply doesn't. As he himself admits, God is transcen-

---

[17]In a later interview (1982) Levinas makes the distinction between God and human other as follows: "In my relation to the other, I hear the Word of God. It is not a metaphor; it is not only extremely important, it is literally true. I'm not saying that the other is God, but that in his or her Face I hear the Word of God." See Emmanuel Levinas, "Philosophy, Justice and Love," in *Entre Nous*, trans. Michael B. Smith and Barbara Harshav (New York: Columbia University Press, 1998), p. 110.

dent "to a point of a possible confusion." And it seems to me the extent of that possible confusion is deep and wide.[18] I can confuse God with creation as a whole, or with powerful elements within that creation, or simply with human others. Moreover, if God is truly transcendent and cannot be contained by theology or even Scripture, then there is an inherent risk of confusion—one that cannot be "fixed." Were we able to specify the exact parameters of God, then it would be possible to have a pure separation of God from everything else. But if the God of Abraham, Isaac and Jacob is also the God who is infinitely other and resists any totalizing human identification, we human beings cannot draw any absolute line between the true God and all possible claimants to that title. This is not a problem with God or his "being" (if one may speak that way). God knows who he is and who he is not. So his identity is not hindered by our inability. Rather it is a problem with our knowledge of God (as well as a question of the degree of God's knowability), our ability to draw lines. So the first commandment is not what keeps us from circumscribing God; instead it prohibits us from *attempting* to do that which we cannot in principle do. Were we able to draw a line around God, we would effectively *be* God.

Does Levinas Escape Violence?

How successful is Levinas at "escaping" philosophy and its violence? In an early essay on Levinas entitled "Violence and Metaphysics," Derrida questions whether Levinas (or for that matter anyone) is really able to get beyond the reach of philosophy's *logos*. He quotes an ancient Greek philosopher as saying, "If one has to philosophize, one has to philosophize; if one does not have to philosophize, one still has to philosophize (to say it and think it). One always has to philosophize."[19] And then Derrida goes on to *quote Levinas himself* to prove his point.

> One could not possibly reject the Scriptures without knowing how to read them, nor say philology without philosophy, nor, if need be, arrest philosophical discourse without philosophizing. . . . One must refer—I am convinced—to the medium of all comprehension and of all understanding in

---

[18]Specifically, Levinas thinks that there is the possibility of a confusion between God and what he calls (following Heidegger) the "there is" (*il y a* in French; *es gibt* in German), that is, "being" without determination or form.

[19]From the *Protrepticus,* which has traditionally been assumed to have been written by Aristotle.

which all truth is reflected—precisely to Greek civilization, and to what it produced: to the logos, to the coherent discourse of reason, to life in a reasonable State. This is the grounds of all understanding. (*WD* 152)

Yet Levinas seems to think that he can escape philosophy's *logos*. In "God and Philosophy" Levinas claims that "*not to philosophize would not be 'to philosophize still,'* nor to succumb to opinions" (*BPW* 148). Clearly Levinas wants to escape philosophy and all of the violence that it perpetrates, but it is not clear whether he can succeed.

Levinas insists that the face comes to us *unmediated*. The face is a text without a context. While the face is a "manifestation," Levinas is reluctant to call it a phenomenon. At least according to the orthodoxy of phenomenology (which will be examined in detail in chapter seven), a phenomenon must always appear within the confines of consciousness. But Levinas wants to insist that the face does not "appear" and certainly does not appear within the confines of consciousness. The face transcends consciousness, so that consciousness is unable to identify or make sense of its otherness. Yet however much Levinas's insistence on the face's otherness seems appropriate and worthy of commendation, it is not clear how possible or desirable this transcendence ends up being. *Does* the face really escape being a phenomenon? Or does Levinas merely insist that such is the case? Even were we to agree that the face at first comes to us unmediated (which seems highly unlikely), it never remains unmediated. Faces are always reconfigured, categorized, placed in context.

Moreover, and much more important, it is difficult to know what it would be like to treat an other simply as other. If I think there are particular ways in which it is appropriate to respond to God, then I must have some idea of God. Similarly, if I treat another as a human being, then I have an idea of what human beings are and how they should be treated. Even the more neutral category "neighbor" carries with it *some* idea of how responsibility is carried out.

Despite Levinas's insistence that the face of the other must be heard and cannot be suppressed, history seems all too replete with instances of the contrary. One might argue that the very fact that we remember these instances testifies that the face cannot be co-opted or erased. But the memories of faces that have been oppressed (or not truly treated as transcendent others) are likely very few relative to all the forgotten others who cannot be brought to mind. Even the extent to which others who are now "present" are capable of commanding me or anyone else is questionable. Do others always disrupt my consciousness? Or am I actually far less "traumatized" than I ought to be? Of course Levinas recognizes that we need to cultivate sensibilities that are readily traumatized by the other. But if I do not have such sensibilities and do not choose to cultivate them, to what extent does the face of the other really break through to me?

A further question is whether Levinas's philosophy can be squared with his theology. On the one hand, Levinas seems to be uncomfortable with any kind of identification of God. Given that Yahweh is reluctant to identify himself for Moses except as "I AM," Levinas's reluctance is appropriate. On the other hand, Levinas writes not only as a philosopher but also as a Talmudic scholar. Thus he must identity himself with a particular conception of God. Can these two aspects be fused? The problem is that religious believers of any sort must make at least limited suppositions about God's identity and character. Else there is no way to draw a distinction between "orthodoxy" and "heterodoxy." But those distinctions *themselves* run the risk of reducing God to an ideology.

For Levinas, it is not that one is unable to speak of God; rather one cannot speak of God in an adequate way. Moreover, while the *logos* of philosophy is useful in helping us make sense of what we encounter in the world, Levinas insists that there is a way of knowing "otherwise" than by way of philosophical concepts that have their origins in ancient Greece. Levinas is often interpreted as bringing together Jewish and Greek elements (so that his philosophy has been described as "Jewgreek" or "Greekjew"),[20] but note that he should be seen, at least in an important sense, as setting up an *opposition* between the all-encompassing Greek *logos* and faith.

Of course "faith" here does not refer to what is "left over" from philosophy's conception of reason or knowledge. To define faith in this way is to allow philosophy's *logos* to set the agenda. Instead faith is a different way of thinking—one that does not submit to philosophy's *logos*. Faith is an order of thought that attempts to "think" the other while renouncing mastery or control. It is not part of philosophy's *logos*.

I do not mean to imply that Levinas is unaware of these difficulties. Rather they are central to his thinking. But they are not difficulties he

---

[20]This terminology comes from James Joyce's *Ulysses*.

"solves." Such difficulties are inherent to the project of sounding out idols—and we will not "solve" here either. At best, one wrestles with them and keeps them at the forefront of one's mind.

We shall return to these difficulties in later chapters. In the next chapter we turn to three key concepts—deconstruction, undecidability and *différance*—that guide Derrida's early and later thinking. Although these concepts have sometimes been read as ways of dismissing or denying the possibility of metaphysics and epistemology, read in light of Levinas, they can be seen as ways of reformulating that project and attempting to deal with the difficulties raised by Levinas.

5

DECONSTRUCTION
AND JUSTICE

In the opening remarks of his essay "Force of Law: The 'Mystical Foundation of Authority,'" Jacques Derrida rightly points out that deconstruction and justice would not seem to go together naturally. As he puts it, "Do the 'deconstructionists' have anything to say about justice, anything to do with it?" (FL 231). Obviously it is a rhetorical question. This seeming incompatibility extends far beyond matters of justice. For has not deconstruction (at least sometimes) proved destructive not merely to morality but also to theology and even philosophy? Given the early texts and themes of Derrida, it might be difficult for many to imagine him not just writing on justice (and also caring deeply about it) but also (and much more surprisingly) giving a reading of the Gospel of Matthew as a way of thinking about what constitutes true morality.

Few notions of the last two decades of the twentieth century caused as great a storm—or were open to such widely varying definitions—as "deconstruction." A speaker in chapel at my institution summed up the typical view by telling us that "deconstruction is the theory that says you can make texts mean anything you want them to mean." But perhaps that chapel speaker himself was guilty of a sort of deconstruction: making deconstruction itself mean anything you want it to mean. Of course he was hardly alone in denouncing deconstruction by way of such "deconstruction." Derrida speaks of those who have "carefully avoided reading" his work, but such avoidance hasn't necessarily kept them frt tm commenting.[1]

There is an interesting structure to such denunciations. The danger is that one constructs deconstruction, using one's own *logos,* and thus does it a kind of injustice. It is what philosophers call building a straw man. Note that the structure is rather similar to that of idolatry, for the resulting construct usually mirrors more one's own *logos* than the thing or person that is supposedly being depicted. One must be careful, then, to allow deconstruction to be what it is rather than a construct of one's own mind. Deconstruction, argues Derrida, is designed to *keep* us from building straw men (though whether Derrida actually succeeds in regard to "religion" and "dogma" is, of course, open to question).

Deconstruction, Undecidability, *Différance*

So what *is* deconstruction, and how does it relate to these notions of "undecidability" and *différance?* Derrida insists that "deconstruction is not a philosophy or a method, it is not a phase, a period or a moment. It is something which is constantly at work and was at work before what we call 'deconstruction' started."[2] On Derrida's account, deconstruction *happens*. It is not something one does per se; if anything, it is something that happens *to* texts and systems and ideas—and even us. Thus texts are not deconstructed; rather they deconstruct themselves. To "deconstruct a text," then, is to see complications and contradictions that are already there. But there is more to deconstruction. Derrida claims that "undecidability is the *condition* of all deconstruction: in the sense of condition of possibility."[3] Thus deconstruction is the continual modification and reformulation of all formulations, so that it is constantly at work in human understanding, explaining and questioning. The possibility of questioning or reformulating or deepening is precisely what deconstruction is.

---

[1]Jacques Derrida, *Points . . . : Interviews, 1974-1994* (Stanford, Calif.: Stanford University Press, 1995), p. 218.

[2]Jacques Derrida, "Hospitality, Justice and Reponsibility: A Dialogue with Jacques Derrida," in *Questioning Ethics: Contemporary Debates in Philosophy,* ed. Richard Kearney and Mark Dooley (London: Routledge, 1999), p. 65.

[3]Jacques Derrida, *Memories: For Paul de Man* (New York: Columbia University Press, 1986), p. 135.

Technically Derrida is right that deconstruction is not a method. But technically neither is phenomenology. In its most basic sense, phenomenology is the fact that phenomena appear and define themselves. Thus phenomenology *too* is something that happens, something that is fundamental to the way the world is. And yet phenomenology can be termed a method in the sense that one pays particular attention to how phenomena appear and makes that attention the basis of theorizing. To the extent that phenomenology can be called a method, perhaps to that same extent we can call deconstruction a method. Without doubt, it has functioned as one among some philosophers and literary theorists.

As a "method" it seems simple enough. The term can be read as a translation of Heidegger's notion of *destruktion* and of Edmund Husserl's notion of *Abbau*. Although the former sounds formidable, Heidegger has in mind a careful (and respectful) analysis of the history of philosophy, in order to see what philosophers have said and to bring to light what has been left unsaid.[4] *Abbau* is, literally, the "unbuilding" of a complex structure into its component parts. Such "unbuilding" is remarkably similar to what philosophers call analysis.[5] In fact the term *analysis* (which comes from the Greek noun *analusis,* with the corresponding verb being *analuō*) means the "breaking up of anything complex into its simple elements."[6] Given this definition, it is not at all clear what truly constitutes a fundamental difference between analytic philosophy and deconstruction (despite the fact that many practitioners of each would be loath to admit any similarity). Perhaps we might contrast them in terms of their focus. Like analysis, deconstruction attends to what a text (or idea or statement or theory) says and the way it is structured. But deconstruction puts particular emphasis (to a degree philosophical "analysis" usually does not) on what the text or theory does *not* say (i.e., whatever is assumed but not explicitly stated), as well as on the

---

[4] See *BT* ¶6.

[5] Analytic philosophers have often argued that what they do is quite different from what Derrida does. The most famous of protests against deconstruction by analytic philosophers is a letter to the *Times* (London), written at the time that Cambridge University was about to give Derrida an honorary doctorate. The writers of that letter claimed that "Derrida's work does not meet accepted standards of clarity and rigour." See *"Honoris Causa:* 'This Is *Also* Extremely Funny,'" in Derrida, *Points,* pp. 419-21, (and Derrida's commentary, pp. 399-419).

[6] *The Oxford English Dictionary,* 2nd ed., s.v. "analysis."

points at which its structure or content is vulnerable.[7]

Given this emphasis, there is at least the potential for arriving at inter-
pretations that are peripheral at best or completely contrary to the text at
worst. If truth be told, many deconstructive "readings" tend in the latter—
which is to say "violent"—direction. Although some of them turn out to
be harmless and amusing (like the "explication" of Thomas Paine's *Common Sense* I once heard in which it was argued that *food* was the primary
issue behind the American Revolution), such has not always been the
case. Thus conservatives who view deconstructionists as having it in for
everything they hold dear are not merely paranoid. It is far too much to
claim that deconstruction is the ruin of academe, but it is likewise hard to
argue that deconstruction's effect on the academy and thinking in general
has been completely positive or even positive overall.[8] On that point I
clearly side with the critics. Yet is deconstruction itself somehow evil or
atheistic? I don't think so. Of course a method that concerns itself with
aporia can easily get out of hand. In any case, it is difficult to know how
much deconstruction has been to blame for irresponsibility versus its
having been simply the handy tool of the moment.[9] Any method—however seemingly benign—can be used for violent purposes, as David
Hume showed us long before deconstruction.[10]

Though Derrida sometimes makes some rather startling claims, a
careful reading of his texts shows that he usually qualifies them. Here

---

[7]Admittedly, even this distinction cannot be pushed too hard, since *analysis* can also
mean "the tracing of things to their source" (ibid). Perhaps the "difference" between
analysis and deconstruction is the difference of *différance.*

[8]Still, it is hard to take seriously the sort of claim made by Amy Gutman, who argues that
deconstruction is basically responsible for virtually everything bad in the American academy (and culture at large). See her "Relativism, Deconstruction and the Curriculum," in
Campus Wars: Multi-culturalism and the Politics of Difference, ed. John Arthur and Amy
Shapiro (Boulder, Colo.: Westview, 1995), pp. 57-69.

[9]Again, Derrida would not agree with my characterization of deconstruction as a "tool,"
but it clearly has functioned as such.

[10]Can Derrida himself be considered irresponsible in his reading of texts—has he done
them violence? Such a question cannot simply be answered through assessment of the
"accuracy" of Derrida's explications. As it turns out, specialists in Husserl, Plato, Heidegger and Joyce (to name just a few of the figures Derrida has explicated) disagree as to
the "accuracy" of readings of these figures. For instance, while some Husserlians vigor-
ously maintain that Derrida's reading of Husserl is simply a misreading, others (including
Rudolf Bernet, the current president of the Husserl Archives) think that Derrida's reading
is largely justified. One could, of course, simply write off Derrida's supposed (and also
very real) excesses with the admittedly politically incorrect (not to mention violent)
observation that hyperbole is the stock-in-trade of French philosophers, "just one of
those French things."

are three particularly illuminating examples. Claim one: "There never was any 'perception.'"[11] Claim two: "There is nothing outside of the text *[il n'y a pas de hors-texte]*" (*OG* 158). Claim three: There is no "center which arrests and grounds the play" (*WD* 289). As should be immediately evident, the implications of these claims are far-reaching for human perception, knowledge, reason, morality and metaphysics—to name just a few aspects.

What should we make of these claims? To take the first, it is important to note that Derrida's surprising pronouncement comes only *at the end* of an extended analysis of Husserl's notion of perception as "intuitive givenness" (which, as was shown earlier, means that when I perceive something that thing itself is present to my consciousness). Derrida's claim is that *if* we take Husserl's conception of perception as the standard of what counts as perception, then human perception does not live up to that standard. Thus Derrida's claim is in regard to a particular— and also a very strong—notion of perceiving. Only in that context can his statement be understood. Even if one were to conclude here that Derrida's interpretation does an injustice to Husserl's view, that would not necessarily invalidate Derrida's general point about the limits of human perception.

What about the phrase "there is nothing outside of the text"? Some have read this as a statement of "creative antirealism," a term used to describe the belief that what we call "the world" is merely a construct of our minds. While it has never been clear to me what "creative antirealism" could possibly mean, it doesn't seem to be Derrida's view. Consider Derrida's own gloss of that statement: "'There is nothing outside the text' means nothing else [but]: there is nothing outside context" (*L* 136). He goes on to criticize anyone who would read this phrase as implying that "all referents are suspended, denied, or enclosed in a book" as "naive" (*L* 148). Moreover, he points out that in the very paragraph before the one where "there is nothing outside of the text" appeared, he had emphasized the need for a careful "doubling commentary" of a text with "all the instruments of traditional criticism" to serve as an "indispensable guardrail" (to protect the meaning of the text). Otherwise "critical production would risk developing in any direction at all and authorize itself

---

[11]Jacques Derrida, *Speech and Phenomena and Other Essays on Husserl's Theory of Signs*, trans. David B. Allison (Evanston, Ill.: Northwestern University Press, 1973), p. 103.

to say almost anything." Of course Derrida also reminds us that good commentaries do not content themselves with merely repeating the text and also that even "doubling commentaries" are never absolutely "pure" in the sense of having no interpretive aspect at all, however much the commentator might try. Yet he still warns that the interpreter must treat the text with "respect." So it would be difficult—if one has any respect for *Derrida's* text—to argue that "there is nothing outside the text" means either that "the world is a construct of my mind" or that "I can make a text mean anything I want."

In regard to the third claim, the notion of a "loss of center," there is a great deal at stake. Whereas human thought and endeavor have been characterized by the belief or at least the hope that they are (or could be) guided by and grounded in something like an *eidos* (essence), a *telos* (purpose) or *alētheia* (truth), if Derrida is right then such assumptions might seem to be unfounded. While Derrida has often been read as suggesting that some sort of indeterminate "free play" replace traditional metaphysics, epistemology and ethics, that is a careless reading of his text. Derrida clearly maintains that "there is no sense in doing without the concepts of metaphysics" (*WD* 280). In fact it is not too much to say that we human beings *are unable* to think apart from these concepts (or at least something *like* them). But having said that, he thinks there is still good reason to deconstruct these ideas, not to eliminate them but to attempt to reformulate them. Why would one want to reformulate them? Because as helpful as they have been in aiding thought, they are (being human) inadequate.

Further, to say that such concepts do not provide a center is to say at least two things. First, even if we take (say) a particular *telos* as the center of our thinking or philosophizing, that center cannot be itself grounded. If it could be, then it would no longer be the "center." Something else would have effectively taken its place, since whatever proves to be the "ground" is effectively the "center."

Second, Derrida could be taken as saying that the "center" is just all over the map, or simply that any talk about centers is misguided. But such does not seem to be the case. Rather the center cannot be pinned down exactly, given that thinking—whether secular philosophy or Christian theology—is continually in development. Being historical by nature, thought grows, and so the center is never quite stable. As an example, even though we say (rightly) that the *Logos* Jesus Christ is the center not just of our thought but our very being as Christians, *how we conceive that center* is always in development. Christ may not change, but we do. Indeed we and our thinking *must* change, for part of "growing in grace" is undergoing continual refinement of our conception of, say, "Christlikeness." Or to put this in terms of concern for idolatry, we can assume that our current understanding of Christ and his teaching is at least somewhat inaccurate and unfounded, at least somewhat idolatrous. That is to say that it is more a reflection of us than of him. So *not to grow* would be to accept idolatrous images of him (or portions of our images of him).

Ultimately Derrida would agree with Nietzsche's contention that the basic ideas of metaphysics are "dogmatic." Yet this lack of grounding does not for Derrida signal the need to abandon metaphysics or even philosophy as it has been traditionally conceived.[12] Instead the task as he sees it is somehow to hold on to philosophy's vision and yet be open to ways of rethinking and reformulating that vision. Derrida claims (*L* 115) that he has never proposed anything so simple as an "'all or nothing' choice between pure realization of self-presence and complete free-play or undecidability" (i.e., between pure knowledge and no knowledge at all, between an absolute metaphysic and the abandonment of metaphysics). Whereas John Searle characterizes Derrida's view as "indeterminacy," Derrida responds by claiming that he has never held such a view. On his account, such a view would mean that no distinctions could be made, that things are neither "themselves" nor "anything else," and that there can be no "right" or "wrong" and no "good" or "bad." To make his point, Derrida accuses Searle of misunderstanding him and also of simply being wrong. As Derrida puts it, the characterization of the deconstructionist as "skeptic-relativist-nihilist" is "false (that's right: false, not true) and feeble; it supposes a bad (that's right: bad, not good) and feeble reading of numerous texts, first of all mine" (*L* 146).

It is understandable that Searle takes Derrida as undermining the possibility of all distinctions. If deconstruction shows us anything, it is that the simple distinctions we believe quite obvious turn out to be less obvious (and also more dangerous) than we had assumed. But even more important, the possibility of deconstruction suggests that there is no

---

[12]Derrida is sometimes criticized by his French colleagues for being too "conservative" on this point.

"solution" to the problem of indefinability. One can only be vigilant. Like Jean-Paul Sartre's reformed gambler who has no assurances that he might not fall back into the trap of "gaming" (as we now euphemistically call it),[13] one has no fail-proof formula for success. Yet while it is true that Derrida has paid particular attention to instances where distinctions break down, his conclusion is not that we are left with the indeterminacy of "freeplay" in which no meaning distinctions can be made. Probably Derrida is guilty of overemphasizing that indeterminacy and having helped give rein to moral, epistemological and metaphysical anarchy. But Derrida at least can also be read as reminding us of the fragility of our distinctions. Indeed it would seem that he wishes to be understood in this way. Speaking particularly of moral distinctions, he claims, "This does not mean that we should not calculate [morally]. We have to calculate as rigorously as possible. But there is a point or limit beyond which calculation must fail, and we must recognize that."[14]

Derrida insists that his view is better characterized by the term *undecidability*. In saying that all decisions are undecidable, Derrida points to the ultimate impossibility of their calculation. We should still calculate, but we should also be clear as to the actual status of that calculation. If, for example, I decide to do x rather than y, I can provide reasons for so doing, but not in the sense of a mathematical calculation explaining my action. I can only say that, in my judgment, one of those choices seemed to be the right one to make. This is not to say "I just felt like doing x" or "I can give no reason at all." But there is only so far that one can go. Eventually one runs out of reasons for one's reasons. On Derrida's view, it is this undecidability—the fact that decisions can be calculated only to a point—that gives my decision the character of being a *decision* made by a rational agent, as opposed to a quasi decision made by a machine programmed by logic or rules. Were I able to formulate a calculus for my action, I would not be making a decision. Machines operate by way of calculus; people make decisions.

In his later texts Derrida explicitly argues that his notion of undecidability is and has always has been about avoiding violence. Yet as noted in the previous chapter, he sees this goal as problematic, since he thinks

---

[13]Jean-Paul Sartre, *Being and Nothingness,* trans. Hazel Barnes (New York: Philosophical Library, 1956), pp. 32-33.

[14]John D. Caputo, *Deconstruction in a Nutshell: A Conversation with Jacques Derrida* (New York: Fordham University Press, 1997), p. 19.

human beings cannot help but do violence of a conceptual sort. Why so? Assuming that philosophy can be more or less characterized by the ideal of *adaequatio intellectus ad rei,* then Derrida's early and later philosophy can be read as a serious questioning of this ideal of mental adequation. The solution (as if there were such a thing) is not to look for concepts that give us perfect *adaequatio* (for there aren't any such *human* concepts) but to attempt to find better concepts than the ones we have.[15] But if such an ideal remains forever unrealized, then do not all human concepts do some sort of violence to that which they purport to describe, precisely because they are inadequate?

Given Derrida's phenomenological background, he speaks of adequation in terms of *presence.* His questioning of adequation is put in terms of the goal of having truth fully present to one's consciousness. In place of the ideals of adequation and presence, Derrida suggests the notion of *différance* (spelled with an *a* to indicate its difference from the French term *différence*). Note that *différance* does not involve substitution of the ideal of "absence" for that of presence (as some interpreters have accused Derrida of doing). Rather it is Derrida's way of rethinking the ideal of philosophy as a kind of presence mingled with absence, or an adequation that is never fully adequate in the sense of *adaequatio* even though it may be still adequate in the sense of being "good enough." In perception I never fully get "the thing itself" present to my consciousness, but only a trace (Derrida borrows Levinas's term). Derrida reminds us that the French word *différer* has two senses: (1) "to differ," in the sense of there being an inequality or inadequation between two terms and thus nonidentity or nonpresence, and (2) "to defer," the putting off of presence and adequation until a later time. Given this latter aspect, then, *différance* has implications not merely for violence but for the "messianic," in that it points to a time when there *will* be presence. Of course, as we shall see in the following chapter, for Derrida the time of full presence is always deferred and the messiah never comes.

How might one apply these ideas practically? And more important for our concern here, how might we use them to think about (and, one hopes, avoid) idolatry? Let's first consider how these ideas get worked out in terms of being moral in a practical sense.

---

[15]Of course the notion of "better" itself opens up significant questions: Better for what? Better for whom? Better in which respects?

Foundations as Antimorality

Although the phrase "the mystical foundation of authority" comes from the French skeptic and atheist Michel de Montaigne, it is actually cited by the Christian believer Pascal with approval. According to Montaigne:

> Laws remain credible, not because they are just, but because they are laws: that is the mystical foundation of their authority, they have no other [foundation]. . . . Anyone who obeys them because they are just is simply not obeying them the way in which they ought to be obeyed.[16]

This claim by Montaigne (and Pascal) is less about laws (or rules or any other specific moral injunctions) than about how those moral prescriptions get their force. When Pascal says that "anyone who tries to bring [a law] back to its first principle destroys it," he gives us a similar argument to that which I noted in Nietzsche. The attempt to "ground" a "first being" or "morality" proves its undoing, since *we* become the ground.

Shortly I will turn to the *aporias* raised by following rules or laws. But here the question is "What gives laws their force?" which can be translated as "Why should I follow a given law?" What might seem an unimportant point turns out to be crucial, for my motivation is at stake. In the same way that only a slight difference can make visiting a dying relative in the hospital either virtuous (I care about the person and wish to make his dying days as bearable as possible) or unvirtuous (I hate the person but want to make sure he leaves me his fortune), so my motives can determine whether I am following the law or just happen not to go against it. There is a significant difference. Christian morality has a similar structure. God does not say, "Thou shalt not steal, for stealing leadeth to bad consequences." Rather the commandment is simply "Thou shalt not steal." Even where there is a reward attached to a command, following the command is *different* from going for the reward. To "follow" God's laws for a reason other than the fact that they are laws is not to follow them in the strongest possible sense, even if one is following them in a limited sense. If I say, "I don't care what God says, for I don't even believe in God; it just so happens that I think stealing is not in my best interests," then I am not really following God's law. Similarly, I might

---

[16]Montaigne, *The Essayes of Montaigne,* trans. John Florio (New York: Modern Library, 1933), p. 970 (translation modified). Also see Blaise Pascal, *Pensées,* trans. A. J. Krailsheimer (Harmondsworth, U.K.: Penguin, 1966), no. 60: "Custom is the whole of equity for the sole reason that it is accepted. That is the mystic basis for its authority. Anyone who tries to bring it back to its first principle destroys it."

drive down the highway not knowing the speed limit and just happen to stay within it, but I would not actually be "following" the speed limit.

So what should our motivation be? One possible answer comes from Kant, who describes the "force" of morality as a "categorical imperative." A "hypothetical imperative" has an if-then character. *If* you'd like to drive, *then* you must get a driver's license. But perhaps you'd rather not drive. In such a case you don't need a driver's license (except if you want to cash a check at the supermarket). But a categorical imperative is simply "Do this" (and don't waste time asking whether you really must). Further, to be truly moral on Kant's account, one must follow the categorical imperative *for itself.*

At first glance, Kant might seem to endorse Pascal's idea that one must follow the law simply because it is a law. Yet the situation is more complicated. Where Kant differs is in his justification of the categorical imperative. According to Kant, acting morally is the hallmark of a rational being. And since we are moral beings, we obviously want to act rationally. To use the Kantian formulation, the ethical is defined by whatever can rightly be accorded the status of a universal law. And something can be a universal law only if it is *logical.* On Kant's read, my decision not to lie is justified because I can rationally will the universal law "Always tell the truth." So I can explain my action in terms of a more general law that grounds my action. Of course, even this justification proves problematic in the end, for we cannot really "justify" reason. In other words, at some point the line of argumentation just stops. Even Kant would admit that the grounding for moral laws ends up being reason, which itself cannot be grounded. Kant's ultimate response to the person who does not wish to be moral is "Well, don't you want to be rational?" If the answer is no, then there is no place to go from there. One can hardly give a rational argument to the effect that one ought to be rational, for what is being assumed is precisely the point of the argument.

It is not that Kant is necessarily *wrong* in recognizing that acting morally is rational, even though it should be noted that Kant is not saying (as do Plato and Aristotle) that acting morally is also in your best interest. Kant recognizes—and finds it quite disturbing—that acting morally may not lead to personal happiness.[17] But if acting morally to bring

---

[17]Indeed this recognition leads Kant to postulate an afterlife in which one is appropriately rewarded.

about one's own personal happiness is suspect, so is acting morally in order to be a rational person. Indeed if we look at the formula that Nietzsche thinks sums up the ancient Greek conception of morality found in Plato and Aristotle (reason=virtue=happiness), it should be clear that Kant's motive of being rational and Aristotle's motive of being happy aren't very far from each other. For Aristotle, virtue is equivalent to rationality, and rationality leads to happiness. For Kant, virtue is equivalent to rationality, and while rationality may not lead to happiness, it leads to the next best thing—the satisfaction of knowing that one acted rationally. Moreover, if heaven is the place where the score is finally settled, then the only real difference between the happiness of Aristotle and Kant is *when* you get the reward.[18]

We might argue that there is a hierarchy of levels of motivation, beginning with the least worthy and ascending to the most worthy (though even speaking in those terms is problematic).

The lowest level is that of the hedonist or consequentialist. It is the level of pure economic calculus. While Aristotle and Jeremy Bentham, the founder of utilitarianism, may differ on particulars, they agree on one thing: "moral rightness" is—ultimately—based on economics.[19] While Aristotle has his "golden mean" that requires a complex set of virtues and Bentham his comparatively crass "hedonistic calculus," both construe morality economically. For each, the "right" is either directly (in Bentham's case) or indirectly (in Aristotle's case) defined in terms of consequences.

It seems to me that the next level is that of the Kantian. This is the level of duty to ethical law or rationality. Note that this is a move away from a sheer calculus and a purely economical system to a much less (or perhaps we might say less obviously) economic system. The "good will," says Kant, acts out of a pure regard for the moral law. But there is still a kind of calculation here—one is motivated by the desire to be rational, and the moral is precisely the rational thing to do (and can be shown to be such). For Kant, the ultimate motivation for human action is duty, but duty construed in a particular way: I have a duty to the moral law because I am a rational being, for reason informs me that it is rational to

---

[18]Actually, even in Aristotle there is often a delay between being virtuous and being happy, so the difference really has to do with how *great* a delay.

[19]While this is not immediately clear in Aristotle (as it is in Bentham), they ultimately agree. Of course, Aristotle's ethics are valuable in many other respects.

follow the moral law. But if I do someone a good turn in order to fulfill the demands of duty, then is not that person whom I helped my means to my duty? So isn't that person being used by me? To do one's duty to God, then, it would seem that one cannot be acting out of a duty to the moral law. To put this in Kantian terms, if one is doing one's duty because it is the rational thing to do, then one is doing *what* duty requires but not *because* duty requires it. To do one's duty to God is precisely not to act out of "duty."

The third level is what we might ascribe to the Old Testament. One acts out of duty not to a "general law" or "reason" but to God. We follow God out of an absolute duty, simply because God commands us to do so. Here we have left the realm of the ethical and the economic; we are now following the categorical imperative not of "rationality" but of God. The reason for following God is "God says."[20]

The fourth level of obligation is what I take to be the highest Christian level, one that moves beyond both economics and duty. It is love. We follow God because we love him ("If you love me, you will keep my commandments"). We likewise treat others kindly because we love *them*. If we were to treat them well only because of a love for God, then we would be using them as means to display our love for God.

The last of these—love—is the "highest" motivation. To act in a fully moral sense is to act out of love. And love is simply the end of the line of explanation. To love for some other reason is not really to love. When John says, "We love because he first loved us" (1 Jn 4:19), he is not setting up an economic formula for love.[21] We do not love God to pay him back, nor do we love others as a way of paying God back. The love that God infuses in us enables us to love him and others.

Do we (or should we) love God because he is worthy of being loved? And is our love for others based on their deserving? It stands to reason that loving God is appropriate because of who God is. Clearly he is an "object" (obviously this is a woefully inadequate term for God) who is worthy of being loved. Moreover, it would seem that we "owe" him our

---

[20] While "God says" is the ultimate *motivation* of moral action on this account, such a view is substantially different from a "divine command theory" in which the *definition* of morality is dependent on God's volition.

[21] Although certain later manuscripts read "we love *him*," early manuscripts only read "we love." Note that loving God inevitably involves loving our neighbor also. As John goes on to say, "Those who love God must love their brother and sister" (1 Jn 4:22; see also Mk 12:29-31).

love. Yet the question here is, should one love God because of that worth or because of our debt to him? I think the answer must *ultimately* be no. These are fine motivations as far as they go, but they don't "adequately" define *love*.

There are at least two problems here. First, if we appeal to some sort of worth as the basis for loving God, then we have set that worth and—more important—our valuation of that worth above God. Second, the danger is that love is turned into economic return and so loses its character as love. These two problems are likewise to be found in loving others for some sort of "reason." In the same way that God could be loved for his worth, human beings could be loved because they are made in God's image and so possess a kind of worth. While that is undoubtedly true, it cannot be the *ultimate* basis for love. Perhaps we might argue that it works for *duty* (if we construe a duty to others as warranted because of who they are), but not for love. Loving one's neighbor does not rest on the neighbor's being made in God's image. One loves one's neighbor for no other reason than that the neighbor is *there*. Certainly the good Samaritan has no *reason* to love the Jewish traveler in need. Similarly, God loved "while we were still weak" (Rom 5:6), "while we still were sinners" (Rom 5:8), "while we were enemies" (Rom 5:10). As Paul puts it, "Rarely will anyone die for a righteous person" (Rom 5:7), so we can hardly make sense of Christ's dying for God's enemies. But that is precisely the point. Christ dies for us despite all of these "rational" objections.

There are two important caveats to add. First, calculating motivations may be appropriate as initial motivations. In fact we may often appeal to them simply to accomplish certain worthwhile goals in society. But as we mature as persons, those motivations take on a decreasing role. As noted in chapter one, in persuading people around us to be moral, we may indeed argue that morality is both rational and, at least ultimately, in our best interest (and both arguments are also *true*). That sort of argument, though, should cause us some uneasiness, as should arguing that people ought to be Christians because they will profit in certain ways—escaping punishment or gaining some reward. This kind of argument unravels itself. To follow Christ *because* one will profit in some anterior way is to set up an idol, to put something in Christ's place. I am not really following Christ; instead I am ultimately following another object put there by myself. Christ becomes the means to my end, and *I* have become God. So "economic" reasons may be satisfactory in the beginning, but they are not the motivations of a mature Christian believer.

Second, not only are motives difficult to know, they are usually quite mixed. The psychological egoist's position is problematic if for no other reason than because it reduces all motives to a single motive. But I am not arguing for something that is simply the opposite of psychological egoism. I assume that motives are mixed, and so my position is simply the following: the more we are motivated by love, the more our actions are in line with those of God. Indeed the more we act out of love, the less the category of "morality" matters. Acting out of concern for oneself, acting out of duty and acting "because God commands" are all moral to *some* degree. There is nothing wrong with them per se. But they do not represent the highest motivation out of which one can act. We have seen that Jesus does not overturn the law; rather he simply ups the moral ante. So Jesus himself gives us an example of what being truly moral is. Similarly, after talking about the "utility" of various gifts of the Spirit, Paul says, "I will show you a still more excellent way" (1 Cor 12:31)— and goes on to speak of love.

What we have considered so far is the "practical" implication of law's having no justification. There is a slightly different, though very similar, problem. It is more a theoretical issue. In the same way that Nietzsche thinks that "life" cannot be justified (and that such an attempt represents a fundamental misunderstanding of what life is), Derrida thinks that justice cannot refer to something beyond that is just, or else we have an infinite regress. Justice just is. So what is "justice"? Derrida is not quite sure, and he is reluctant to attempt an answer. He situates himself somewhere between what he calls "substantialism" (the idea that justice is either a "thing" or a fixed and stable "concept") and what he calls "irrationalism" (that there is no such "thing" as justice—a position that might be termed skepticism or relativism).

For Derrida, justice is a kind of absolute that is "not deconstructable" because it is beyond deconstruction. Justice is what makes deconstruction possible. Human beings are such (existentially) that they *always do* presuppose that there is something like "justice," and pragmatically they also cannot function without it. We cannot say that the founding moment of "justice" is just, or else we open the door to an infinite regress. For if justice needed to be defined in terms of something that is just, then does not that defining term need a further definition? Whereas a given law can be justified by way of justice, justice cannot be justified by anything further.

A possible (and I think right) Christian response to Derrida on this point might be that justice is justified by God's character. Yet all we would do then is push the problem back a step. For then what justifies God's character? In the end, we have to say that justice simply is just (and, similarly, that God is just because he is just). The problem is that if we attempt to provide a justification for justice, then we in effect make *ourselves* the definitions of justice. Similarly, any attempt to justify God and justice effectively makes us higher than God. So the line *must* stop. For Derrida, the line stops at "justice." For the Christian, the line stops at God's character. Any attempt to take it further than God is to be guilty of idolatry. Note that *were* Derrida to put justice *above* God, then we could (and should) read him as guilty of idolatry.

Being Just

Law—by its very nature—is always an interpretation of justice. Precisely in the name of justice, the law can and must be deconstructed. Or else it turns into an ideology. But why so? While laws are always attempts at instantiating justice, they always fail (no matter how close they come) at doing justice to justice because of the lack of adequation between law and justice. Thus we must continually ask such questions as: What is the aim of a given law? Does it achieve this aim? Has it come into existence because of motives ulterior to the stated aim?

Derrida explains this difference between law and justice by way of the notion of "translation." On the one hand, translation allows something to be in a place it could not previously be (such as an English-speaking context, if the text is originally in French); so one does "justice" to a text by making it available. On the other hand, precisely in making something available, translation does a kind of violence to what it translates. For however careful and well-intended the translation, it never completely or perfectly renders the meaning of what is translated. This *aporia* of translatability is likewise found in instantiating justice: on Derrida's account, justice is a kind of universal that must be translated into the particularities of laws and cases. If we apply this notion of translation to law, it becomes clear that law is always an interpretation of justice, not justice itself. But Derrida thinks that even in making laws and rules—that is, applying justice to specific sorts of actions—one *always* does a kind of "violence" to justice. Of course if we as Christians think that justice is defined by God, then to the extent one does a violence to justice, to that extent one does a violence to God.

Deconstruction attempts to show the *aporias* of justice: that justice is experienced and not experienced, that every instance of justice proves to be both an instance of justice and a falsification of justice, that every experience of justice shows the impossibility of doing justice here on earth.

> There is no justice without this experience, however impossible it may be, of aporia. Justice is an experience of the impossible: a will, a desire, a demand for justice the structure of which would not be an experience of aporia. (FL 244)

Whereas law is calculable, justice escapes all calculation; whereas law is ensured by a rule, justice surpasses all rules. The reason that deconstruction is justice is that it exposes (or at least *can* expose) rules and laws as less than full justice. And the reason that laws are less than justice is that they are (as surprising as this may sound) always at once both too specific and too general. Derrida does not put his critique in exactly these terms, but I think they help capture the problem(s).

First, laws are too specific because they specify justice of a particular sort and in a limited way, even though justice always has a much fuller meaning. A law concerning fire hydrant violations may tell us something about justice, but it doesn't tell us very much. Laws about murder tell us considerably more. But justice is a much richer concept than any law— or even a well-crafted set of laws—could do justice to. So simply to make laws and rules, to apply justice to specific sorts of actions, is to do justice to justice; but it is likewise to do justice an injustice. To use phenomenological language, it makes justice present but also keeps it absent. One honors justice by making rules, but one also and always distorts justice by making rules. So can an action or a rule ever be just? It would seem that we must conclude that justice always—by nature— eludes the attempt to instantiate it. Any attempt to "do" justice does it an injustice. Between law and justice there is never true *adaequatio*.

Second, laws—however helpful and "just"—are too general. They are never specific enough (we might say "adequate enough") for any particular situation. A law is about general categories, not a specific instance. My parking violation may be classified under the law concerning "parking in front of a fire hydrant," but that law isn't really about *me,* nor did its writer(s) have my *particular* violation in mind. It covers the general category of "parking in front of a fire hydrant," but it doesn't cover *my* parking in front of a fire hydrant. And that problem is not merely an expression of personal hubris along the order of "Since I'm so important, there ought to be a special law just about *me.*" Perhaps there are extenuating circumstances that lessen the severity of my crime. What if I actually park only two inches too close, two inches over the yellow part of the curb, as opposed to that really "bad" person who parked directly in front of the hydrant? Aren't I "less" guilty?

As it turns out, those who administer justice in a court of law (and on the street) do take certain circumstances into account in determining both guilt and punishment.[22] But the application of rules/laws to particular instances is still problematic. The problem with treating the other aright is that the other must be treated *as other.* If justice did not entail treating the other as other, one could conceivably "master" the situation so there would be a perfect adequation between justice and the specific instance. As we have seen, Levinas points out that to treat the other merely as an instance of a group or class—in other words, to force the other into our system or way of thinking about people—is to treat the other unjustly. Since each case is unique, no case could ever be "just another instance" of, say, rule number 427.

This is why Derrida speaks of the need to continually "reinvent" laws:

> To be just, the decision of a judge, for example, must not only follow a rule of law or a general law but must also assume it, approve it, confirm its value, by a reinstituting act of interpretation, as if, at the limit, the law did not exist previously—as if the judge himself invented the law in each case. . . . In short, for a decision to be just and responsible, it must, in its proper moment, if there is one, be both regulated and without regulation: it must preserve the law and also destroy or suspend it enough to have to reinvent it in each case. (FL 251)

But if each case must be decided and the law newly "reinvented," then one can see why Derrida thinks all decisions end up being, at least in some sense, undecidable. We have already seen that choices, on Der-

---

[22]When I asked the driver of a tow truck as he was hitching up someone's car in front of our apartment in Manhattan, he said, "The law says that you have to be at least fifteen feet away from the fire hydrant, but I'll leave a car that's only nine feet away alone. Seven feet, though—that's just too close."

rida's view, cannot be made in a mechanical, calculable, programmable way. Certainly moral choices have no algorithms. Instead each case must be weighed, and then one must decide.

There is a further and more disturbing aspect of making moral choices. At least some moral decisions (and perhaps ultimately all) are undecidable because the demands of justice are far more than one can possibly meet. For instance, I have responsibilities to a whole host of people—my wife, my wider family, my students, my neighbors—and Jesus considerably complicates this last category by implying that everyone is my neighbor. How could I possibly satisfy all of those demands in a perfectly "just" way? In this case it is not that I have no sense of morality at all; if anything, it is that I have too *much* of one. Part of becoming morally attuned is that one becomes aware of more and more cases of injustice and greater depth of personal responsibility. It is a very poignant example of how ignorance would be bliss. The more self-centered I am, the less I am able to see my moral responsibilities to others.

But despite all of these complications, I cannot postpone acting. It is an old existentialist truism that "not to decide is to decide." Aristotle thought that right action requires a thorough knowledge of the circumstances. For him, the morally well-developed person *(phronimos)* has the necessary practical wisdom *(phronēsis)* to make just the "right" decision, the one that achieves the golden mean. Yet even Aristotle admitted that one is never quite a perfect *phronimos* (though he seems to think that he himself is rather close). And, even if we grant the possibility of anyone's having perfectly developed *phronēsis,* it is hard to imagine a situation in which all possible aspects of a given situation are known. How could you ever be sure that there wasn't at least one additional salient fact? Yet even though one will never have enough knowledge and enough understanding of the context, person and circumstances to act perfectly aright, one must make just decisions. One is required to act, but one never has enough information to make a completely and fully calculated (completely "just") decision. Frankly, one sometimes has precious little information and so makes a bad decision, through no fault of one's own.

In the logic of *différance,* we can say that just acts always differ from justice itself and that justice is always deferred. One still must calculate as rigorously as possible, but one must likewise realize that one's calculation always falls short of the mark. Oddly enough, if one cannot calculate exactly how close one's action comes to perfect justice, one can also never be quite sure how short one falls of the mark. Whatever justice or shalom we currently experience is mingled with and thus corrupted by injustice and war. While the Christian can rightly insist that there really *is* justice (even if we are not exactly sure what it means to make that statement), the danger comes in insisting that one's particular conception of it is adequate to it. Even that great proponent of natural law Thomas Aquinas realized that human law only imperfectly mirrors natural law and that natural law only imperfectly mirrors the eternal law.

Of course Derrida does recognize that his is a "hypersensitive" understanding of justice, one that can ultimately never be satisfied. But that, thinks Derrida, is the point. We can never rest; we can never be satisfied in either our acting or our moral thinking. To do so would to be *self*-satisfied, and that would be idolatrous. If I am "adequate" to virtue and if virtue is defined by God, then I am adequate to God. Thus I *am* God.

Derrida has no solution to such *aporias*, but that lack in no way implies that one ought to give up the quest of being moral. Quite the opposite. Derrida insists that we need to maintain a "hypervigilance," keeping our actions ever open to question. And there is much to commend in Derrida's exhortations. We are always inclined to see our parochial conceptions of justice as "justice itself."

Does Derrida himself escape this danger? Is deconstruction always justice? Even if we are willing to grant that deconstruction is *at times* justice, can we say that it is always justice? Since deconstruction is primarily (though not exclusively) a method of interpreting, it all depends on what it is used for. To deconstruct is to examine the underlying presuppositions and the consistency of a political, ethical or theoretical position; therefore one can further justice by deconstructing that which is unjust or unrighteous, or simply by using deconstruction as a tool to explain and understand. Deconstruction can be a way of taking responsibility, as one attempts to carefully think through ideological implications and assumptions.

But one can also use deconstruction not for justice but for antinomianism—escape from all law. Thus one must be careful about the claim that deconstruction is justice, for the veracity of the claim will depend largely on who is deconstructing what and why. We are probably well advised to be just a little suspicious of the claim that "deconstruction is justice"—and that suspicion is advised in the name of "hypervigilance." Derrida is right that we need to be vigilant, but that vigilance needs to be in his direction also. Derrida's equation of deconstruction with justice seems just a little too uncomfortably similar to the Pharisees and scribes' inclination to equate their own rules with justice. True, he says that deconstruction is something that was at work long before him. Yet that disclaimer only goes so far. It is all too easy for me to equate my view with "the way things are." And Derrida is no different.

6

FAITH
AND DOGMA

One thing is clear: whatever it is that Derrida believes, it is something neither Jewish nor Christian. To use his own description, it is a "religion without religion" (*GD* 49), "about which nobody understands anything."[1] As we shall see later, perhaps some understanding of that "religion" may actually be possible. But even though the faith of the orthodox Christian is clearly not that of Derrida, there is much to be learned from his reflections on the meaning of speaking of God and believing in him.

---

[1]Jacques Derrida, *Circumfession,* in Geoffrey Bennington and Jacques Derrida, *Jacques Derrida* (Chicago: University of Chicago Press, 1993), p. 154. Personally, Derrida is a circumcised Jew, married to a Gentile wife, whose sons are not circumcised. Is he an "atheist," an agnostic or some sort of believer not readily quantified? This is a difficult question to answer, and I won't attempt it here. For more on Derrida's religious life, see *Circumfession* and the interview with Derrida titled "A 'Madness' Must Watch over Our Thinking," in Jacques Derrida, *Points . . ., Interviews 1974-1994* (Stanford, Calif.: Stanford University Press, 1995), pp. 339-64. Whether or not one agrees with the interpretation of Derrida in John D. Caputo, *The Prayers and Tears of Jacques Derrida* (Bloomington: Indiana University Press, 1997), there can be no question that Caputo's is the most significant treatment of Derrida's "religion" to date.

Saying God's Name

Traditionally, the name of God—Yahweh—has been deemed so sacred among Jews that it must not be written or even said. That concern is symbolic of the particularly difficult *aporia* that is at the heart of both Jewish and Christian theology.[2] By its very definition, theology is a *logos (-ology)* of *theos,* the Greek term for God. But if *logos* is by nature something human, how can it adequately characterize the divine? Can there be a theology that remains uncorrupted by *logos?* As we shall see in chapters eight and nine, Jean-Luc Marion argues that God is able to reveal himself to us apart from any human *logos,* in a fundamentally uninterpreted or unmediated way. Whether Marion succeeds is a question I will have to reserve for later. But the difficulty is clear. Any *logos* by nature is (at least partially) intelligible to human beings. So how can there be a *logos* that rightly reflects God rather than merely human reason?

There is a further *aporia* at work in theology. Both the Old and New Testaments emphasize two aspects of God, and it is difficult to get them in proper balance. On the one hand, Scripture makes it clear that God can be known to us. In the Old Testament, God reveals himself in quite a variety of ways: as a stranger who visits Abraham, as an angel appearing to Jacob in a dream, as a burning bush to Moses. In the New Testament, Christ is even said to be the Word of God *himself* (Jn 1:1), and John (1 Jn 1:1) and Paul (1 Cor 15:5-8), for instance, claim to bear witness to what they have seen and even touched with their hands. Christ plainly says that those who have seen him have seen the Father (Jn 14:9). On the other hand, there is no question that God is still "Other," that he has revealed himself but not in his fullness.

So there are two risks. On the one hand, we run the risk of "domesticating" God (to borrow William Placher's memorable way of putting it): we can think that our descriptions and the descriptions of the Bible correspond exactly to who and what God is. We can easily forget that our descriptions of God and even those found in the Bible are truly analogies and metaphors. The reason for the commandment not to make images of God is that our images of him (and these can be literal images or simply our imaginings) can become substitutes for God. This, of course, was a reason why Plato thought that the images created by rhetoricians and artists were bad. As long as it is remembered that they are

---

[2]I shall limit my discussion here to Christian theology.

merely images, then they have some value; but, says Plato, we can easily forget, and then they become dangerous. On the other hand, we can
become so paranoid of human statements made about God that we do
not accept any statements and we silence both God and any who wish
to talk about God.

A way of taking this *aporia* seriously is "negative theology," which
has a long tradition going back at least as far as Augustine. The anonymous sixth-century "Dionysius"[3] provides us with a conception of God
as "hyper" (in Greek, *hyper*), which is to say above and beyond "being"
and thus above predication (which is to say beyond either affirmation or
negation). Properly speaking, God cannot be "named" or "characterized"
or "conceived," for he goes beyond all names, character traits and conceptions. Of God's name, Dionysius says:

> there is no speaking of it, nor name nor knowledge of it. Darkness and
> light, error and truth—it is none of these. It is beyond assertion and
> denial. We make assertions and denials of what is next to it, but never of
> it, for it is both beyond every assertion, being the perfect and unique
> cause of all things, and, by virtue of its preeminently simple and absolute
> nature, free of every limitation, beyond every limitation; it is also beyond
> every denial.[4]

From the viewpoint of negative theology, whatever one says of God
must be placed in quotation marks. It is simultaneously said and denied.
Since God occupies a "space" beyond being, nothing that can be said
about being can truly be said about God. "Since the unknowing of what
is beyond being is something above and beyond speech, mind, or being
itself, one should ascribe to it an understanding beyond being."[5] Dionysius in no way wishes to say that one cannot say anything about God.
But one must recognize that one speaks in a strange sort of way regarding God, saying and "unsaying" at the same time.

---

[3]Earlier known as "Dionysius the Areopagite" since he was thought to have converted as a
result of Paul's apology to the Athenians recorded in Acts 17, this anonymous Syrian
monk (who is judged today to have written actually between 485 and 510) is now called
Pseudo-Dionysius or simply Dionysius. For more on Dionysius and his importance in theology, see Paul Rorem, *Pseudo-Dionysius: A Commentary on the Texts and an Introduction to Their Influence* (Oxford: Oxford University Press, 1993).

[4]Pseudo-Dionysius, *The Mystical Theology* 1048a-b, in *The Complete Works,* trans. Colin
Luibheid and Paul Rorem (New York: Paulist, 1987).

[5]Pseudo-Dionysius, *The Divine Names* 588a, in *The Complete Works,* trans. Colin Luibheid
and Paul Rorem (New York: Paulist, 1987).

These difficulties of "speaking" about God or saying his name are the subject of Derrida's essay "How to Avoid Speaking: Denials." On Derrida's read, even the gesture of not talking, of ceasing to talk about God, has significant theological implications and "says" something. The recognition of the complexity of God-talk should not cause us to stop talking—any more than awareness of the complexity of our motivations should cause us to stop acting—but should lead us to be circumspect. As we shall later see, such worries over "identifying" God lead Derrida to take a position with which orthodox Christians are likely to disagree deeply and adamantly. Yet that does not mean his cautions ought to be ignored.

Already in the discussion of Nietzsche—let alone those of Heidegger and Levinas—I noted that the origin of the *logos* is problematic. Nietzsche thinks that philosophy's *logos* always arises from *within us,* so that all truth claims end up being ways of exalting ourselves. The problem of talking about God is not significantly different from the problem of the limits of human reason, speech, perception or knowledge in general. Even though Christians rightly claim that our belief is grounded on a claim of special revelation (that, say, Platonism does not make), there is still the construal of that revelation by theology. More pointedly, it would seem that God's revelation to us is always *itself* an interpretation of himself. Indeed what else could it be? Since God reveals himself to human beings, he reveals himself in human terms. To respond "But that's a theologian's problem" is to miss the undeniably *interpretative* aspect of human understanding that characterizes human belief— whether religious, scientific or otherwise—and to miss the fact that God's own picture of himself (say, when he reveals his "back" to Moses) is not identical to his being. This problem should concern every believer, for it goes to the very heart of what religious belief is all about. If I believe, in whom am I believing? Obviously the possibilities for idolatry are significant. But can they be avoided?

So the problem of *adaequatio* raised by negative theology is, as we have seen, a general one. This point is often either unnoticed or else not taken seriously enough in many discussions of negative theology. To what degree are we able to grasp (by what we say, how we think, how we perceive and the ideas that we use) "ultimate reality"? Understanding God is truly beyond our grasp. But isn't our understanding of much else likewise problematic? For example, do scientific theories describe the world *exactly* as it is? I'm assuming here that they describe it to a greater or lesser extent (an assumption that has been questioned by some), but the question at issue is whether the sense of adequation is complete or less than complete.

To take another example, when I perceive something, is that all there is to it, or is there something beyond what is perceived? "Substance" for John Locke ends up being "that which we know not what." This turns out to be fancy philosophical talk for "I know there's something there, but I haven't the foggiest idea what it is." On Locke's view, whereas we "know" what he calls "primary qualities" (e.g., size and weight) and "secondary" qualities (e.g., color and temperature) of a thing, we don't know what it really is "materially." This is a shocking admission. Isn't it the case that if we know anything about the objects we encounter in the world, we at least know that they are made of matter? Perhaps we do. But having said that, what have we really said? Just how much of a sense of adequation is there between our concepts and the reality that they are supposed to represent? I know the desk at which I am writing really "is" there. Yet if you were to ask me exactly what I mean by that statement, I could not go very far in explaining it. The adequation between my statement and the actual existence of the desk is limited—at best.

Thus is reality "as it really is"—not to mention God—just inaccessible to us? One can follow the lead of Levinas and Derrida by using the notion of the trace. As noted in the previous chapter, Derrida adopts this Levinasian notion as an alternative to Husserl's notion of intuitive givenness. Perception and speech do not give us "the thing itself" but a trace of the thing—a partial vision of the thing, with much left out. Many have interpreted Derrida as saying that there is no presence at all, but I take that to be a significant misinterpretation. At most, Derrida's argument against presence proves that there is no complete presence. However, lack of complete presence in no way means complete absence (whatever that could possibly mean).

The notion of the trace would seem to lend itself quite naturally to both the Hebrew and the Christian tradition. Thinking of God by way of something like the trace would seem to go back to the Pentateuch. When God shows his "back" to Moses, a trace of God is made known to Moses. The very idea of God's having a back is in one sense almost comic. Could God have anything like a body part correlative to a back? Obviously this is Scripture's way of letting us know that whatever Moses saw, it was not the fullness of God. Indeed, as noted in the introduction, Moses is warned quite specifically that he cannot see God in all his glory (Ex 33:18-23). The concept of the trace is a way of thinking that that always slips away, remaining an other that cannot be "sublated" or systematized. The trace presents itself but does not make itself fully present. In light of *différance,* Derrida would point out that whatever we say about God, he is always different from that saying, not merely in the trivial sense that God and the saying are ontologically different—which should be obvious—but in the important sense that the saying is inadequate to the thing it represents.

This idea that one can talk about God only in terms of a trace both is and is not similar to negative theology. There is no question that *différance also* has a logic similar to that of negative theology. As early as the essay *"Différance,"* Derrida points out that *différance* resembles negative theology "occasionally to the point of being indistinguishable" from it; yet he goes on to say that the "aspects of *différance* which [he delineates] are not theological."[6] What separates theology from deconstruction, at least on Derrida's account, is that the former is concerned with establishing God's "hyperessentiality" beyond the realm of predication and being. Such is not the concern of *différance,* even if its logic is similar. Derrida elsewhere explicitly says, "No, what I write is not 'negative theology'" (HAS 77). Moreover, *différance* is not found beyond predication and being but within. Thus it is not quite correct to say that negative theology is simply a "form of deconstruction," even though it is helpful to recognize their similarities.[7]

We have noted that negative theology is the attempt to theologize about God by talking about what God *is not.* The logic of negative theology is clear, even if the content is not. All statements about God must be made with the qualifier "without" *(sans).* The reason is twofold. First, if we say that God "has" wisdom, then there is something that is higher than God. According to negative theologians, in order not to place wisdom above God, we should say only that God *is* wise. Here one need

[6]Jacques Derrida, *"Différance,"* in *Margins of Philosophy,* trans. Alan Bass (Chicago: University of Chicago Press, 1982), p. 6. *"Différance"* was first given as an address and later published (in French) in 1968.
[7]Such is the claim of Kevin Hart in *The Trespass of the Sign: Deconstruction, Theology and Philosophy* (Cambridge: Cambridge University Press, 1985), p. 186. See Graham Ward's discussion of this point in *Barth, Derrida and the Language of Theology* (Cambridge: Cambridge University Press, 1995), p. 226.

merely recall Nietzsche's argument about philosophers who claim to know the meaning of life. Just as to make such a claim is to set oneself above life, so ascribing to God a characteristic is to make God subordinate to the characteristic and to oneself. Second, if we say that God has "wisdom," then it would seem that he partakes in the realm of being. If God is not part of "the world," then he is beyond the realm of being (i.e., beyond the world of substantiality).

It is understandable that a religious believer might be suspicious about negative (or "apophatic") theology. After all, negative theology almost sounds like a refusal to say anything (making it negative in another sense). If negative theology is just a wholesale denial *(apophasis)*, why should anyone take it seriously? More poignantly, how *could* one take it seriously? Take *what* seriously? There are two possible directions such criticism might go. On the one hand, if we refuse to say anything positive about God, might not *any* talk—whether about table lamps or cabbages or deposed South American dictators—turn into talk about God? If God's being can in no way be defined, then there is no way to separate it from anything else. The possibilities for idol creation would seem to be endless. I noted a similar problem in Levinas. On the other hand, perhaps *nothing* qualifies as God-talk. In such a case we have the possibility of creating a kind of "anti-idol," the god who is not God; we could even make a god of our refusal of allowing anything to be God.

So there are two dangers of negative discourse, and they cannot simply be eliminated. But as we have seen again and again, dangers abound. Apophatic theology can be praised for being cautious, but one can always be *too* cautious (despite the common aphorism to the contrary). Moreover, whatever one may say (positive or negative) about negative theology, one is never forced into a situation of having to choose between negative and positive theology. Both are possible ways of talking about God, and both have advantages and disadvantages.

Indeed "positive theology"—the articulation of God's characteristics— is subject to its own complications. First, and perhaps foremost, even positive theology—however strongly a particular view or attribute of God is articulated—is always implicitly or explicitly, wittingly or unwittingly, tempered by something like negative theology. When I say "God is all-knowing," I am forced to add, willingly or not, a disclaimer along the lines of "But God doesn't 'know' in the sense that human beings know." Were I to speak of God as knowing "just like me except a whole lot more," I would be dangerously close to heresy (or would have already crossed the line). One quite properly says, "God is our Father," and then quickly adds, "But not exactly." The danger of positive theology is that one can easily take one's own thoughts on God to be definitive and one thus runs the risk of making an idol: one holds up one's image of God and says, "Here is God."

There is a very strange logic at work in both positive and negative theology. One affirms something but denies it, because to affirm it too strongly would be heretical and to deny it completely would also be heretical. However much the negative theologian attempts to deny by way of a negative preface ("Don't take what I say too literally"), Derrida rightly points out that one cannot get away with this, for speaking in denials always leads to affirmations. Even to speak in denials means to assert God in some sense. Negative theology continually points us back to God as the source of our theologizing, so that we should not merely open our theologizing with prayer but make the entire project one long prayer.

So is the recognition of one's lack of understanding in speaking about God simply a negation of reason in religious belief? I take it that the answer is no. The believer recognizes that reason itself always begins and ends with faith. In presenting one of the most rationalistic of all arguments for God's existence, St. Anselm begins by admitting that his argument is only possible after he believes: "For I do not seek to understand that I may believe, but I believe in order to understand. For this also I believe,—that unless I believed, I should not understand."[8] Prayer is not just a way of spiritualizing or blessing an ordinary secular argument. It is not as if Anselm says, "Let's open in prayer," and then gets on with the real business of hard-core philosophical argumentation, so that the prayer functions merely as religious window-dressing. Rather it is the very context of the argument. We might even go so far as to say that prayer provides the very structure of what counts as "reason."

Derrida describes the move as follows:

Here prayer is not a preamble, an accessory mode of access. It constitutes an essential moment, it adjusts discursive asceticism, the passage through

---

[8]Anselm, "Proslogium," in *Basic Writings,* 2nd ed., trans. S. N. Deane (LaSalle, Ill.: Open Court, 1962), p. 53.

154 ————————————————————————— GRAVEN IDEOLOGIES

the desert of discourse, the apparent referential vacuity which will only avoid empty deliria and prattling, by addressing itself from the start to the other, to you. But to you as "hyperessential and more than the divine Trinity." (HAS 110)

But even prayer requires an affirmation. To pray to someone is not to pray to someone else. Thus there is a necessary postulation of identity even in prayer—or else there cannot be prayer. To pray to God the Father is not to pray to just any god or spirit. True, one may pray without knowing exactly to whom one prays. "Foxhole prayers" are often offered up without much of an idea to whom one is praying. But even to pray to "whoever might happen to be listening" is to give some form of address, however vague and imperfect. Or, rather, since prayer is a form of address, one must have an addressee—a someone or something or someplace. A *whatever* or a *whoever*.

However foggy all of this may be, it should at least be clear how difficult it is to conceptualize "otherness," and that is exactly the point. If we could reduce the other to a generality or image of our own making, it would not be other. To be truly other, it must be ultimately irreducible to any general category (even if we can and *must* use categories in some sense, as I have argued previously). God is the ultimately Other, the One who exceeds all the categories (including even "being"), and this is part of what makes him God (indeed the most important aspect of his "being"). It is this concern for protecting otherness that leads Derrida to speak of "saving the name." *Sauf le nom* can be translated as "save the name" or as "except the name." One saves the name, says Derrida, by refusing to say it, by excepting it from discourse. This is what negative theology attempts to do.

Yet there is something quite unsatisfactory about Derrida's account, at least for the religious believer. Whereas for Emmanuel Levinas there is a distinction between God and neighbor as others (even though both are truly other), for Derrida there is clearly a danger that God becomes "just another other" rather than the ultimate Other. As he puts it, "The other is God or no matter whom, more precisely, no matter what singularity, as soon as any other is totally other" (*ON* 74). Elsewhere Derrida gives us two possibilities. Where Levinas "keeps in reserve the possibility of reserving the quality of the wholly other, in other words the *infinite other,* for God alone," there is also the possibility that one "recognizes in this infinite alterity of the wholly other, every other, in other words each,

each one, for example each man and woman" (*GD* 83). Derrida clearly opts for this second possibility, claiming that *tout autre est tout autre*—the other is wholly other. But once one makes such a claim, it becomes impossible to make a distinction between God and human beings. Isn't that to lose the very distinction that negative theology works so hard to save? Has the name really been saved? To make God into anything less than the ultimate Other is to make him into an idol.

Whether Derrida truly falls into this trap is perhaps open to question, but it is a danger to which he seems particularly susceptible. What *may* save him is his notion of the gaze (God's gaze) that sees me and the hands that hold me (*GD* 91, 93), which seem to allow for a difference between the human others. We turn to these aspects shortly.

Faith and Its Reasons

The Czech philosopher Jan Patočka sets up an interesting and instructive dichotomy between secrecy and responsibility.[9] Religion sides with the latter, thinks Patočka, whereas the demonic or pagan sides with the former. Religion is open, having nothing to hide. Moreover, it operates on the basis of logic: one makes a rational choice in being religious. Being able to articulate one's course of action is precisely the bringing of it into the open. In contrast, the sacred is connected to mystery and esotericism: one is bidden to follow but not given any information. And the choice one makes as a follower of a cult is one that cannot be articulated or defended, at least not to someone who is not a follower. Although many of us are inclined, as children of the Enlightenment, to think that we have gone beyond the stage (assuming it can be so termed) of the cultic or mystical, Derrida warns that the logic of overcoming or "surpassing" the "outmoded" is a strange one indeed. We may think that we have overcome the cultic or mysterious, but we have certainly not done so in a *simple* way, if we have done so at all. Like the magician whose rabbit never really goes away, the believer—however rational and respectable—never simply does away with the mysterious.

Derrida thinks there is something more than a little "mysterious" about responsibility. On the one hand, responsibility would seem to be

---

[9]Jan Patočka, "Is Technological Civilization Decadent, and Why?" in *Heretical Essays in the Philosophy of History*, ed. James Dodd, trans. Erazim Kohák (Chicago: Open Court, 1996), pp. 95-118.

tied to the rational and the universal. On the other hand, it seems hard to connect responsibility to some abstract thing like "reason." Am I "responsible" to reason, or even some universal moral law? Does not responsibility require a *someone* to whom I am responsible? Yet if I am responsible to a someone, a singular other, then how can I characterize that responsibility? I cannot characterize it in terms of a universal, or at least not in terms of a universal alone or even primarily. And if this other is truly other (rather than just a version—however cleverly disguised—of *me*), then can I ever adequately characterize the otherness of this other to whom I am responsible? What does it mean to be responsible to someone who is other to myself, someone who cannot be mastered or controlled by me? Can responsibility, then, have anything like "its reasons," or does it simply boil down to "faith"? Which is to say: does faith have its reasons?

Donner la mort is the rather euphemistic French expression for suicide, but Derrida uses it to illuminate the idea of responsibility to the other.

> How does one give *oneself* death *[se donner la mort]?* How does one give it to oneself in the sense that putting oneself to death means dying while assuming responsibility for one's own death, committing suicide but also sacrificing oneself for another, *dying for the other,* thus perhaps giving one's life by giving oneself death . . . ? (*GD* 10)

The vagueness of the phrase *donner la mort* is important. For sacrificing oneself for another can be seen as praiseworthy—or simply stupid and senseless. If it is the former, we call the act martyrdom; if it is the latter, we call it suicide. If one thinks that dying as a martyr for Allah is a key to eternal reward, then being a "suicide bomber" makes sense. If not, it is hard to imagine a more senseless sacrifice. But this raises an important question: can a sacrifice be truly a sacrifice if it can be made "sensible" as part of a larger economy? In other words, if the suicide bomber is a martyr, is he really sacrificing anything at all? Or is there a shrewd, more secret sort of calculation going on that turns the supposed sacrifice into a calculated economic move?

At the heart of Christianity, asks Derrida, is there a sense of genuine sacrifice—one that is not calculated in an economic sense, one that is not structured around a reward? As a kind of contrast to a Christian notion of responsibility, consider Heidegger's notion of

Eigentlichkeit (authenticity). To be authentic in the sense of *Eigentlichkeit* is to be true to oneself. So Heidegger's sense of moral responsibility is based on the call of one's own conscience. Even if we grant that there is some sense in which Heidegger's idea of responsibility is valid, it clearly is not synonymous with a Christian conception of responsibility. The proper Christian view is that I am also (and, probably better put, first and foremost) responsible to God and to my neighbor. Christianity in effect announces a new sort of death. If I am responsible to God and my neighbor, then there must be some sense in which I "die" to myself. Even if we say that there is still room for one to be responsible to oneself, the extent to which I am responsible to God and my neighbor requires a death on my part. I give God and my neighbor the gift of (my) death. From a Christian view, responsibility becomes a kind of dying to self and dying for the other. Properly defined, Christian responsibility moves away from the Platonic in that its focus is no longer on universality (as in Platonism) but on particularity. I am not responsible to some general law or even (as in Kant's case) to rationality or logic; rather I am responsible to someone.

How, then, are we to construe responsibility? Can we make sense of it? On the one hand, responsibility would seem to be predicated on explanations. I am deemed responsible if I can *explain* my actions to others. If the only answer I can give to the question "Why did you do that?" is "I don't know," then I am unlikely to be deemed responsible. Since the realm of ethics is not particulars ("what's right for me") but universals ("what's right for everyone"), the ethical order is open to scrutiny. One cannot very well say, "The motivation for my actions is private," for to be ethical is to open one's actions up to inspection by others. Even the claim "God told me to do it" is often questionable, for the rest of us don't know if God actually did issue such a command.

On the other hand, I noted in the previous chapter that following Christian morality is ultimately not based on benefit, "rationality" or calculation. Abraham's near-sacrifice of Isaac is perhaps the quintessential example of the renunciation of the calculable in favor of the incalculable. If he were to speak, he would be giving a justification of his action, and that would put him in the realm of the calculable (*GD* 59). Derrida, following Kierkegaard, makes the admittedly bizarre-sounding claim that to provide a justification for one's actions is to renounce one's responsibility:

> As soon as one speaks, as soon as one enters the medium of language, one loses that very singularity. One therefore loses the possibility of deciding or the right to decide. Thus every decision would, fundamentally, remain at the same times solitary, secret, and silent. Speaking relieves us, Kierkegaard notes, for it "translates" into the general. (*GD* 60)

It is important to be clear on what Derrida (and Kierkegaard) means here. In effect, speaking means that one places the blame on someone else. "I was just following the rule," one might say, as if to move responsibility away from myself and onto the rule. Anyone who has ever dealt with petty bureaucrats ("petty" both literally and figuratively) knows that the invocation of "the rules" is designed *precisely* to take the responsibility off themselves. "It's not my fault that you can only get a visa for three months. Those are the rules. I'm just following them." If someone is "just following the rules," then the consequences of that person's actions are the responsibility of someone else (and since the rules are written by an anonymous group of bureaucrats, then no one in particular can be held responsible). If *I* do what I am supposed to do (i.e., follow the rule), that is the end (in more than one sense) of my responsibility. As many of the Nazi concentration-camp guards said at the war trials, "We were just following orders." Even if they were willing to admit that there was something wrong with the orders, that was not *their* responsibility. So they weren't "responsible."

The problem is that responsibility is aporetic. It is somewhere between accounting for one's action (the ethical, the general, the open) and not being able to account for one's action (the nonethical, the singular, the secret). One cannot simply renounce all explanation and still be "moral," but one cannot simply act on the basis of explanation and still be "moral." What should be clear is that one faces the danger of irresponsibility either way: either in taking refuge in the ethical or in acting for no reason at all. Consider the dilemma Abraham faced when commanded to sacrifice his son Isaac. On the one hand, the demands of ethics are such that he must not sacrifice his son (an act that by the standards of virtually all cultures would be considered barbaric); on the other hand, God has called him to act, to do what sounds barbaric. The dilemma comes not in the renunciation of ethics (which would be a simple solution of the dilemma), but in recognition of the validity of *both* ethics *and* the singularity of God's call to sacrifice Isaac.

Such an *aporia* is to be found in religious faith.[10] On the one hand, it is always possible to give "reasons" for one's faith. There really are reasons to which one can appeal (and, yes, those reasons do demand some kind of verdict). On the other hand, if faith is really "faith," then reasons can only go so far. Of course religious faith is hardly alone in this dilemma. Even the ultrarational logical positivists ended up having a central tenet that could not itself be justified. Instead it was an article of faith.[11] So—properly speaking—faith is always characterized by undecidability. If one could "ground" one's ground, then one could turn faith into pure reason. If one could spell out *exactly* who God is, then one would in effect be turning religious belief into a metaphysical explanation. But to do so would be to destroy not only its character *as faith* but God's character *as God*. For then we would be putting ourselves above God, and so committing idolatry.

My responsibility to God is based on a kind of dissymmetry, which can be worked out in a number of senses. I briefly noted earlier that Derrida speaks of God's seeing me with a gaze that I cannot return and that I cannot even see (*GD* 91). We have seen that the recognition of this gaze is partly responsible for Nietzsche's rejection of God. Nietzsche was unwilling to admit that any God could and did see him. Why? Because God sees that which I do not want him to see, all my shortcomings. Moreover, I cannot see myself in the gaze of God upon me: that is, this gaze is not a reflection of me. To put that another way, the gaze cannot be appropriated in an idolatrous way. This dissymmetry puts our relationship outside the realm of economic relationships. There is no way to calculate with a gaze that cannot be seen.

Derrida connects this idea of secrecy to "God paying back in secret." God gives Abraham back his son, but God does not *pay* Abraham. Theirs is an exchange, but it is not an economic exchange: "God decides to *give back*, to give back life, to give back the beloved son, once he is

---

[10]There is a problem with even making a distinction between moral action and religious belief. In Abraham's case there really isn't a distinction between the "faith" demonstrated in the offering of Isaac and that evidenced in "religious belief." When Abraham is commended in Hebrews 11:8-19 for his faith, the offering up of Isaac is included as a component of that faith. One could say that Abraham's action in this case is a particular instance of his faith. But the writer of the Hebrews implies that it just *is* that faith.

[11]The logical positivists insisted that one must accept only analytically or empirically demonstrated theses as true. But the insistence that "one must accept only analytically or empirically demonstrated theses as true" is itself neither analytically nor empirically demonstrable.

assured that a gift outside of any economy, the gift of death—and of the death of that which is priceless—has been accomplished without any hope of exchange, reward, circulation, or communication" (*GD* 96). It is only *after* renouncing all rights and expectations that Abraham is rewarded: indeed it is even improper to speak of a "reward," for it is a reward "in secret"—which is to say it is not really a reward.

The strange economy of heaven is a breaking with the economy of reciprocity. It might be termed an economy of absolute loss—one simply gives and expects nothing in return. In place of payment or repayment, one gives. That is all. The logic of the *Logos* is the logic that renounces all calculation and remuneration. And the logic of sacrifice is the logic that destroys or at least suspends logic: it calls on us to go beyond anything rationally calculable. Derrida describes this "logic" by saying:

> If there is gift, the *given* of the gift (*that which* one gives, *that which* is given, the gift as given thing or as act of donation) must not come back to the giving (let us not already say to the subject, to the donor). It must not circulate, it must not be exchanged, it must not in any case be exhausted, as a gift, by the process of exchange, by the movement of circulation of the circle in the form of return to the point of departure. If the figure of the circle is essential to economics, the gift must remain *aneconomic*. Not that it remains foreign to the circle, but it must *keep* a relation of foreignness to the circle, a relation without relation of familiar foreignness. It is perhaps in this sense the impossible. Not impossible, but *the* impossible. The very figure of the impossible. (*GT* 7)

One gives without expectation of reciprocity. So the circle is broken. Or, rather, one avoids the circular logic of economy altogether.

Of course Derrida points out that this is really impossible. One can at best *try to* transcend the circular economy, to give with just a little abandonment. *Human* giving would seem to be always connected to the circle, whether closely and explicitly (as in "Here is your birthday present, and I expect one just as nice on my birthday") or more disconnectedly, implicitly, less obviously.

So can anyone really give in a noneconomic way? Perhaps the best answer, from a Christian perspective (not Derrida's), is the one Jesus gives to the disciples, who ask, "Then who can be saved?" Jesus replies: "For mortals it is impossible, but for God all things are possible" (Mt 19:25-26). The grace that true giving requires is beyond our capacity. To whatever extent we are able to extend grace, it is only on the basis of having been extended grace ourselves. Grace does not come from within us but from without. It is a gift that one has been given and can exist only in the form of a gift.

Even justice requires something like this character of being a gift. In order for acts of justice to be truly "just," they must be done without expectation of reward. If I treat others in such a way that they will treat me well in return, I have not really done justice. In fact I have put myself in their place, making myself the real reason for moral actions ("I will be just to you, but I'm really only doing this so you'll be just back to me"). Ultimately the effect of my action is that I attempt (however unsuccessfully) to put myself in God's place. How? I try to make myself the "justification" for moral action. To be just to others in order to have justice done to me is not to be just. It is to use the other. When Jesus says, "In everything do to others as you would have them do to you" (Mt 7:12), he is not giving an economic formula ("Do to others *so that* they will do to you").[12] He is giving a guideline, a way of measuring our actions. Thus "when you give alms, do not let your left hand know what your right hand is doing, so that your alms may be done in secret" (Mt 6:3-4). If one truly wishes to give, then giving must be done with self-forgetfulness. One cannot give a gift and focus on one's giving at the same time—else the gift becomes part of an economic exchange. One must keep the secret even from oneself.

Such renunciation of the economy of the world is how Christianity is *supposed* to work. It is entirely possible, though, to envision someone renouncing the world and its economic system and all the while secretly holding on to it. In other words, one could renounce it in order to get it back:

> In its essential instability the same economy seems sometimes faithful to and sometimes accusing or ironic with respect to the role of Christian sac-rifice. It begins by denouncing an offering that appears too calculating still; one that would renounce earthly, finite, accountable, exterior, visible wages *(merces)*, one that would exceed an economy of retribution and exchange only to capitalize on it by gaining a profit or surplus value that was infinite, heavenly, incalculable, interior, and secret. (*GD* 109)

---

[12]The Revised Standard Version actually renders Jesus' exhortation better: "So whatever you wish that men would do to you, do so to them." In effect Jesus says, "You want to know the right thing to do? Just ask yourself, *What would I want others to do to me?* Then do that."

I have already shown (in the previous chapter) that motivations are never pure and that Scripture uses rewards to motivate us to good actions. But in Matthew 6:3-4 Jesus is not setting up a higher reward. Instead, he reveals "a still more excellent way." Consider the strikingly different placement of the terms "so that" in Jesus' depiction of the hypocrites and his instructions to his disciples on giving alms. Whereas the hypocrites give "so that they may be praised" (Mt 6:2), Jesus speaks of the left hand not knowing what the right hand is doing "so that your alms may be done in secret" (Mt 6:4). Verse 4 continues with the phrase "and your Father who sees in secret will reward you. In other words, the reward to Jesus' disciples is not linked with a "so that." Rather, the reward is just something given as a gift.

Of course on Nietzsche's account Jesus simply gives his followers a bigger and better "so that." Nietzsche reads Jesus as giving us the ultimate reward strategy: "Avoid doing good works publicly. That way you'll get an even greater reward." One gets the benefit of appearing to have pure motives *and* a bigger bonus. Such is the Nietzschean account of Christianity—that Christians give us the sneakiest formula for selfishness. "Unselfishness" is used as a cover for selfishness of the most insidious sort. Christian secrecy may be clever (and even Nietzsche would admit that it is), but it is still motivated by the will to power.

Yet if Nietzsche's read is right, it is odd that Jesus goes on in the very next verse to warn his disciples against being hypocrites *(hypokritai)*. One could perhaps read Jesus' admonition as "Don't be like the dumb, obvious hypocrites (actors); be smart, shrewd, calculating ones instead." That is, if you want to be a great actor, you can't look like an actor. However much that might seem a possible reading to Nietzsche, Christians are rightly apt to protest that it completely misses Jesus' point. Instead Jesus gives us an (almost) impossible prescription: do your good works in such secret that even *you* forget about them and you will be rewarded. In other words, one gives up any hope of reward—and so is rewarded. One gets by giving. But one doesn't give *in order to get*. Or else one gets nothing other than the immediate approval of others who happen to see one give.

The renunciation of the economy of the world is the adoption of grace. While grace is not properly the destruction of justice, it is the suspension—or, better yet, fulfilling—of the economy of justice. Grace too is aporetic, and this is seen most obviously in God the Father's sacrifice of Christ for us. God, as creditor, demands the payment of a debt. But in paying the debt himself, he steps outside of the economic system. Or we might say that he institutes a new economy—the economy of love. God openly shares the "secret" of the secret economy and yet keeps it secret—for the why is never given to us. Without rhyme or reason, God simply loves us and redeems us, and so leaves us with the ultimate secret. The only thing we can do is respond to God, not in an economic way but in love.

Everything has a danger. And grace is probably the most dangerous thing around. It's also the best thing around. But aren't most good things quite susceptible to misappropriation and distortion, perhaps even proportionately to their goodness? Grace certainly is. It is so wonderful that we generally want as much of the stuff as we can get. So much so that Paul actually has to write to the Romans and warn them that although the formula "more sin=more grace" is true, they still ought not to "continue in sin in order that grace may abound" (Rom 6:1). Grace is good, but it should not be provoked. We could even say that if grace is provoked, there is the danger that it can lose its quality as grace and become part of an economic exchange. The danger of the logic (or lack of logic) of sacrifice is that it can degenerate into a logic of economy in which sacrifice is sacrificed. Grace can become a cover or justification for irresponsibility. We can excuse our failings by appealing to grace. And then grace is just a means to our ends. It is reconfigured in our own image.

Dogma *Against* Idolatry

I think Derrida's call to vigilance can be ignored by Christians only at our own peril. But there is a danger against which we must be equally vigilant. One can easily become so worried by the prospect of doing violence to God and to neighbor that one is left in inaction. To be fair to Derrida, he clearly points out that the demands of morality cannot wait; so I take it that the demands of belief likewise cannot wait. However, Derrida seems so reluctant to say much of anything positive that he is, I think unduly, critical of even the relatively circumspect attempts of Marion to consider ways of thinking about God which either do not do violence or minimize violence to him. We can, I think, heartily agree with Caputo on the need for deconstruction when he says, "The idea of deconstruction is to break all such locks, to unlock texts and institutions, beliefs and practices, not in such a way as to say that you cannot have

such things, but only to say that you cannot have a lock on them."[13]
After all, at least those of us who are Protestants owe our heritage to the
protesting of such locks.

Derrida seems to lead us in the direction of the opposite danger—
being so afraid of violence that we would eschew not only locks but
texts and institutions and beliefs and practices themselves. For
instance, he is so insistent on making God *tout autre* (wholly other)
that God ends up being beyond *any* determinable faith. The result is
Derrida's faith without religion, what he calls a "nondogmatic doublet
of dogma . . . a *thinking* that 'repeats' the possibility of religion without
religion" (*GD* 49). What is this "religion" "about which nobody understands anything"? Although Derrida says, "I quite rightly pass for an
atheist,"[14] one can hardly argue that he has no belief at all. After all, he
claims, "Not only do I pray, as I have never stopped doing all my life,
and pray to him, but I take him here and take him as my witness." He
prefaces this remark by saying, "I am addressing myself here to God,
the only one I take as a witness, without yet knowing what these sublime words mean."[15] Whatever the content of Derrida's religion ends up
being, both in the present and in the evolution of his thinking, Caputo
is clearly right in arguing that it is "more Jewish than Christian, more
religious than theological, more concerned with the ethico-politics of
hospitality than with mystical or negative theology" (*GGP* 200).

Given the present study's concerns with the practical problem of idolatry, determining the exact contours of Derrida's "indeterminate" religion is much less important than considering the implications of his
thought for idolatry. It is hard to argue with Derrida that faith runs the
risk of being too clear, too certain, too dogmatic. On that point he is
undoubtedly right. But is it really possible to have faith without dogma?
Isn't dogma what faith is all about—or at least what makes it possible?
When I say "I believe," there is something *in which* I believe. Moreover,
given that I am a Christian, there is a someone *in whom* I believe. True,
belief in something and someone can and should be always open to the
questioning of deconstruction. The image of Jesus Christ that I worship
can begin to look like me or be merely an extension of my wants and
needs, so that Jesus becomes the grantor of my wishes rather than the

---

[13]Caputo, *Prayers and Tears,* p. 53.
[14]Derrida, *Circumfession,* p. 155.
[15]Ibid., pp. 56-58.

Lord of my life. Such idols are prevalent enough. But note that the danger from which deconstruction would seek to protect us is one that dogma is also designed to address. When Derrida argues that "the apophatic design is also anxious to render itself independent of revelation . . . independent of all history of Christianity, *absolutely* independent" (*ON* 71), that seems to me Derrida's own particular read of negative theology, with which believers are likely to disagree strongly. The deconstructive logic of negative theology is a helpful tool; but it is not necessarily at odds with dogma. The insistence of the early church upon careful formulation of creeds and doctrines was *precisely* about keeping our image of Jesus pure and unstained, rather than being remade in our image. If such is the case, then we are left with the recognition that the church needs both dogma and deconstruction. It is not a question of choosing but of holding them in tension.

Derrida continually warns of the danger of false dilemmas, of thinking that one must choose between two simple alternatives. Here he could take his own warning to heart: for there is no need to choose deconstruction to the exclusion of dogma. From the viewpoint of historic Christian orthodoxy, if we are going to err on one side or the other, we are advised to err on the side of dogma. Woe to anyone who would take up doctrinal deconstruction lightly!

Perhaps we should read Derrida here in light of his own idea (doctrine?) of undecidability. It almost seems as if he has already *decided* that dogma is just human *logos*. But must it be that? Or must it be *only* that? Might not such a decision itself be a kind of dogma? Christians are likely to agree with Derrida that mixed in with their dogma is an unhealthy dose of idolatrous thinking. While we would like to think that the idolatrous chaff can be easily separated from the orthodox wheat, things aren't so simple. And they are no more simple whether one is a famous French philosopher or a learned Pharisee.

On the one hand, Derrida wants to insist that undecidability ought not to prevent us from deciding. Decisions, he stresses, are not based on decidability. At least to a point, he's right. On the other hand, it seems that Derrida's unwillingness to commit himself to anything like "dogma" is an example of not taking the idea of undecidability seriously enough. True, dogma can be a way of avoiding responsibility if one says, "I believe whatever it is the creeds say. I really haven't thought about it myself. I just believe the stuff." But dogma can also be a way of taking responsibility, of saying "Here I stand." In saying "Here I stand," one does not necessarily say "All that I believe is 100 percent right; I am unwilling to think about this any further." One does say, "I am making a commitment to a body of belief and, more important, to God." After all his talk of responsibility as something that one cannot ultimately justify, it seems odd that Derrida would be so afraid of dogma. For dogma just is that which cannot be ultimately justified. And commitment to it is a way of taking responsibility.

The fear of commitment to anything that smells like dogma is at the heart of Derrida's distinction between the messianic and messianism. For Derrida, all thought, language, morality, religion—everything—has the structure of the "not yet but still to come." He thinks that human beings cannot help but think of our lives and actions as pointing to a time to come in which there is true shalom (a view that has similarities with that of Kant in one of his late texts). Derrida is all for faith but is extremely squeamish about anything that smacks of religion, even his own Jewishness. He is in favor of the "messianic," which he defines as pointing toward a time yet to come in which there is true shalom. But he is very wary of any concrete "messianism," any particular version of who this messiah might be and what the time to come might look like (whether the messianism of Judaism, Christianity, Islam or Marxism). The messianic for Derrida is a time that always "is to come" but never arrives.

It is important to remember Derrida's own qualification in *The Gift of Death* that he is merely spelling out a logic that at bottom

> has no need of *the event of a revelation or the revelation of an event*. It needs to think the possibility of such an event but not the event itself. This is a major point of difference, permitting such a discourse to be developed without reference to religion as institutional dogma, and proposing a genealogy of thinking concerning the possibility and essence of the religious that doesn't amount to an article of faith. (*GD* 49)

In other words, Derrida thinks that the logic of Christian morality can be appropriated without its commitment to a specific event or particular revelation. In effect, he wants the benefits of Christianity's morality (of which he generally seems to approve) without the disadvantages of dogma (which requires a kind of commitment). But can Derrida really do that? Is Christianity's logic not tied both historically and logically with an event and a person?

But wait a moment. Isn't Derrida the one who has been telling us of the irreducible singularity of responsibility? And isn't he now attempting to generalize the singularity not just of Christianity but of the singular event of Christ's incarnation? Such would seem to be a "losing of the name," a violence done to a singularity in the name of a generality.

Oddly enough, I think Derrida's problem is that, in an important sense, he is too (for lack of a better term) *Platonistic.* For everything of value turns out for Derrida to be a kind of ideal object that can never be properly instantiated. Not only is justice so transcendent that all its instantiations pale in comparison, but the content of faith is likewise so transcendent that all attempts to spell it out fail miserably. Like Plato, then, Derrida seems to be very uneasy with any kind of incarnation. But whereas this fear keeps him from making any commitment, it is affirmation of the incarnation that underlies the Christian commitment—the affirmation that Jesus Christ truly instantiates God with us.

I think Christians must both disagree and agree with Derrida. On the one hand, Christ is the Messiah who has already come. We do not point to a Messiah who only is to come, nor do we point to one who never is to come, whose coming is announced but infinitely delayed. On the other hand, Christ's advent is double-sided, for Christ has come and yet still *is to come.* Christ has come; Christ has returned to the Father; Christ will come again. So we live in a time between the two advents.

In the end, does Derrida merely help us in a negative way, by exposing problems with theories but not really offering anything to replace them? Such criticism has been frequent, and Derrida admits that the critics have a point:

> I don't think deconstruction "offers" anything *as* deconstruction. That is sometimes what I am charged with: saying nothing, not offering any content or any full proposition. I have never "proposed" anything, and that is perhaps the essential poverty of my work. I never offered anything in terms of "this is what you have to know" or "this is what you have to do." So deconstruction is a poor thing from that point of view.[16]

There are at least two issues at stake here. First, to what extent ought philosophers to build theories and systems, and should we be critical of Derrida for not having done so? Certainly philosophers over the last cen-

---

[16]Jacques Derrida, "Hospitality, Justice and Reponsibility: A Dialogue with Jacques Derrida," in *Questioning Ethics: Contemporary Debates in Philosophy,* ed. Richard Kearney and Mark Dooley (London: Routledge, 1999), p. 74.

tury have been less inclined toward grand theorizing, and perhaps there is nothing wrong with that per se. Moreover, one could argue that accusing deconstruction of not being constructive is rather like criticizing a screwdriver because it makes an ineffective hammer. Deconstruction was not designed to be constructive.

Yet perhaps there is a more important question here. Might Derrida actually end up "offering" more than is readily apparent? Is he guilty of substituting a *logos*—however scaled down, however modest—of his own? His rejection of Christian dogma in favor of "religion without religion" could just end up being a dogma itself. Perhaps that nondogmatic *logos* is less "totalizing" than others in the history of Western philosophy, but it still seems to be a dogma. If there is anything that Derrida shows us, it is that everyone has a dogma—even Derrida. But he seems less than willing to own up to his.

So does Derrida lead us into just a different sort of idolatry? Perhaps that is undecidable, but there is certainly a danger of his setting himself up as the deconstructor who is never deconstructed, the center of logical discourse who questions all centers, the reminder of the need to be vigilant who is considerably less practiced at self-vigilance. In so doing, might Derrida turn himself into the center that all are forced to respond to?

By turning at this point to Marion—with a short detour on the problem of "otherness" in Husserl and Heidegger—we in no way leave behind the questions raised by Derrida. If anything they will become more acute, for Marion attempts to provide a way of thinking about God's appearing to us that escapes the *logos* of philosophy. Whether he succeeds, of course, remains to be seen.

7

HUSSERL AND HEIDEGGER ON OTHERNESS

Jean-Luc Marion's philosophical training and tradition are deeply phenomenological and thus strongly indebted to Husserl and Heidegger. Even though Marion applies phenomenology to topics that are not typically Husserlian, *God Without Being* is a very phenomenological text. In the same way that Husserl wishes to allow the *logos* of the phenomena to arise from the phenomena themselves, so Marion hopes to refrain from imposing unwarranted conceptual schema on God. Thus Marion attempts to point us to ways of speaking about and relating to God that are not idolatrous, that do not succumb to ideology.

Is there a way to speak of God that both makes God present and allows God to remain other to us? Before we can begin to answer these questions, in this chapter we need to consider some basic aspects of Husserl's and Heidegger's thought that complicate this move.

The Problem of the Transcendental Ego in Husserl

There is no question that at the very heart of phenomenology is a strong desire to allow the phenomena to be manifest "just as they are." In the *Logical Investigations* Husserl speaks of a *"pure phenomenology of the experiences of thinking and knowing"* (*LI* 249). "Pure" here means "free-dom from metaphysical, scientific and psychological presuppositions" (*LI* 265). And I have noted Husserl's "principle of principles," in which he stipulates

> that *everything originarily . . . offered* to us *in "intuition" is to be accepted simply as what it is presented as being,* but also *only within the limits in which it is presented there.* (*ID* 44, Husserl's italics)

So there ought to be no "hermeneutical moment," no added interpretive aspect to our perceiving and knowing.

To achieve this purity, Husserl insists that we need to "bracket out" any ideas or concepts that we may have already connected to the phenomena. He attempts to "suspend" those beliefs (and thus purify the phenomena) by what he calls the phenomenological reduction, explicit suspension (*epoché*) of any metaphysical ideas concerning their "reality" or "ideality" (realism or idealism), as well as any other "added" concepts (*ID* 61). In other words, instead of worrying about the true "being" of phenomena, we are concerned only with their features. To the phenomenological reduction Husserl adds the "eidetic reduction," the analysis of phenomena for their "essential" features. Rather than focusing on the particular features of a given phenomenon, we focus on its essence. Thus the phenomena are likewise "purified" of everything that is merely "accidental" or contingent.

As Husserl's thought developed, he called for an even further reduction, one that makes the basic goal of phenomenology ("to the things themselves") increasingly problematic—though of course it was problematic from the start. In this somewhat revised formulation of phenomenology, the appearance of the phenomena is grounded in my transcendental ego, which constitutes both the field on which the phenomena appear and their very possibility conditions. The transcendental ego—consciousness or the "I"—is the "horizon" on which phenomena appear, which means that the transcendental ego provides both the limits of what can be seen and *how* it is seen. Even in the "principle of principles," Husserl says that the phenomenon appears *"within the limits in which it is presented there."* But what are these limits? As it turns out, they are limits not just of the phenomenon itself but of the intentional act in which that phenomenon is contained. In *Ideas I,* the same text in which Husserl insists on "the principle of principles," he makes the now almost infamous claim that whereas the world could be annihilated and the transcendental ego would be unscathed, there would be no world if the transcendental ego (*my* transcendental ego) were to stop constituting it. To quote Husserl: *"The world of transcendent 'res' is entirely referred to consciousness and, more particularly, not to some logically conceived consciousness but to actual consciousness"* (*ID* 110, Husserl's italics). In addition to the phenomenological and eidetic reductions, then, there is the "transcendental reduction" in which phenomena are reduced to the transcendental ego. Through the transcendental reduction, we see that the world is ultimately reducible to the transcendental ego—or ultimately reducible to *me*.

Given the transcendental reduction, it is hard to escape the idea that phenomena are somehow "mine," a part of my own consciousness and thus dependent on that consciousness for their existence. Moreover, since those phenomena appear for me, they appear within the limits that my transcendental ego imposes. We can still speak of them appearing as they are, but "as" now takes on a whole new meaning. For their state of being "as they are" is at least partially dependent on me the knower and ultimately the constituter of both their meaning and their existence. With such a conception of my knowing of the phenomena and even of their very being, whether they can be truly other—whether they can escape my seemingly all-encompassing interpretive gaze—becomes increasingly problematic in Husserl's thought. In the introduction I noted that the goal of phenomenology is to have the phenomena "intuitively given" to consciousness in such a way that they are fully immanent rather than transcendent. Husserl characterizes the genuinely immanent phenomenon as one that "'points' to nothing 'outside' itself, for what is here intended is fully and adequately given in itself."[1] But if there is nothing left over, if there is no "pointing" to something that is other to consciousness, can there be any genuine sense of otherness? Husserl confronts this problem—specifically, the problem of the *human* other— in the fifth of the *Cartesian Meditations*.

The problem of otherness can be worked out as follows.

First, in order for phenomenology to be a truly "transcendental" philosophy (i.e., scientific and systematic), it must be all-encompassing.

---

[1] Edmund Husserl, *The Idea of Phenomenology*, trans. William P. Alston and George Nakhnikian (The Hague: Martinus Nijhoff, 1973), p. 3.

Thus phenomenology must be able to describe the phenomena, as well as provide the very possibility conditions for the appearance of phenomena, not to mention the possibility conditions for the doing of phenomenology.

Second, Husserl's transcendental possibility condition for the appearance of the phenomena is the transcendental ego, the unidentified consciousness standing behind all apprehensions of phenomena. But if the transcendental ego is the possibility condition in the sense of being the horizon and ground of consciousness, then how can any kind of otherness be constituted from this perspective? In other words, the other would seem to be constituted from the point of view of the transcendental ego, even *by* the transcendental ego, so the other would not seem to be so very other. Indeed the other at least seems to be almost an extension of *me.*[2]

Third, while the phenomenological reduction is advanced by Husserl to allow for the possibility of the phenomena's appearing "purely," one could argue that it actually serves to distort them. To reach the place of phenomenological purity, we must bracket all our beliefs concerning the existence of the natural world; our concern must be only for objects as they *appear to us in consciousness,* not for their being-in-themselves. What remains, then, after this reduction is (1) the ego, (2) its acts of consciousness and (3) the objects of its consciousness (phenomenal objects). But note what this perspective implies: if all objects of consciousness are detached from their relation to a so-called outside world, then these objects become objects for me—for my transcendental ego—and thus I am, at least to some degree, the author of them. Even more important, they are also "objects for me" in the sense that it is through the interpretive activity of my consciousness that they have their "sense." Interpretation is the act of *Sinngebung,* "giving sense" to the phenomena. Among these sense-giving acts are those that apprehend what is "alien" *(fremd).* But even for the appearance of the *fremd* to be possible, I must be the possibility condition, both for the appearance of the other and for the constitution and characterization of the other *as* other. So whereas the other would seem to be something beyond me, something I cannot possess, something that would not submit to my categories or any of my attempts to contain it, possession—in terms of intuitive

──────────────────────────────

[2]To complicate this even further, Husserl is aware that even the self is other to itself.

givenness and immanence—seems essential to phenomenology.

What does all of this mean for idolatry? If idols are defined as entities or concepts made in our own image which we worship, then it would seem that there can *only* be idols on Husserl's account. For *everything* seems to be made in my own image, or at least to bear my stamp. Thus Husserl's view poses a grave difficulty for the possibility of avoiding idolatry.

But Husserl's emphasis on the transcendental ego also turns out to pose a problem for his own conception of phenomenology. The very postulation of a dichotomy between the "same" and "other" raises a fundamental *aporia* for the possibility of a *logos* of phenomenology.[3] On the one hand, if the other is dependent on me for its identity as an other, in what sense can it truly be other? Husserl says that the human other is "constituted as 'alter ego,'" which is to say that the other is pictured as a kind of image of me. On the other hand, if the other is really other, then how can it be meaningful to me? How can I possibly relate to such an other, one who is simply otherness to me? Husserl's "solution" to the problem of the human other is that we postulate the existence of the other on the basis of analogy. Since I know that behind my phenomenal body (one that, as a phenomenon, can be sensed by others) is a transcendental ego (which cannot be sensed by others), I can assume that behind the body of the other stands a transcendental ego.

One might rescue phenomenology from the danger of solipsism by insisting, as does Alfred Schutz, that the background of consciousness is a fundamental "we-community."[4] Yet such a move at best reformulates the problem of sameness and otherness from an individualistic into a social problem. Perhaps the we-community of my culture helps me to understand the members of that particular group, but it does not necessarily help for understanding those of other groups. We might be able to solve (or at least ameliorate) this problem by saying that we-community consists of all human beings past, present and future. Yet even if these reformulations were to solve the problem of otherness of human others (which I don't think is the case), the problem of divine otherness remains. Perhaps we are now less likely to fall into a purely personal sort of idolatry, but idolatry of a corporate sort is still possible.

---

[3]There are other ways to formulate this *aporia,* but we won't consider them here.
[4]Alfred Schutz, *Collected Papers* (The Hague: Martinus Nijhoff, 1966), 3:77. Solipsism is the view that only I exist.

Heidegger and the *Logos* of Phenomenology

The danger of "reducing" the otherness of the other is not merely a problem for Husserl. Rather than overcome this problem of phenomenology in *Being and Time,* Heidegger's account of "Dasein" manifests this same sort of tendency. Of course, much like Husserl's, Heidegger's conception of phenomenology is explicitly against any imposition upon the phenomena which would distort them. He points out that the Greek term *phainomenon* "means that which shows itself" (*BT* 51). Whereas "appearing is a *not-showing-itself*" (*BT* 52), a true phenomenon can be defined as "the showing-itself-in-itself [*das Sich-an-ihm selbst-zeigende*]" (*BT* 54). The very point of a phenomenology is to let the phenomena themselves appear, just as they are.[5]

Such a goal is compromised by Heidegger himself. While there are a number of elements of *Being and Time* which have at least the potential to diminish or simply obliterate the otherness of the other, Heidegger's idea that Dasein (human being) is fundamentally interpretive proves particularly problematic. According to Heidegger, Dasein "projects its Being upon possibilities" (*BT* 188). We might say that Dasein sees the world in terms of itself or in terms of its own possibilities. Admittedly, the world is not *simply* composed of Dasein's possibilities, for any particular Dasein encounters the world and entities existing within the world as already there and already given meaning by other Daseins in the world. So Dasein cannot give the world just any meaning it wishes. Yet Heidegger insists that Dasein interprets the world in a particular way, one that cannot be reduced to something like "the way things really are in themselves."

> An interpretation is never a presuppositionless apprehending of something presented to us. If, when one is engaged in a particular concrete kind of interpretation, in the sense of exact textual Interpretation, one likes to appeal to what "stands there," then one finds that what "stands there" in the first instance is nothing other than the obvious undiscussed assumption of the person who does the interpreting. (*BT* 191-92)

Thus while an interpretation is not *just* a matter of one's own presuppositions (note that Heidegger adds the qualifying phrase "in the

---

[5]Heidegger gives a similar locution in a work roughly contemporaneous with *Being and Time.* In *History of the Concept of Time* (trans. Theodore Kisiel [Bloomington: Indiana University Press, 1985]) he speaks of "letting the manifest in itself be seen from itself [*das an ihm selbt Offenbare von ihm selbst her sehen lassen*]" (p. 85).

first instance"), there is always a foreconception or forestructuring that takes place. In other words, Dasein always applies a *logos* to the phenomena. In explaining how phenomenology is possible, Heidegger claims that the *logos* "lets something be seen," since the *logos* effectively serves to "point out" that which is there (*BT* 56). But the pointing of the *logos* is always of a particular sort. One never points out something in a noninterpretive way. Heidegger points out that pointing out is always a "letting [something] be seen *as* something" (*BT* 56). Heidegger speaks of this as the "as-structure" *(als Struktur)* of perception and knowledge. That is, we always perceive or know things "as such." When I see the tree outside of my window, I see it *as a tree*. But if knowledge and perception always function by way of a hermeneutical "as" or "as such," then it is difficult to take seriously Heidegger's comment that "the function of the *logos* lies in merely letting something be seen" (*BT* 58). There is nothing "mere" about the interpretive function of the *logos*.

This interpretive aspect is fundamental to Dasein's existence, so much so that Heidegger claims that "meaning is an *existentiale* of Dasein, not a property attaching to entities, lying 'behind them,' or floating somewhere as an 'intermediate domain.' . . . *Hence only Dasein can be meaningful or meaningless*" (*BT* 193, Heidegger's italics). There are at least two ways to work out this claim. First, without Dasein there is no such thing as "meaning." A rock lying on the ground has no meaning in itself. For its meaning to be brought forth into being, there must a relation between that rock and a meaning-giver (Dasein and, I will add, God). Although Heidegger's conception of the relation between Dasein and the world does not fall neatly into either realism or idealism, it is idealistic in the sense that the world needs Dasein in order to have meaning. Heidegger's claim that *"there is' truth only in so far as Dasein is and so long as Dasein is"* could equally be said of meaning (*BT* 269). Since truth for Heidegger is "disclosedness" and disclosedness requires the *logos* of interpretation, both truth and meaning require Dasein.

Second, Heidegger claims that the meaning of entities in the world is determined by their relation to Dasein. As he puts it, "the ready-to-hand is always understood in terms of a totality of involvements" (*BT* 191). The "ready-to-hand" *(zuhanden)* is a thing that has a hermeneutical "as-structure" determined by Dasein's purposes and needs, making its meaning very much dependent on what is useful to Dasein.[6] Heidegger underscores the centrality of Dasein in interpretation when he says that "understanding is either authentic, arising out of one's own Self as such, or inauthentic" (*BT* 186). An "authentic" *(eigentlich)* interpretation is one that arises from *me,* from my perspective and for my purposes.

Yet Dasein is central not merely to meaning in the world but to the world's very being. "Only as long as Dasein *is* (that is, only as long as an understanding of Being is ontically possible), 'is there' Being" (*BT* 255). What exactly is Heidegger asserting here? He does *not* simply reject the category of "realism," nor does he simply discard the idea of "objectivity." It is less clear exactly what Heidegger (or, for that matter, Husserl) puts in place of objectivity and realism, though.[7] Heidegger goes on to argue in *Being and Time* that there are ways in which both realism and idealism are correct and incorrect. He ultimately ends in a view that is probably best described as being somewhere beyond the realism-idealism (or, for that matter, the realism-antirealism) continuum. Even though Heidegger clearly does not hold a purely idealistic position (or an antirealist one), there is no question that Dasein is central to both the constitution and the meaning of the world. For clearly Dasein clearly has a good deal of *interpretive* control. The only question that remains open here is how *much* control.

Given the centrality of Dasein for meaning and even Being, just how *other* can the ready-to-hand or even Being be? Is not the so-called other determined in advance by Dasein's projection? And would that not mean that everything becomes an idol made in Dasein's image?

There are a variety of reasons that Heidegger moves from the position of *Being and Time* to his later notions.[8] Surely one of the most important is his realization that not only the entire philosophical tradi-

---

[6]One might try to let Heidegger off the hook by pointing out that entities within the world are also designated by Heidegger as *vorhanden*—"present-at-hand." But there are at least two problems with this route. First, if the *vorhanden* only have meaning "as" involved with Dasein, then all *vorhanden* would seem to end up being *zuhanden* (in *some* sense). The difference threatens to collapse. Second, whether *vorhanden* or *zuhanden,* entities for Heidegger always have their meaning in relation to a *hand.* Either way, their meaning and their very being seems highly dependent on *human* being.

[7]Certainly Husserl can be read in a number of ways on this issue, particularly depending on which texts one emphasizes.

[8]Although Heidegger identifies the move from his earlier to his later thought as *die Kehre* (the turning), the extent of difference between the two is open to question. Briefly put, my own view is that there is more continuity than discontinuity between them.

tion but even his own early philosophy tends toward subjugation of Being *(Sein)* by particular beings *(seiende)*—more pointedly, by the particular being which he calls Dasein.[9] Heidegger comes to see philosophy as characterized by an attempt to use thinking in order to control and master Being, and ultimately God. In later writings he comes to criticize this move as "onto-theology." But how might this "subjugation" relate to the immediate problem of otherness in phenomenology, as well as to the overarching concern for idolatry? To answer these questions, we need to consider the genesis of metaphysics and how it (at least according to Heidegger) quickly turns into an idolatrous onto-theology. I will use Heidegger's more complete formulation of metaphysics as being "onto-theo-ego-logical" in nature as a guide.

Let's begin with ontology. Already in *Being and Time* Heidegger was concerned with explicating the difference between Being and beings (Being itself versus particular entities), what he comes to term "the ontological difference."[10] There he argues that the very question of what Being is—seemingly the most obvious and basic of philosophical questions—has been overlooked by the tradition. True, it was raised by early Greeks such as Aristotle, who distinguishes between the "science which investigates being as being" and what he calls the "special sciences," which focus on particular entities.[11] But even Aristotle, and certainly subsequent philosophers, quickly became preoccupied with the question of "beings," so much so that the study of beings effectively *became* the study of Being.

Despite Heidegger's explicit wish to avoid losing sight of the *Seinsfrage* (the question of Being), his insistence in *Being and Time* that ontology "must be sought in the *existential analytic of Dasein*" (*BT* 34) proves problematic. *Being and Time* ends up being far less about Being and far more about Dasein, so that whatever we learn about Being is strongly colored by the hermeneutical "as" supplied by Dasein. If

---

[9]Even the English translation of these terms is in dispute. Although the noted Heidegger scholar William Richardson advocated these translations (see his *Heidegger: Through Phenomenology to Thought* [The Hague: Martinus Nijhoff, 1963]), other scholars have questioned their accuracy.

[10]Although the term *ontological difference* never occurs in *Being and Time*, the idea is implicit in Heidegger's thinking. Just a year later, though, in a course of 1928, Heidegger spoke of the ontological difference as a basic problem of phenomenology. See Martin Heidegger, *The Basic Problems of Phenomenology*, trans. Albert Hofstadter (Bloomington: Indiana University Press, 1982), p. 17.

[11]Aristotle *Metaphysics* 4.2.1003b.

Heidegger is right when he claims that ontology is *"blind and per-verted"* when *"it has not first adequately clarified the meaning of Being"* (*BT* 31), one must wonder whether such a characterization applies to his own early ontology. Is not ontology all the more "blind and per-verted" when it attempts to clarify Being by way not merely of beings but of only one particular being? Has not a profound sense of otherness been removed from Being?

The ontological difference and the idea that metaphysics quickly turns into "onto-theology" come together in Heidegger's late work *Iden-tity and Difference,* specifically the section titled "The Onto-theo-logical Constitution of Metaphysics." Heidegger argues that the ontological dif-ference forms the basis of Western metaphysics, since particular beings have always been defined in terms of their own "particular" Being and Being itself, even though that difference has gone largely unnoticed.[12] But he goes on to point out that the ontological difference in metaphys-ics has always been *theological* in nature.

> Metaphysics is theology, a statement about God, because the deity enters into philosophy. Thus the question about the onto-theological character of metaphysics is sharpened to the question: How does the deity enter into philosophy, not just modern philosophy, but philosophy as such? (OCM 55)

Heidegger's answer is that God provides the ultimate foundation or ground for philosophy, in more than one sense. On the one hand, as the first or highest being (the *ens realissimum*), God serves as the final entity in the "chain" of beings. He can thus be designated as "first cause" *(causa sui)*. On the other hand, since even Being itself has its ground in God, the highest entity becomes the ground of Being. The result is curi-ously twofold: (1) Being has its foundation in a particular being, and (2) metaphysics is somewhere between ontology and theology. Regarding this second aspect, Heidegger points out that "when metaphysics thinks of beings with respect to the ground that is common to all beings as such, then it is logic as onto-logic. When metaphysics thinks of beings as such as a whole, that is, with respect to the highest being which accounts for everything, then it is logic as theo-logic" (OCM 70-71). But since God

---

[12]Note that the ontological difference is not the basis of only Western metaphysics. If meta-physics (the study of being) is foundational to philosophy per se, then the ontological difference proves foundational to Western philosophy in general.

is both the ultimate ontic and ontological answer to the question "What is being?" then "onto-logic" actually collapses into "theo-logic."

Heidegger's account of onto-theology is grounded in Aristotle, but it also reflects the subsequent tradition of Western metaphysics. In the *Metaphysics* Aristotle says that the "science which investigates being as being" attempts to discover "the first principles and highest causes."[13] Although Aristotle does not use the term *first philosophy* at this point in his writing, when providing a hierarchy of sciences (natural, mathematic and divine) he says that first philosophy is that which considers "being *qua* being."[14] Note that the science of "being *qua* being" is clearly linked with the divine. Aristotle claims that "if there is no substance other than those which are formed by nature, natural science will be the first science; but if there is an immovable substance [God], the science of this must be prior and must be first philosophy, and universal in this way, because it is first."[15] Thus already in Aristotle God becomes the *ens realissimum*. But this conflation of theology with metaphysics is even more obvious in Aquinas, when he speaks of a single science with multiple names: "It is called *divine science* or *theology* inasmuch as it considers the aforementioned substances . . . *metaphysics* inasmuch as it considers being . . . *first philosophy* inasmuch as it considers the first causes of things."[16]

At this point it might be tempting for a religious believer not only to affirm an "onto-theology" in which God grounds both beings and Being but to consider it the triumph of religion over philosophy. Yet Heidegger cautions us to step back and examine the way God came to serve as the *logos* for metaphysics. As he puts it, "The deity can come into philosophy only insofar as philosophy, of its own accord and by its own nature, requires and determines that and how the deity enters into it" (OCM 56). In other words, there is a more primordial *logos* at work, one that decides if, when and how God becomes an integral part of the metaphysical story. Thus God ends up being turned into an idol, a creation of thought that is used for our purposes. As we saw in Nietzsche, the true God is *reduced* to being merely *causa sui* and *ens realissimum,* the

---

[13]Aristotle *Metaphysics* 4.1.1003a.
[14]Ibid., 4.1.1026a.
[15]Ibid.
[16]Thomas Aquinas, *Commentary on the Metaphysics of Aristotle,* trans. John P. Rowan (Chicago: Henry Regnery, 1961), 1:2.

result being the entity known as "the God of the philosophers." Heidegger reminds us that "before the *causa sui,* man can neither fall to his knees in awe nor can he play music and dance before this god" (OCM 72). King David "danced before the LORD with all his might" (2 Sam 6:14), but that dancing was before the God of Abraham, Isaac and Jacob—the God of Christian faith. The God of the philosophers is really no more than a metaphysical explanation, invoked whenever it suits the metaphysician's purposes. If we dance before such a god, we are really dancing only for ourselves.

Sometimes overlooked is the fact that Heidegger's charge against onto-theology is almost identical with that of Ludwig von Feuerbach, even if it is given a different twist. Although we define "God" as "highest idea" and "sum of all realities," Feuerbach argues that "the understanding is the *ens realissimum,* the most real being of the old onto-theology."[17] As noted in chapter one, on Feuerbach's view "God" is simply a projection of our own qualities taken to the highest perfection. Thus the real end of the chain of being is us. Feuerbach goes on to say, "The measure of thy God is the measure of thy understanding."[18] Not only are we the creators of the notion of "God," then, but his limits are imposed by our minds. So the move of "onto-theology" for Feuerbach might be more properly termed "onto-theo-anthropo-logical" in nature (though Feuerbach doesn't use this terminology).

The difference between Feuerbach and Heidegger can be summed up as follows: for Feuerbach, "God" is merely an idol, and that is the end of the story; for Heidegger, the God of onto-theology is an idol, but that is not necessarily the end of the story. Although Heidegger's own faith commitments are murky at best, he distinguishes between the "God of the Philosophers" and the "God of Faith." The death of one does not necessarily result in the death of the other.

Has metaphysics always been ontotheological in nature?[19] Heidegger seems to detect a shift in modernity.

> The inquiry into the *on* was onto-logical ever since its beginning with the ancients, but at the same time it was already with Plato and Aristotle onto-

---

[17]Ludwig von Feuerbach, *The Essence of Christianity,* trans. George Eliot (New York: Harper & Row, 1957), p. 38.

[18]Ibid., p. 39.

[19]The term *ontotheology* can found at least as far back as Kant's *Critique of Pure Reason,* A632/B660.

theo-logical, even if it was correspondingly not conceptually developed. Since Descartes the line of inquiry becomes above all ego-logical, whereby the ego is not only crucial for the logos but is also co-determinant for the development of the concept of *Theos* as it was prepared anew in Christian theology. The question of being as a whole is onto-theo-ego-logical.[20]

On Heidegger's read, metaphysics has been ontotheological virtually since its inception. Modernity, however, proves to be the point at which the line of onto-theology turns "ego-logical." If we take Hegel as an instance (and note that Heidegger's remarks here are taken from his explication of Hegel's *Phenomenology of Spirit*), then there is no question that the *logos* of onto-theology veers in the direction of an "ego-ology," for the notion of "absolute spirit" merges knowledge, ego and God. A similar reading, admittedly with somewhat different particulars, might be given of, say, Descartes or Kant.[21] So it seems difficult to avoid saying that modernity (or at the very least some of the most influential thought in modernity) is characterized by a strain of ego-ology. But a much more important question is, just how new is this ego-logical aspect to onto-theology? Although there was a nasty outbreak of the ego-logical virus in modernity, hasn't it been lurking all along? What Heidegger says is that "since Descartes the line of inquiry becomes *above all* ego-logical" (my italics), implying that it may have been a feature of onto-theology from the start. Certainly this aspect is found in Husserl's later phenomenology (from whom, as Heidegger points out, he borrows the term *ego-logical*).[22] But as we have seen all along, importing the *logos* of phenomenology from someplace other than "the things themselves" is hardly a problem unique to Husserl's brand of phenomenology or even to phenomenology per se.

Any attempt to describe the world can fall prey to this possibility. If metaphysics can be properly described as the science in which "Being becomes present as *logos*" (OCM 69), then there has always been the question of where metaphysics gets its *logos*. Moreover, if the *logos* of onto-theology has been god as *causa sui* and *ens realissimum* from the start, then has metaphysics *ever* been structured around the God of

---

[20]Martin Heidegger, *Hegel's Phenomenology of Spirit,* trans. Parvis Emad and Kenneth Maly (Bloomington: Indiana University Press, 1988), p. 126.
[21]Though we have seen that Descartes's conception of God points to an infinite otherness.
[22]Heidegger, *Hegel's Phenomenology,* p. 125.

Christian faith? It is difficult to avoid the conclusion that such a god has always been a human invention. It should come as no surprise, then, that Heidegger claims that "the god-less thinking which must abandon the god of philosophy, god as *causa sui,* is thus perhaps closer to the divine God. Here this means only: god-less thinking is more open to God than onto-theo-logic would like to admit" (OCM 72). Of course for the Christian believer the goal is not "god-less" thinking but a kind of thinking that attempts to think God without reducing him to a philosophical concept.

However this goal is worked out, it must be pursued with a caveat in mind. As Heidegger reminds us, the difficulty of overcoming onto-theology is closely tied to language.

> Our Western languages are languages of metaphysical thinking, each in its own way. It must remain an open question whether the nature of Western languages is in itself marked with the exclusive brand of metaphysics, and thus marked permanently by onto-theo-logic, or whether these languages offer other possibilities of utterance—and that means at the same time of a telling silence. (OCM 73)

Actually there are at least two open questions. The first one Heidegger raises here: is human language (or at least Western language, which is tied to Western metaphysics) so distorted by ontotheological ways of thinking that it is unable to break free from such ways of thought? If language is the medium in which theology is done, and if language is thoroughly permeated with metaphysics, *can* one speak theologically without metaphysics—or, more generally, philosophy—intruding into the discourse? Even if we decide that it is not completely subverted by such logic, clearly it is markedly infiltrated by it. So any attempt to break free will be difficult. A second question is one that Heidegger raises elsewhere, but it is closely related to the issue of the relation of metaphysics and language. Can philosophy still have an important role in theology, or ought theology to pull away from philosophy altogether?

Let's start with this second question. In "Phenomenology and Theology," which is roughly contemporaneous with *Being and Time,* Heidegger gives us an account of the relation of philosophy and theology which is complicated, to say the least. Briefly put, Heidegger seems to hold two conflicting ideas, which can be only partially reconciled. On the one hand, faith and philosophy are so opposed that there is no common ground and no possibility of mediation; on the other hand, not only can theology *not* avoid metaphysics and philosophy, but they can serve as important aids to theology. Heidegger opens by reminding us that the relation of faith and knowledge has historically been "a tension and struggle between two world-views" (*P* 40). Heidegger seems to affirm the opposition when he goes on to say that "faith is so absolutely the mortal enemy that philosophy does not even begin to want in any way to do battle with it" and that "there is no such thing as a Christian philosophy; that is an absolute 'square circle'" (*P* 53).[23] "Faith" and "philosophy" are not simply different entities but entities that can in no way be brought together, else they risk compromise. Of course this threat seems to be more significant from one direction than the other. Perhaps philosophy could be infiltrated with faith, but certainly not the other way around.[24] In a later context, Heidegger claims:

> Were I yet to write a theology—to which I sometimes feel inclined—then the word *Being* would not occur in it. Faith does not need the thought of Being. When faith needs this thought, it is no longer faith. This is what Luther understood. Even within his own church this seems to be forgotten.[25]

Even more strikingly Heidegger elsewhere asks, "Will Christian theology make up its mind one day to take seriously the word of the apostle and thus also the conception of philosophy as foolishness?"[26] Merold Westphal rightly argues that in linking himself to Luther, Heidegger places his critique in a tradition that has stood against the infiltration of faith by pagan philosophy, one that "looks back to Augustine and ahead to Pascal, Kierkegaard, and Barth."[27]

But on the other hand, Heidegger sees a need for theology—and thus a need for philosophy. As he puts it, "If faith does not need philosophy, the *science* of faith as a *positive* science does" (*P* 50). Note how Heideg-

---

[23]Elsewhere Heidegger also speaks of the impossibility of a "Christian philosophy." See his *Introduction to Metaphysics,* trans. Ralph Manheim (New Haven, Conn.: Yale University Press, 1959), p. 7.

[24]It seems to me that the threat works both ways, but Heidegger's concern is much more with preserving faith from infiltration than keeping philosophy pure.

[25]Martin Heidegger, *Seminare [Gesamtausgabe* 15] (Frankfort: Klosterman, 1986), p. 437. Note that this is Heidegger's response to the question, "May Being and God be posited as identical?"

[26]In *Existentialism from Dostoevsky to Sartre,* ed. Walter Kaufmann (New York: Penguin, 1975), p. 276.

[27]Merold Westphal, "Overcoming Onto-theology," in *GGP* 157. Westphal provides a fine assessment of Heidegger's conception of onto-theology.

ger defines the entities of faith, theology and philosophy. Faith is the lived experience of the Christian believer, mediated by revelation and Christian history. Theology is "the science that faith motivates and justifies" (*P* 46). Thus the task of theology is to understand the experience of faith. Faith is the content (what Heidegger refers to as the *positum*), and theology merely supplies the form. Now, "if faith would totally oppose a conceptual interpretation, then theology would be a thoroughly *inappropriate* means of grasping its object, faith" (*P* 45). Yet Heidegger clearly thinks that faith does not oppose (and should not oppose) the attempt of theology to make sense of faith. For faith needs the "formation" supplied by theology.

What role, then, does philosophy play in theology? It seems to me that Heidegger has in mind at least two roles, distinct though closely tied. First, philosophy helps us understand the experience of faith. To use Heidegger's example, though guilt is a central aspect of the Christian doctrine of sin, it is even more fundamentally a feature of human experience. Embedded within the particular experience of guilt felt by the Christian believer is this more general experience of guilt, one that Heidegger thinks can "be grasped purely rationally" (*P* 51).[28] Thus philosophy is able to analyze *"the pre-Christian content of basic theological concepts"* (*P* 53). While this general philosophical explication of guilt in no way replaces the specific Christian experience, it provides a larger experiential context and a better understanding of the particular experience. Of course, the question here is the extent to which philosophy can *truly* understand the religious experience and at what point philosophy simply ends in mystification.

Second, Heidegger points out that *"theology itself is founded primarily in faith,* even though its statements and procedures of proof derive from the formally free operations of reason" (*P* 49). The intrusion of philosophy in this respect seems much harder to categorize and thus more problematic. In effect, Heidegger says that theology equals "faith plus something else." If we take Heidegger literally here, we must conclude that theology—in terms of its method and how it states its conclusions—equals "faith plus the 'formally free operations of reason.'" But which operations or which reason? It's hard to keep from thinking that "reason" here equals "Western metaphysics." And Heidegger's com-

---

[28]This is exactly what Heidegger attempts to do in *BT* ¶58.

ments only seem to support such a read.[29] But then theology isn't really assisted by "formally *free* operations of reason" based simply on disembodied logic. It is corrected by a particular *sort* of reason.

Moreover, Heidegger complicates the relationship by speaking of philosophy as relating to theology in two different ways.[30] The least intrusive way is "correction." Philosophy, says Heidegger, helps clarify theology and thus acts in a "corrective" capacity. But philosophy—or, more specifically, ontology—also assists theology by "co-directing." Thus ontology—which Heidegger elsewhere insists is contrary to faith— ends up supplying what faith lacks. Does it, then, put the *logos* in theology? Heidegger would likely be loath to admit that such is the case, but it is difficult to see how philosophy's *logos* does not at least affect the *logos* of theology. Historically, theology has always borrowed at least some of its concepts from philosophy. If theologians are "in the world," however much they might seek not to be "of it," theology is never going to be a philosophy-free zone. And that influence is not wholly lamentable. Yet while philosophy perhaps can help clarify theological concepts, we have seen that it has (at least sometimes) served rather to *distort* than to correct theology, and thus faith. So the real issue is *how* the "conceptualization" of philosophy is employed.

Regarding the first question, Heidegger gives a clue to how one might speak of God without succumbing to philosophy's *logos* with his conception of a "non-objectifying thinking and speaking." If, for example, we experience a rose in a garden or a statue in a museum in terms of its chemical composition—that is, in natural scientific terms—we "objectify" it by reducing it to a set of artificially imposed categories. In one sense, of course, such objectification is perfectly acceptable; there is nothing "wrong" with such thinking, so long as it is acknowledged for what it is.[31] The danger of objectifying thinking is that it misses fundamental

---

[29]For instance, Heidegger interchanges "philosophy" and "ontology" and even defines phenomenology as "the procedure of ontology" (*P* 53). While it is possible to imagine non-Western ontologies, ontology is a "science" that is distinctly Western in origin, and phenomenology even more so.

[30]Heidegger seems to think these two ways are actually the same. He writes: "The function of ontology here is not to direct, but only, in 'co-directing,' to correct" (*P* 49). But "co-directing" and "correcting" are not identical.

[31]Although it might seem that philosophers enjoy bashing scientific thinking in general, their more nuanced criticism is usually against the sort of scientific thinking that takes itself to be giving an exhaustive account of reality, when it is really, philosophers would argue, giving merely a partial account of reality (and an interpretive one at that).

aspects of the true being of such objects, precisely because it imposes a foreign category on them. It is not hard to see that an experience of a rose that is strongly mediated by the category "chemical composition" misses other aspects (and probably the most important aspects) of a rose. In contrast, "non-objectifying thinking" is the attempt to experience the object as other, without determination.

> When, for example, we sit in the garden and take delight in a blossoming rose, we do not make an object of that rose, nor do we even make it something standing-over-against us in the sense of something represented thematically. When in tacit saying we are enthralled with the lucid red of the rose and muse on the redness of the rose, then this redness is neither an object nor a thing nor a standing-over-against like the blossoming rose. . . . All the same we think it and tell of it by naming it. There is accordingly a thinking and saying that in no manner objectifies or places things over against us. (*P* 58)

Of course it is too much for Heidegger to say that such a way of relating to a rose "in *no* manner objectifies" the rose, for it would seem that a sensuous experiencing of a rose still employs the hermeneutical "as," however unobtrusively or appropriately. So the rose is not *purely* other, and my experience is not a pure, unmediated experience unaffected by my categories and "ontologizing." And yet there can be no question that such an experience is significantly less objectifying and far more open to the "being" of the rose.

Applying this conception of nonobjectifying thinking to theology, Heidegger says that, properly speaking, theology should "place in discussion, within its own realm of the Christian faith and out of the proper nature of that faith, what it is to think and how it is to speak" (*P* 61). But how does one do that? Heidegger cites poetry as an example to follow.

> Poetic thinking is being in the presence of . . . and for the god. Presence means: simple willingness that wills nothing, counts on no successful outcome. Being in the presence of . . . : purely letting the god's presence be said. Such saying does not posit and represent anything as standing over against us or as object. There is nothing here that could be placed before a grasping or comprehending representation. (*P* 61, Heidegger's ellipses)

Although Heidegger's conception of poetic thinking is not completely clear (and he would likely argue that this lack of clarity is even central to poetic thinking), it seems to be a kind of speaking that employs a double gesture. On the one hand, it explores (to quote an earlier phrase from Heidegger) "other possibilities of utterance." I take it that these other possibilities are ways of speaking and thinking that objectify neither God nor the phenomenon of faith. On the other hand, it attempts to maintain "a telling silence." That is, one affirms God's existence and the believer's experience of God without "objectifying" them or claiming to give the last word. Thus overcoming onto-theology—and idolatry in general—requires the twofold move of learning how to speak aright *and* how to keep an appropriate silence.

Such is what Jean-Luc Marion attempts to do.

8

THE OBJECTIFYING
IDOL AND THE
TRANSCENDING ICON

W e have already seen four of the primary aspects in which Marion's thought must be situated: (1) Nietzsche's proclamation of "the death of God," (2) the *aporia* of Husserl's insistence on the phenomena providing their own *logos* with his notion that the phenomena are ultimately grounded in the transcendental ego, (3) Levinas's concern that the otherness of the other be taken seriously and (4) Heidegger's condemnation of onto-theology. Now we need to see how these are worked out in Marion's thinking.

For Marion, "the death of God" has long been overdue and Nietzsche does Christian believers a great service in exposing what turn out to be merely "metaphysical 'idols'" (*GWB* xxi). Marion thinks these idols have taken many forms, such as Plato's Form of the Good, Aristotle's Nous, Plotinus's One, Kant's "moral founder" and Hegel's *Geist* (*IAD* 10-11).[1] On Marion's read, these have been attempts by philosophers (more specifically, metaphysicians) to name God. But once all candidates for the

---

[1]Regarding Descartes, see Jean-Luc Marion, *On Descartes' Metaphysical Prism: The Constitution and Limits of Onto-theo-logy in Cartesian Thought*, trans. Jeffrey L. Koskey (Chicago: University of Chicago Press, 1999).

title "God of the Philosophers" have been shown to be ontotheological creations designed to serve human needs, we are in a better position to see our conceptual idols for what they are. Clearly Marion is drawing upon Heidegger's criticism of onto-theology. Earlier I noted that Heidegger challenges Christian thinking "to take seriously the word of the Apostle and thus also the conception of philosophy as foolishness." To this challenge Marion responds by saying, "To take seriously that philosophy is a folly means, for us, first (although not exclusively) taking seriously that the 'God' of onto-theology is rigorously equivalent to an idol" (*IAD* 18).

Having our blinded eyes now opened, how do we proceed? Is there a way of following the phenomenological orthodoxy that the phenomena provide their own *logos* without somehow slipping in a *logos* that we instead supply? How do we take the otherness of God seriously and yet still maintain the possibility of meaningful theological discourse?

Marion employs two sorts of strategies in thinking and speaking about God, and as with Levinas these strategies stem from his dual role as both theologian and philosopher.[2] On the one hand, whereas Levinas was a Jew who wrote extensively on the Talmud, Marion can be classified as a Roman Catholic theologian who bases much of his thinking about God on a careful reading of Scripture and a sacramental theology. This Marion makes actual Christian faith and experience central to his thinking. One finds this more theological Marion in *God Without Being* and *The Idol and Distance*. On the other hand, again like Levinas, Marion is a philosopher who is highly indebted to phenomenology (however much his thinking might be said to depart from it). Thus in *Reduction and Givenness* and *Etant donné* he argues for an apprehension of God on the basis of a creative rereading of Husserlian and Heideggerian phenomenology. Whether these two perspectives are truly compatible is a question we shall take up later. For the moment, though, let's consider Marion the theologian.

Central to Marion's attempt to spell out a conception of thinking and speaking of God that does not "objectify" him is the distinction between

---

[2]"I always make a clear distinction, in what I write, between philosophical and confessional texts," says Levinas in an interview with Richard Kearney in *Face to Face with Emmanuel Levinas,* ed. Richard Cohen (Albany: State University of New York Press, 1986), p. 18.

idol *(eidōlon)* and icon *(eikōn)*. Marion's way of distinguishing them is often insightful and instructive, although we have seen that the distinction in no way originates with him.

Icons Versus Idols

Picking up on etymological connection between *eidōlon* and the Greek term *eidos,* Marion centers the existence of the idol in what he terms "the gaze." In one sense "the idol never deserves to be denounced as illusory" (*GWB* 9). Idols can always be seen, whether literally or metaphorically, since that is their reason for existing. We create idols in order to satisfy our gaze, and their continued existence is completely dependent on that satisfaction. Should our fascination with a particular idol cease, it ceases to be an idol for us; it becomes "just" an idea or material object. Note that the idol is the effect and the gaze the cause, rather than the other way around. As Marion points out, "If the gaze did not desire to satisfy itself in the idol, the idol would have no dignity for it" (*GWB* 10). Further, not only is the idol created by us, we are reflected in it. Instead of being a window to something beyond us, it acts as a mirror. Of course it is an "invisible mirror," for we are unaware of its mirrorlike quality. In the idol we think we see God, but we see mainly (or even *only*) ourselves.

In the introduction I noted the strong similarity between the *eidōlon* and the *kenēs apatēs* of which Paul warns in Colossians 2:8. Both are empty, or at least they are empty of what they purport to contain. But they are not *fully* empty. Although Feuerbach speaks wrongly of God in denouncing him as mere projection, his description aptly characterizes idols. Indeed Marion quotes Feuerbach as saying, "It is *man* who is the *original model* of his idol" (*GWB* 16). We have seen all along that the problem with idols is that they often have a grip on us that is difficult to break. But that grip on us is understandable. *From the very beginning* we see exactly what we want to see: ourselves. We are indeed deceived, but the deception is self-induced.

It seems to me that idols are often based on the kind of lying Nietzsche has in mind when (as noted earlier) he says, "I call a lie: wanting *not* to see something one does see, wanting not to see something *as* one sees it" (*A* 55). Lying to oneself is a strange phenomenon, for it requires both sight and blindness. One must first see (however imperfectly or incompletely) in order to discern the need for a lie. And one is often if not usually aware—at some level—that one is lying.[3] If idolatry involves the self-deception of thinking oneself or one's creation to be God, then one must have some awareness of not being God in the first place—and perhaps all along. But of course the longer one plays the role of the *hypocritēs,* the actor playing the part of God, the less likely one is to recognize one's action as mere acting.

In contrast to the idol, which is limited to the visible, "the icon summons sight in letting the visible . . . be saturated little by little with the invisible" (*GWB* 17). As the image or icon—the incarnation into visible flesh—of the invisible God, Christ "must serve as our norm" of a proper icon (*GWB* 17). The icon, though, is a curious sort of phenomenon. While it "appears," its appearance is always only a shadow of its full reality. That is not to say that it does not really appear—an icon really does make something present to us. So the icon is not to be confused with a sign that merely points to something that it is not. Although Marion does not make explicit reference to the Levinasian notion of the "trace," an icon can be defined as a trace of a greater reality, one present but far from wholly present.

The icon is an example of what Marion calls a "saturated phenomenon." Although Marion well recognizes the *aporia* that Husserlian phenomenology presents, he argues for a way of thinking beyond it. I noted earlier that Husserl himself points out that the phenomena "offered to us in 'intuition'" always have certain "limits." But if, as Marion points out in his essay "The Saturated Phenomenon," "not everything is capable of being given perfectly" (*PTT* 181), then there must be something beyond those limits. Exploiting what Husserl terms the "ambiguous" nature of the phenomenon—which can be defined both as "appearance" and as "that which appears"—Marion argues that even in Husserlian phenomenology there is the possibility of something that goes beyond the appearance (i.e., is not reducible to that appearance).[4] Such a phenomenon is "saturated" in that it contains much more than what appears. In other words, there is a fundamental lack of *adaequatio* between the

---

[3]This phenomenon of knowing and yet not knowing is sometimes also found in cases of insanity. One of my acquaintances, a psychiatrist in Belgium, tells of a patient who signed his letters with a locution that translates into English as "king of the world." After much analysis, it became apparent to the therapist that at some level this patient realized that such was not really the case.

[4]Edmund Husserl, *The Idea of Phenomenology,* trans. William P. Alston and George Nakhnikian (The Hague: Martinus Nijhoff, 1973), p. 11.

intuition of the object and the object itself.[5] But whereas Husserl reads this inadequacy in terms of intention outstripping intuition, Marion contends that intuition exceeds intention. Rather than being able to master the phenomenon, consciousness is surprised, overwhelmed and drawn up short by its inadequacy. Moreover, the rules and order that consciousness has imposed (by way of its horizon) are shaken and, depending on the particular phenomenon, perhaps overthrown. Our experience is "bedazzlement," a characteristic not merely incidental but fundamental to the experience of the saturated phenomenon.[6]

> It is in fact a question of something visible that our gaze cannot bear; this visible something is experienced as unbearable to the gaze because it weighs too much upon that gaze. . . . What weighs here is not unhappiness, nor pain nor lack, but indeed glory, joy, excess. (*PTT* 200)

The very "excess" of the saturated phenomenon keeps it from becoming merely an object, in the sense of being controlled by my gaze. It remains invisible to my gaze, being what Marion terms "invis*a*ble."[7] Conversely, any concept of God or picture of God claiming to present us with God in his fullness is clearly idolatrous.

This lack of "objectivity" also brings about a transformation in the very status of the transcendental ego. No longer is that ego "transcendental," for there is now something above it, something that transcends even it. In effect, the transcendental ego is "detranscendentalized." Whereas the transcendental ego was previously the source of all identity and meaning, being decentered it now becomes subject to the identity and meaning of something above it. "The gaze of the invisible" is directed at the now nontranscendental ego (*GWB* 19).

For Marion, the saturated phenomenon can be rightly described as a "revelation." Since it is an "appearance that is purely of itself and starting

---

[5]Note that this idea of an inadequation between intuition and object is central to Kant's conception of an aesthetic idea, which Marion discusses at length in "The Saturated Phenomenon." Kant speaks of "a concept to which no *intuition* (presentation of the imagination) can be adequate." See Kant, *Critique of Judgment*, p. 182.

[6]Both the idea of "saturation" and the experience of "bedazzlement" come from Plato's metaphor of the cave. Were one of the cavedwellers to be freed and let outside into the light, Plato says that such a person would be bedazzled. See *Republic* 518a. Descartes likewise speaks of God as producing such a sensation at the end of his Third Meditation. See René Descartes, *The Philosophical Writings of Descartes,* trans. John Cottingham et al. (Cambridge: Cambridge University Press, 1984), 2:35-36.

[7]Marion coins this term to indicate that which not only cannot be seen but also cannot become the "object" of the gaze. See *GWB* 201 n. 8.

from itself," it is not subject to any "preliminary determination" (*PTT* 215). It comes wholly from without and is not subject to our control.

The move that Marion makes here is similar to that of Levinas. Not only is the otherness of the saturated phenomenon much like the infinite otherness of *to heteron* and the face (a concept to which Marion makes explicit reference), both Marion and Levinas attempt to keep theology from being subjugated by philosophy. Their appeal, then, is to a kind of revelation that stands so outside of us that it is not subject to any sort of prior determination. Marion's conception of the saturated phenomenon sounds much like Levinas's "idea of the infinite," which "does not allow itself to be reduced, without remainder, to the act of consciousness of a subject" (*BPW* 156). In both cases this "other" comes to us wholly without any hermeneutical "as," presuppositions or *logos*. It creates its own *logos* and forces us to be subject to it. Thus what we might call the "revelatory phenomenon" (to unite Marion and Levinas) has a kind of force upon us, one that we are unable to overcome and turn into a force of our own.

However much Marion wishes to draw—or thinks he actually succeeds in drawing—a hard-and-fast line between idols and icons, it tends not to stay put. In the following chapter we will consider whether the postulation of a purely revelatory phenomenon is even a possible move on the part of Marion and Levinas. For the moment it is enough to observe that the distinction between idols and icons tends to come undone. This is less a feature of Marion's thinking than a general problem of the relation between the two. Marion speaks of an "antagonism that infallibly unites" idol and icon. But there is more to their connection than merely a play of difference in which the one serves to define the other. The problem with all icons is that they have a tendency to morph into idols. Properly speaking, of course, it is not *their* tendency so much as *our* tendency to take icons and turn them into idols. That transformation occurs whenever we "refigure" an icon into an idol.

It is probably too much for Marion to say that "the idol *always* marks a true and genuine experience of the divine" (*GWB* 27, my italics), since not all idols necessarily connect to the divine in some way. Certainly many do. But even if we were to argue that they always *start* that way, they often end up being very removed. Thus Jesus may begin as the *Logos* who cannot be mastered, who continually confronts us with hard sayings. But we usually (as opposed to merely "sometimes" or even "often") find ways to explain (away) those confrontational passages and experiences, or at least to soften their blow. Sometimes with one fell swoop, more often little by little, we learn to "massage" that message in order to sooth our consciences and relax our guard. Of course if icons can turn into idols, perhaps idols can sometimes turn back into icons.

On Marion's account, Nietzsche's death of God is actually the death of a particular idol, "a determination of God that formulates him in a precise concept" (*GWB* 29).[8] It is thus "the God of the philosophers"—a god who is limited by human discourse or intelligibility—that dies. Note that Nietzsche himself says that "it is only the moral god that has been overcome" (*WP* 55). In chapter one we saw that "morality" for Nietzsche is the formula "reason=virtue=happiness," with reason as the source and motivation for morality. This is also what happens in Kant's account of religion, in which reason becomes the ultimate source of duty and God merely the lawgiver. God as "moral god" can die precisely because he is a creation of reason.

When Marion speaks of needing to overcome a "double idolatry," the first sort of idolatry he has in mind is clearly onto-theology, with its attempt to formulate God as *causa sui* and *ens realissimum.* Oddly enough, those who affirm this god (theists) and those who deny his existence (atheists) are alike in that they buy into the same concept. In both cases "God" is circumscribed by human limits. Yet Marion thinks that Heidegger introduces a second idolatry as well. As Marion puts it, "Beyond the idolatry proper to metaphysics, there functions *another* idolatry, proper to the thought of Being as such" (*GWB* 41). Although Heidegger rightly criticizes onto-theology's postulation of God as an entity, Heidegger still submits God to Being in the sense that "any access to something like 'God' . . . will have to determine him in advance as a being" (*GWB* 43). Of course I have noted that Heidegger at times says what sounds to be just the opposite, such as when he maintains that "faith does not need the thought of Being." But we have likewise seen that Heidegger insists on philosophy's acting as a "corrective" to and "co-director" with theology. So while Heidegger speaks of the possibility of a God who is outside the bounds of being, Marion is right in saying that he "can never seriously commit himself to it" (*GWB* 43). In fact at

---

[8]In chapter one I argued that "the death of God" for Nietzsche actually involves four deaths. Thus while Marion is right that the death of God spells the demise of "God of the philosophers," I think he is wrong in suggesting that this is all that is at stake.

times Heidegger clearly says (rather than merely implies) that God is part of the realm of being. For instance, he claims that "God is a being, who by his essence, cannot not be."[9] And if God must be, then he must be subject to the bounds of being, which means he is subject to the bounds of metaphysics. Note that even when Heidegger says that "Being and God are not identical," he goes on to say that insofar as God appears as a phenomenon (i.e., is made manifest) he must do so within "the dimension of Being." So even if God is not a being, he comes before us on the horizon of Being or within the limits of Being.

Thus, at least according to Marion, we have two sorts of idolatries. The first makes God into a "being"; the second submits him to the category "Being." But is there really much of a difference between the two? After all, if God is subject to the category Being, then must he not end up being a being, as Heidegger himself says? On that read, then, Heidegger's conception of an ontological difference between particular beings and Being itself seems hard to maintain, for it is difficult to see how, once we place God under the category of Being, God does not become "a" being. Further, even if these two idolatries can be said to be distinct, they are variations on the theme we have been exploring all along—philosophy's insistence that its *logos* takes precedence. So the problem in both cases ends up being simply another example of the same old problem.

How do we rethink God's "being" so that we can (to quote Levinas) "hear a God not contaminated by Being" (*OTB* xlvii). Marion puts it as follows: "To reach a nonidolatrous thought of God which alone releases 'God' from his quotation marks by disengaging his apprehension from the conditions posed by onto-theo-logy, one would have to manage to think God outside of metaphysics" (*GWB* 37). This goal of thinking God "outside of metaphysics" is clarified by Marion as "to think God without any conditions" (*GWB* 45). In other words, it is to apprehend God—or somehow relate to God—without the *logos* of philosophy (or for that matter any other *logos*) dictating the conditions under which God may appear. Thus God is removed from the realm of metaphysics or ontology.

---

[9]Martin Heidegger, *The Basic Problems of Phenomenology*, trans. Albert Hofstadter (Bloomington: Indiana University Press, 1982), p. 79. Elsewhere Heidegger says, "And the gods likewise: to the degree that they *are*, and however they are, they too all stand *under 'Being,'* " in "On the Being and Conception of *phusis* in Aristotle's *Physics* B,1," trans. Thomas J. Sheehan, in *Man and World* 9 (1976): 222.

There are at least two implications of this move. First, technically speaking, we can no longer ascribe "being" to God. Of course it is not that God's "existence" is really in question. As Marion puts it in answer to some of his critics, "God is, exists, and that is the least of things" (*GWB* xix). But if God is not limited by ontology or metaphysics, then what does it mean for God to "be"? Clearly he "is" in a very different sense from the way the world or human beings "exist." Second, if ontology is a realm controlled by human thought and God is outside of that realm, then God is beyond the reach of human thought. What does it mean to think about a God who cannot be thought? One could read Marion as suggesting that we simply go "beyond" thought. But Marion has in mind something very similar to what Levinas intends when he speaks of knowing and thinking "otherwise."

How Should We Speak of God?

For Marion, theology is "good" when it helps us to be addressed by God and remembers that its talk about God is necessarily incomplete. Conversely, it is "bad" when it makes us think that we have captured God conceptually. The kind of conceptualizing that thinks it has captured God stems from us and places us in the center. Marion suggests we find ways of "thinking" about God that do not tempt us to idolatry. Earlier I noted that Levinas employs various ways of thinking about the other that allow the other to remain truly other, such as the face, infinity and "sense." Likewise Marion provides us with various strategies: the St. Andrew's Cross, God as *agape,* the parable of the prodigal son, good and bad "silence," and the Eucharist.

Marion's antidote to the fear of speaking in negative theology is to suggest a concept of God that is "crossed out" by the sign of the crucified. Such a sign of God both makes God present and at the very same time announces the limitation of that presence:

> The cross[ing out of the name of God] does not indicate that G⨯d would have to disappear as a concept, or intervene only in the capacity of a hypothesis in the process of validation, but that the unthinkable enters into the field of our thought only by rendering itself unthinkable there by excess, that is, by criticizing our thought. . . . We cross out the name of G⨯d only in order to show ourselves that his unthinkableness saturates our thought—right from the beginning, and forever. (*GWB* 46)

The crossing out of God's being utilizes the logic of the trace: G⨯d is a presence that precisely in being present points to something that is absent. Thus God is "given" to us as a phenomenon that dazzles us but that we do not possess. It is God who gives himself to us, who "offers the only accessible trace of He who gives" (*GWB* 105).

Marion appropriates what he takes to be an appropriate biblical way of speaking of God: *agapē*. First, we have seen that love is something that by nature goes beyond any limit or restriction. But its transcendence is not a "problem" or shortcoming of love. It is rather love's greatest strength. Marion points out that "love does not suffer from the unthinkable or from the absence of conditions, but is reinforced by them" (*GWB* 47). The very essence of love (if we can use such a baldly metaphysical term as *essence*) is that "love loves without condition, simply because it loves" (*GWB* 47). Second, love is not based on understanding but on faith: one does not comprehend but one loves anyway. God is given to us as a gift that we do not deserve, cannot comprehend and do not own. If God loves us for "no reason at all," then how can such love be comprehended? The God who reveals himself as love, who demonstrates that love by the gift of his Son, cannot be confused with the God of the philosophers (*GWB* 52), precisely because the latter *can* be controlled and used.

Of course, in that we human beings are *not* fully characterized by love (more often we are characterized by an absence of love), we do not take naturally to the "noneconomy" of *agape.* There is even something "horrifying to us" about love (*GWB* 109): we want to know and possess *agape,* to make it part of our economy and theories. In place of knowing, there is trusting and faith. In place of possessing, there is the gift. God and his love are given to us, but not in a way that would make either one ours, not in the sense that they become our personal property.

Marion well illustrates our desire to "own" the gift by his striking reading of the prodigal son. Instead of focusing on the prodigal's return, Marion concentrates on the beginning of the story. The prodigal is able to go off on his own only after asking for his "share" in the goods *(ousia)* of the father (Lk 15:12). Admitting that his reading of the text is influenced by Greek philosophy, in which the term *ousia* can be translated as "substance" or "being," Marion points out that the key concept here is *possession*. The son asks for nothing less than that he might possess these goods.

He asks that one grant that he no longer have to receive any gift—precisely, no longer have to receive the *ousia* as gift: He asks to possess it, dispose of it, enjoy it without passing through the gift and the reception of the gift. The son wants to owe nothing to his father, and above all not to owe him a gift; he asks to have a father no longer—the *ousia* without the father or the gift. (*GWB* 97)

We want the same: to have God's gifts without owing him anything, without feeling that we need to give him an account. Of course the ending of the story is that the father gives the gift all over again, without taking account of the dissipation of the earlier gift. This is precisely the move of love: it gives again and again. Love is profligate.

What can one "say" about such gift giving and such a gift giver? Certainly the prodigal son would not have had anything "adequate" to say.[10] Of course in regard to our heavenly Father it is not enough simply to say that one must be silent. Following Heidegger, Marion distinguishes between "silencing" and "keeping silence."[11] Therein lies the difference between a good and a bad silence. A bad silence is where all God-talk is silenced, or else where one simply gives up on speaking about God. In contrast, a good or wise silence recognizes the limitations of one's speech and is cautious about what one says, but does not simply say nothing. We might take Marion even further and say that one keeps an appropriate silence by attempting to say *why* it is that one cannot speak. But any saying we deem possible still ends up in praise. As Marion puts it, "Predication must yield to praise" (*GWB* 106).[12]

Having noted the danger of theologizing that makes God into an idol, Marion reminds us that Christ is the Word not as a sign of something (giving mere signitive presence) but as the thing itself embodied. With Christ there is a collapsing of the difference between the thing and the word that represents it:

Christ does not say the word, he says *himself* the Word. . . . [I]n him coincide—or rather commune—the sign, the locutor, and the referent that elsewhere the human experience of language irremediably dissociates, he

---

[10]There is no recorded response of the son. Perhaps that is simply because his response is unimportant for the story. Or perhaps it is at least partially because the father's own prodigality would have resulted in a stunned silence. After all, what could the son have said that wouldn't simply sound trite?

[11]The difference is not really seen in the passive English construction "being silent," but it is evident in the more active German construction "keeping silence"—*schweigen*.

[12]I shall return to the notion of praise shortly.

merits, contrary to our shattered, inspiring or devalued words, to be said, with a capital, the Word. (*GWB* 140)

One cannot provide anything like a real *logos* of this *Logos*. Yet Christ "presents" himself to us such that we have real (even if not full) contact with him. Thus Scripture is not the Word in the primordial sense that Christ is; rather, it presents us with the Word and the event of the Word:

> The text results, in our words that consign it, from the primordial event of the Word among us; the simple comprehension of the text—the function of the theologian—requires infinitely more than its reading, as informed as one would like; it requires access to the Word through the text. To read the text from the point of view of its writing: from the point of view of the Word. This requirement, as untenable as it may appear (and remains), cannot be avoided. (*GWB* 149)

The text of Scripture does not give us Christ himself, in the flesh, though it points us to him. Scripture provides a "trace" of Christ but not Christ in full presence.

So where do we meet Christ? Given Marion's own theological tradition, it should come as no surprise when he says that we truly meet Christ in the place where he becomes present to us—the Eucharist. Marion insists that "theology can reach its authentically *theo*logical status only if it does not cease to break with theo*logy*" (*GWB* 139). As long as we insist on adding on a *logos* from philosophy, we cannot meet the *Logos* himself. Marion insists that this break from the philosophical *logos* takes place in the realm of practice. Like love, theology is most itself when it is *done* rather than spoken or theorized. It is in the breaking of bread that we come to see Christ for who he is, like the disciples on the road to Emmaus (Mt 16:4). Thus it is in the gathering of the community of Christ to celebrate his death and resurrection that true theology takes place. "If the Word intervenes in person only at the eucharistic moment, *the hermeneutic (hence fundamental theology) will take place, will have its place, only in the Eucharist*" (*GWB* 151). For Marion, the presence of Christ in the Eucharist is indeed a "full presence," though we are unable to grasp it in its fullness. Were we so able, the Eucharist would not be a gift.

But there is a fundamental problem with Marion's account, and the Eucharist provides a particularly good example of it. As Marion would have it, the eucharistic moment is when theology takes place and theology is truly itself, when it is *theo*logy rather than theo*logy*. One point at which someone who is not Roman Catholic might be tempted to argue with Marion is when he says that "the Word intervenes in person *only* at the eucharistic moment" (my italics). The response might be: Are there no other moments at which the Word can appear? Isn't this far too limited a conception of Christ's being with us? Might this not even make the Word into an idol that can appear only when we say it may?

And even a Roman Catholic could challenge Marion when he says that "the Word intervenes *in person*" (my italics). Can Marion dispense with all *logoi* in the moment of the Eucharist, so that Christ's appearance is truly without any mediating *logos?* Certainly the Roman Catholic *doctrine* of what takes place in the Eucharistic moment is highly dependent on Aristotelian metaphysics. According to official doctrine, transubstantiation occurs when the essential substance *(ousia)* of the bread and wine is changed into Christ's body and blood, even though the "accidents" determining their appearance remain the same. So this account can make sense only against the background of an Aristotelian view of substance.

But, of course, a doctrine is merely a description of what takes place, not the event itself. Still, could the event take place *and* be meaningful without at least some *logos* from outside? Even if Marion were to opt for a more "mystical'" account of the Eucharist, the problem would not disappear. For the *meaning* of the Eucharistic moment is at least partially dependent on things as diverse as the symbolic meaning of bread and wine for ordinary human existence and the history of the practice of the Christian church. Thus it is difficult to see Christ's presence in the Eucharist as *simply* the suspension or subversion of all other human *logoi,* for the meaning of that presence is partially constituted by them and would be lost without them.[13]

As I will show in the following chapter, this aspect of the *Logos* against *logos* is central to Marion's thought, and proves to be highly problematic.

---

[13]Note that Marion does not take seriously the fact that the horizon for Husserl is *temporally* constituted—that is, it is not simply static but evolves over time, so that the past is incorporated into the present. See Edmund Husserl, *On the Phenomenology of the Consciousness of Internal Time,* trans. John B. Brough (Dordrecht, The Netherlands: Kluwer, 1991).

9

LOGOS
VERSUS *LOGOS?*

Having considered Marion's theology, we need to turn to how Marion backs it up philosophically—more specifically, phenomenologically. As we shall see, the two are inextricably linked. Marion wants to give us a kind of phenomenology that is no longer bound by the phenomenological restrictions I have noted in Husserl and Heidegger.[1] But can Marion succeed in this break with phenomenology? And to what extent is the break necessary?

Getting "Outside of the Text"
It is no coincidence that Marion gives the title *Hors-Texte*—literally, "outside of the text"—to the last section of *God Without Being*. While the section consists of two chapters labeled "six" and "seven," the table of contents would lead us to think that *God Without Being* and *Hors-Texte* are two separate texts. Or, perhaps more accurately, that the former is the "text" and the latter is somehow outside not only of the particular text *God Without Being* but of textuality itself. "There is nothing outside

---

[1]See the introduction and chapter seven.

of the text *[il n'y a pas de hors-texte]*," says Derrida. Marion in effect replies, "There *is* something outside of the text." It is in this text outside of the text—this text that is "not a text"—that Marion tells us that "the 'good news of Jesus Christ' exceeds every metaphysic" (*GWB* 163). That is, Jesus Christ the *Logos* (which can be rendered as "speech" in English, and thus as "text") remains untouched, unmastered, uncontrolled by the *logos* of metaphysics or philosophy in general. As we have seen, metaphysics relies heavily on language. Thus if the *Logos* is outside of textuality, he is likewise outside of metaphysics. And vice versa.

As Marion tells us, "Faith has nothing like a discourse, at least if discourse implies the succession of arguments, the assurance of an object that is defined precisely by the preeminence of a subject. Faith neither speaks nor states; it believes, and has no other end than to believe" (*GWB* 183). There are two crucial aspects here: (1) the status of "discourse" and (2) the role of the subject in shaping discourse. Let's begin with the second of these, returning to the former later on.

As we have seen, a primary problem of phenomenology (not to mention philosophy in general) is that it privileges the self and thus seems to allow no room for otherness. On Husserl's view, the world is a phenomenon of my consciousness. Not only does my ego transcend the world in terms of being the one thing left over after everything else is bracketed out, I also transcend it in being the source of the world's meaning. So I—as subject—am beyond the phenomenological recution. As Marion puts it, "The *I* is excepted from the reduction (because it carries it out)" (*RG* 161). Marion argues that there is an important sense in which the transcendental ego is thus "outside of being." If metaphysics (or ontology) is the study of being, then the *I* seems to be located somewhere beyond metaphysics.

Ostensibly Heidegger breaks with Husserl, for Dasein is first and foremost "being-in-the-world" *(in-der-Welt-sein)*. Dasein is so integrally linked with its world that it is impossible to imagine Dasein's existing apart from it. But there is still a privileging of Dasein over the world in Heidegger. We have seen that Dasein is necessary for the existence not only of truth but also of meaning (by way of the hermeneutical "as"). Even if Dasein is not the sole horizon on which the phenomena of the world appear, Dasein is an essential constitutive factor of that horizon. One could argue, then, that Heidegger's phenomenology is reductive in that the meaning of phenomena reduces to Dasein. As Heidegger puts it,

"Dasein accordingly takes priority over all other entities" (*BT* 34). But if Dasein has an ontical priority (i.e., is a privileged entity) and serves as the source of fundamental ontology, then isn't Dasein likewise prior to ontology (or metaphysics)? Marion calls this move of privileging Dasein "the existential reduction."

In order to break with both Husserl and Heidegger, Marion gives us a "third reduction." Marion claims that beyond the transcendental ego or Dasein is a "something" (clearly not a "thing") that might be termed "pure givenness." We have seen that central to the notion of phenomenology is the idea of givenness—that phenomena are "given" to consciousness. Marion claims that this givenness (*Gegebenheit* in German; *donation* in French) is absolutely prior to the transcendental ego or Dasein. It is a "call" (to use his terminology) that precedes us temporally and ontologically, thus making the two other reductions reducible to it.

> The call thus appears as the originary scheme of the two previous reductions, precisely because it alone allows one to reconduct to . . . , in that it demands that one give oneself over to the deal *(donne)* of the call as such—to render oneself to the call in the double sense of abandoning oneself to it and of moving toward it. As a pure reduction—because a perfect reconduction to . . . —the call that claims for itself belongs eminently to the domain of phenomenology. (*RG* 198)

There are four aspects here worth considering in more detail: the call, the status of *interloqué,* the identity of the ellipses and the idea of "reconduction." Having examined them, we will have a much better idea of Marion's third reduction.

Coming from outside of me, the call displaces me as center of my world. Since the call (vocative case) is *to me* (dative case), I (subject) am now put in the place of receiver (object). No longer do I occupy a privileged position in which I am the actor; instead I am the one acted upon. Marion characterizes this change as being "deposed from autarchy and taken by surprise" (*RG* 201). In this way I become the *interloqué,* the one who is called and must answer.[2] Whereas the "I" was once the source of the *logos* of reason, the *logos* is now given to the "I"—to me. Marion claims that "in delivering itself, the *Logos* delivers the *logia* (i.e. logic)" and with it "the practice of language" (*IAD* 180, 183). Thus *logos*

---

[2] Marion explicitly connects *interloqué* to Heidegger's term *der Angesprochene.* See *RG* 200.

and language are not "properties" of the "I" but are gifts with which it has been "endowed" (*ED* 397). All that the "I" can think and say about what it is given is itself given. But it is given in such a way that the "I" cannot "master" or "possess" it. "Surprise prohibits the *interloqué* from comprehending," says Marion, and he goes on to point out that comprehending is equivalent to "taking possession" (*RG* 201).

Marion also describes the *interloqué* as the *adonné*. The infinitive form *adonner* means "to give oneself over" or "to devote oneself to something." But the *adonné* does not actively give itself over; rather the *adonné* is given over to the gift without its permission. One might conclude from this move that the *adonné* loses its identity. But Marion claims exactly the opposite: in being given over, the *adonné* or *interloqué* actually receives its identity. It is actually given birth (*ED* 400). Marion says that the "proper" name is "given to *me* before I could choose it, know it or even hear it; it was given to *me* because in fact *I* was given [*interloqué*]."[3] Indeed he goes so far as to say that my identity "can be proclaimed only when called—by the call of the other" (*RG* 201). Thus my authenticity is *given to me*—and so is "mine" only as a gift that I do not own. In strict Heideggerian terms, then, I am made *inauthentic* because this gift that comes from outside of me defines me, instead of my defining myself. I am no longer my own; I belong to the call.

But who is the one calling? If there is a call, must there not be a caller? Here the situation becomes much more complex. For Marion, at least in his role as phenomenologist, wants to leave this caller unidentified, which is why he inserts ellipses at two key spots in the lengthy passage on the previous page. Why? While this may seem a strange move, Marion's reasoning can be worked out in the following ways.

First, if the caller were truly identified, then it/she/he would seem to be in some sense "controlled" by the one called, for the one called has now placed a name or concept on the caller. Marion wants to emphasize the "pure" givenness of the call—it is given to me and so stands outside of my control. This idea of givenness leads to a second way of explaining Marion's move. Earlier we saw Derrida argue that technically speaking it is impossible to give a gift. A "present" can be a gift only if it does not set up any kind of economy between a giver and a receiver. Moreover (and

[3]Jean-Luc Marion, "Le Sujet en dernier appel," *Revue de Métaphysique et de Morale* 96 (1991): 93; "The Final Appeal of the Subject," in *Deconstructive Subjectivities,* ed. Simon Critchley and Peter Dews (Albany: State University of New York Press, 1996), p. 102.

this is key), if a "gift" can be traced back to a specific giver, then it becomes possible for an economy to arise. As long as there are the three terms—giver, gift and receiver—there can be an economy. But, argues Marion, if we eliminate one of those terms, then the economy vanishes.[4]

How exactly does this work, though? Marion thinks the gift can remain untouched by economy if either there is no giver or else that giver remains anonymous.[5] In place of identifying a giver, as just noted, Marion uses ellipses. Further, while *reconduction* literally means "renewal" in French, Marion is claiming to give us a new interpretation of the phenomenological reduction—that is, re(con)duction (*RG* 2). His "new" reduction is to the realm not of the "I" or Dasein but pure givenness itself, in which the gift—or simply *Gegebenheit,* unidentified givenness—is primary.

To reach this horizon, Marion provides us with three specific reductions.[6] If we turn to the experience of the donor, we see that the donor is not really the "cause" of the gift, since the donor is first and foremost recipient. The donor gives out of prior obligation, and so the gift is "prior" (both temporally and metaphysically) to the donor. Similarly, the gift holds sway over the recipient. One might think that receiving a gift is a matter of "deciding" to take it. But Marion claims that the gift has a kind of allure over the receiver, who takes the gift because of its hold on the one who receives. So the gift has a hold on both donor and receiver. Further, the gift is ultimately reducible not to a "thing" that can be given but to "givenness itself" or "gifting." Thus the gift, according to Marion, escapes the cause-effect schema of economy.

But if the giver remains unidentified, how can we speak of the giver? Perhaps this is less of a problem if we are talking about an unidentified *human* giver, for we might be content to allow that one to remain unidentified, as in the case of an "anonymous donor." But it is clearly a major difficulty for a religious believer, who wants to be able to "iden-

---

[4]Not only does Marion think it is possible for there to be gifts without anyone giving, he also thinks there can be gifts without recipients or even without actual "gifts." To quote him: "Thus a gift could still achieve itself with a gift, a receiver, but without any giver; or, in another solution, with a giver, a gift, but no receiver; or, in a third figure, with a giver, a receiver but no *thing* which is given" (*GGP* 65). Giving up any of these terms (or even two of them—e.g., donor and recipient) would result in the possibility of a "pure" gift.

[5]Note that Marion thinks an anonymous giver is virtually the same as no giver. It is not clear to me how the two could be equated.

[6]See *ED* §4 and Jean-Luc Marion, "Esquisse d'un concept phénoménologique du don," *Archivo di Filosofia* 62 (1994): 75-94.

tify" God as this giver. For support, Marion turns to negative theology, or what he prefers to call "mystical theology." Just as Marion points us to a "third reduction," so he thinks mystical theology (specifically that of Dionysius) gives us a "third way" of speaking about God. The first two ways are immediately familiar, since they are essential to predication. On the one hand, in "affirmation" *(kataphasis)* we speak about God by drawing on attributes of finite creatures (e.g., God's love is like that of a human father). On the other hand, "negation" or "denial" *(apophasis)* proceeds by separation of God from the finite (e.g., God's love is *not* like that of a human father).

Yet mystical theology, claims Marion, gives us a third way, what Marion calls *dé-nomination*. Although the French *dé-nomination* translates into English as "denomination" or "name," in setting apart the *dé* Marion intends the idea of "unnaming." Thus *dé-nomination* is a double-sided move of naming and unnaming, of saying God's name in such a way that it is not said, of predication that undoes itself. Even though Dionysius says that "it is necessary at first to impose and affirm all theses of beings insofar as it [God] is the cause of all, then deny them even more radically, as it surpasses all," he then goes on to say that God is "above *[hyper] every* negation and affirmation."[7] Marion insists that Dionysius's version of *apophasis* truly supersedes—rather than merely combines—affirmation and negation. He claims that "the third way does not hide an affirmation beneath a negation, because it means to overcome their duel, just as it means to overcome that between the two truth values wherein metaphysics plays itself out" (*GGP* 26). Whereas metaphysics is confined to affirmation and negation, God—who is beyond metaphysics, since he is beyond being—does not have to "be" or "not be." This is why Marion (interestingly enough, following Thomas Aquinas) considers this way of speaking to be "eminent"—above all predication, conceptualization and metaphysics.[8]

Marion reads these three ways of speaking in Husserlian terms. In the case of affirmation, the intended object is fulfilled by intuition's giving us ("at least partially," as Marion reminds us, *GGP* 39) a measure of adequation between the act of knowing *(noēsis)* and the object known *(noēma)*.

---

[7]I have quoted this using Marion's translation ("In the Name," in *GGP* 24, 26). See Pseudo-Dionysius *The Mystical Theology* 1000b, in *The Complete Works,* trans. Colin Luibheid and Paul Rorem (New York: Paulist, 1987).

[8]Thomas Aquinas *Summa Theologiae* 1a.13.3.

So I "intend" Westminster Abbey and that intention is "fulfilled" by that entity's being present to my consciousness (because I am there). In negation there is no intuitive fulfillment of the intention. Here I may invoke the term "Westminster Abbey," but I have no grasp of it (say, because I have never been there, have not seen a picture of it or do not even know what the term denotes). The "third way" works out as follows:

> The intention (the concept or the signification) can never reach adequation with the intuition (fulfillment), not because the latter is lacking but because it exceeds what the concept can receive, expose, and comprehend. . . . According to this hypothesis, the impossibility of attaining knowledge of an object, comprehension in the strict sense, does not come from a deficiency in the giving intuition, but from its surplus, which neither concept, signification, nor intention can foresee, organize, or contain. (GGP 39-40)

Predication becomes impossible precisely because the object to which it attempts to refer cannot be adequately "captured."

Agreeing with Gregory of Nyssa when he claims that God "surpasses all signification that a name could express" (*GGP* 38), Marion puts forth *de-nomination* as a way of referring to God that acknowledges a lack of comprehension and adequation. *De-nomination,* claims Marion, is a kind of reference or intention that avoids naming or predication. Marion assumes that, technically speaking, in order to "name" God one must be able to name or predicate God's essence. But since God is above metaphysics and cannot be properly characterized as having an "essence," no claims can be made regarding God's "essence." God is "hyperessential" *(hyperousias)*—above all essences and so above all essential claims. As hyperessential, God is beyond the reach of either affirmative or negative statements. Any discourse that destroys this distance between God and us is idolatrous.

What does this *de-nomination* look like in actual practice? Earlier I noted that on Marion's account "predication must yield to praise" (*GWB* 106). Following Dionysius, who puts the verb *hymnein* (to praise) in place of "to say" (*IAD* 184), Marion holds up praise and prayer *(euchē)* as the models of his third way of speaking.[9] In both prayer and praise,

---

[9]Marion uses the terms *prayer* and *praise* interchangeably. There are, of course, important differences between the two, which I examine later in this chapter.

one recognizes that God is beyond the intentionality of the one who prays and so remains radically unidentified. Thus prayer both recognizes and maintains distance and crosses it—at once. Marion claims that "prayer performs distance" (*IAD* 162), in that prayer acknowledges a distance between God and us. But prayer also allows for the "traverse of distance" (*IAD* 160). In prayer there is a "participation" with God but without "assimilation" (*IAD* 158).

The Call and the Horizon

Can Marion truly make this move of insisting on the "purity" of the call? According to Marion, not only are prayer and praise returned (i.e., reconducted) to a God whose identity remains purely anonymous, utterly unidentified, but the call from God is a "pure call."[10] But Derrida asks in reponse, "Is it possible to hear a 'pure form of the call' . . . and, if one does, on what basis?" (*GT* 52). In other words, what are we to make of a call that comes from nowhere and no one? In order for me to have any sense of "call" or claim upon me, don't I need to recognize a call as a call? One might argue that there can be calls that I do not hear or heed because I do not recognize them as such. I take it that others (and the Other) often call to us in vain. If that call is to have a hold on me, I have to recognize it *as such*.

At stake here is both a phenomenological question and a practical question. We have seen that phenomenologically speaking there *must* be a "horizon" or background—a *logos* or *als Struktur*—on which a phenomenon appears. This is clear from Husserl, and it is a tenet to which succeeding phenomenologists have generally given their agreement. In a discussion with Marion, Derrida argues for the "phenomenologically orthodox" point of view that this "as such" is indispensable to phenomenology, not to mention philosophy in general: "I think that phenomenology, as well as ontology, as well as philosophy, implies the *als Struktur,* the as such."

What Derrida says here needs to be placed in context. In the introduction I noted that Husserl himself says, "I can simply look at that which is *intended as such* and grasp it absolutely."[11] But within this seemingly innocuous formulation is something deeply problematic. On

---

[10]"Before Being has claimed, the call as *pure call* claims" (*RG* 197, my italics).

[11]Edmund Husserl, *Introduction to the Logical Investigations,* trans. Philip J. Bossert and Curtis H. Peters (The Hague: Martinus Nijhoff, 1975), p. 27.

the one hand, Husserl emphasizes the "as such" aspect of intentional-ity—that intentions are always on the background of an horizon. On the other hand, Husserl speaks of grasping something "absolutely." But if my grasp of an intentional object (a *noema*) is always by way of a per-spectival act of knowing (*noesis*)—which is Husserl's view—then how can the relation of *noesis* to *noema* be absolute? This problem is even more complicated. While Levinas is right that the act of giving meaning *(Sinngebung)* to an object can be read as a way of reducing its other-ness to the domesticity of the "same," that move *always* fails. Since the other remains other, an "absolute grasp" can never be had.

Marion's response to the problem of the "as such" is much like that of Levinas, but with a twist. In response to Derrida, Marion tells of having said to Levinas at some point that "the last step for a real phenomenol-ogy would be to give up the concept of the horizon" and that Levinas responded by saying, "Without horizon there is no phenomenology." To this claim by Levinas, Marion retorts, "I boldly assume he was wrong." Derrida goes so far as to suggest that here Marion is a phenomenologi-cal heretic: "Would you dissociate what you call phenomenology from the authority of the as such? If you do that, it would be the first heresy in phenomenology. Phenomenology without as such!" Derrida points out that once one gives up the notion of horizon, one is "no longer a phe-nomenologist" (*GGP* 66). So we have here Marion as "phenomenologi-cal heretic" and Derrida as "phenomenological inquisitor."

As noted in the preface, Derrida is not the first to criticize Marion as a heretic of phenomenology. Dominique Janicaud also takes Marion to task, but for the opposite reason. Whereas Derrida criticizes Marion for attempting to deny the "horizon," Janicaud criticizes Marion for import-ing it from theology, instead of being the "neutral" scientific observer that Husserl requires. "Despite all the denials, phenomenological neu-trality has been abandoned" (*PTT* 68). Instead of a "scientific" analysis, Marion's "theological veering" (as Janicaud terms it) "leads to analyses that verge on edification" (*PTT* 69)—*quelle horreur!* Further, on Jani-caud's account, Marion does not take seriously enough the explicit "bracketing" of God stipulated by Husserl in section 58 of the first book of his *Ideas*. There Husserl extends the reduction to the "'absolute' and 'transcendent' being" (*ID* 134). To this latter charge Marion responds in effect that the "God" excluded by Husserl is simply a version of the God of the philosophers, being the "foundation" or *Grund* of the world. Left untouched is the God of theology, the revealed God, the One who is both immanent and transcendent (*ED* 336-37).

Yet the phenomenological question is not solved quite so easily. Derrida is clearly right in insisting that the notion of horizon plays a key role in phenomenology, at least as it is traditionally defined. As far as I can see, something like a horizon (a background, a context or whatever one might call it) seems to be at work in any kind of perception or knowledge. It seems impossible to imagine the appearance of any phenomenon without any background at all. Thus the question is not merely one of phenomenology but of any sort of philosophy. Even Marion's claim in *Reduction and Givenness* that he has "attempted nothing more than to free the phenomenological way of thinking *as such*" (*RG* 3, my italics) requires the "as such," or else even such a claim could not be meaningful. But while there can be no dispensing with the horizon (the "as such") in any phenomenology or philosophy, Marion is likewise right in insisting on the centrality of Husserl's "principle of principles," that every phenomenon *"is to be accepted simply as what it is presented as being"* (*ID* 44). Where Marion goes too far is in insisting on "the unconditional primacy of the givenness of the phenomenon" (*RG* 32).

The problem is that these two emphases of phenomenology—the horizon and the principle of principles—must be given equal due. Or we might simply point out that even the principle of principles itself contains both aspects. Perhaps it can be put as follows: while phenomena must appear on a horizon to be meaningful, those phenomena still "overflow" that horizon (so they are not "limited" by it). Levinas speaks of "the surplus of being over the thought that claims to contain it" (*TAI* 27). Thus we can preserve both the notion of horizon *and* the phenomenon's "exceeding" of that horizon. Clearly it will not do (at least phenomenologically speaking) to give up either one, nor would it be desirable philosophically to give up either. Nor can either be privileged over the other. We must recognize that phenomena indeed appear against a certain cultural background (an aspect of perception and cognition which seems simply undeniable) and yet still emphasize the importance of the phenomenon's defining itself. Simply to dispense with the hermeneutical "as" will not work. So both Marion and Derrida are right in the sense that they emphasize two different but equally crucial emphases of phenomenology.

It seems to me that one neither can nor ought to privilege either of these aspects, for both are essential features of human perception and cognition. And if God is to "appear" to human beings, it is *within* these limits that he must appear. Yet what does it mean to say that neither is to be privileged? On my read, there is a kind of play of one against the other.[12] I take this to be Husserl's position. And it is Husserl's position because it is a phenomenologically accurate account of our experience. It is not that either is simply given priority, though one might be given a kind of momentary priority, with one emphasized over the other. But that priority is never sustained. Rather the equilibrium between the two is maintained by a constantly shifting emphasis.

Thus although Derrida agrees with Marion by saying, "I am also for the suspension of the horizon," it is not clear that he is right when he goes on to say, "for that very reason, by saying so, I am not a phenomenologist anymore" (*GGP* 66). If Derrida means by the phrase "I am also for" that he is in favor of allowing the horizon to be *temporarily* deemphasized or even simply suspended, then I take it he is still within the realm of phenomenology. After all, Husserl himself advocated the notion of the *epoché*—the bracketing of horizonal beliefs. Of course the problem is that while such bracketing may be useful and appropriate momentarily, depending on what and how much is bracketed, such a suspension is only partially successful—and also only partially desirable.[13] Were we to bracket *all* of our previous beliefs, perception and understanding would be impossible. Yet were our beliefs to remain completely intact and undisturbed, it would be impossible to perceive or know anything that had not already been previously perceived or known. In other words, there could be no revelation *either way*.

There are some ways, however, in which I have to part company with Husserl.[14] We have seen that Husserl advocates the transcendental reduction, with everything reduced to the transcendental ego and genuine otherness excluded. Yet all three of the reductions prove to be "reductionistic." Whereas the phenomenological reduction removes the phenomena from the world, the eidetic reduction removes the particularities

---

[12]Here I have in mind something like Kant's idea of "the play of the faculties" found in the *Critique of Judgment.*

[13]As Merleau-Ponty memorably puts it, "The most important lesson which the reduction teaches us is the impossibility of a complete reduction." See Maurice Merleau-Ponty, *Phenomenology of Perception,* trans. Colin Smith (London: Routledge & Kegan Paul, 1962), p. xiv.

[14]Of course Husserl's thought on alterity is much more complex than can be shown here.

of phenomena. What if we were not to follow Husserl on the reduction-
ary path? It may be helpful to examine via the eidetic reduction the
"essential features" of a phenomenon or to consider via the phenomenological reduction a phenomenon apart from ontological views concerning
its "reality." But both can seriously *distort* a phenomenon. Ultimately, in
order to understand a phenomenon aright we need to know about both
its "reality" and its "accidental" features. Moreover, there is no need to
follow Husserl in advocating anything like a transcendental ego that
"grounds" the world—or anything, for that matter. While something *like*
an ego (whatever that may be) clearly is important in the constitution of
horizons, it does not stand as the sole force of the horizon's constitution,
phenomenologically speaking. For the horizon is not simply formed by
me; it is the result of many constituting selves, the product of a mutual
constitution. It is not reducible to me or even other selves. I am not "the
master of my horizon." Moreover, the horizon is not static: it is constantly
in motion and influenced by incoming phenomena—as Husserl himself
was well aware. Most important, as Marion and Levinas remind us, our
horizon is always subject to alteration by forces beyond our control.

On my read, then, both the horizon and the principle of principles
are indispensable, even though the conception of the horizon I have
briefly sketched here is only very partially in my control. The essential
duality of horizon and principle of principles becomes even clearer
when we consider Marion's idea of the call from both practical and theological points of view. Practically speaking, in order to hear a call as a
call, I need to hear it as coming from someone in particular (i.e., by way
of a hermeneutical "as"). Interestingly enough, Marion says that while it
is most important to hear specifically Christian and Jewish calls as coming from one God, he admits that "it is important to maintain the difference between these two calls" (*RG* 197). But how can one make any
differentiation if the call is a "pure call"? Not only does such anonymity
present a practical problem for hearing and answering a call, it threatens
the undoing of theological discourse.

This problem can be worked out in two opposite ways, with the
result of either the elimination of God-talk or else its utter multiplication.
On the one hand, if God (or whoever is doing the calling) cannot be
identified at all, then can there be any theological talk? It would seem
that only if God can be identified can there be theological talk. One
might argue that one positive result of silencing all theological speaking

and thinking would be the reduction or even elimination of idolatry. But *some* sort of idol is very likely to fill that void. Even with all theological talk eliminated, idolatry still remains a threat. In any case, the silencing of God-talk is hardly the purpose of theology. On the other hand, if the caller cannot be named or identified, then does not all talk of a negative nature (in which there is an acknowledged lack of adequation) threaten to turn into God-talk? In other words, if God's primary characteristic becomes the lack of identity, then does not all talk of things that cannot be properly identified have the potential to turn into talk about God? In such a case we could have, as Derrida puts it, "the becoming-theological of all discourse."

> God's name would suit everything that may not be broached, approached, or designated, except in an indirect and negative manner. Every negative sentence would already be haunted by God or by the name of God. . . . Not only would atheism not be the truth of negativity; rather God would be the truth of all negativity. (HAS 76)

But of course, we have already seen that in making everyone *tout autre* Derrida *himself* faces this same problem.

There is a further problem here. Although Marion asserts that the "hermeneutical 'as'" is not a feature of the call to the *interloqué,* he himself puts into jeopardy this purity in *The Idol and Distance* when he says that "*logia* given by the *Logos,* manifesting the paternal distance in demands that coincide with gifts, the *Pater* establishes the language of praise in its site and constitutes the requestant in a request to the Requisite as . . ." (*IAD* 195, Marion's ellipsis). As Marion reminds us, the *Logos* himself teaches us to pray "Our Father." But does not a reference to "Our Father" identify the One to whom we pray? If the words "Our Father" do not serve to do so, wouldn't the term *Abba* do so? Although speaking explicitly of Dionysius, Derrida's question is applicable to Marion.

> How can one deny that the encomium qualifies God and *determines* prayer, *determines* the other, Him to whom it addresses itself, refers, invoking Him even as the source of prayer? How can one deny that, in this movement of determination (which is no longer the pure address of the prayer to the other), the nomination of the *trinitary* and superessential God distinguishes Dionysius's *Christian* prayer from all other prayer? (HAS 111)

Does not a prayer that is explicitly addressed to the God whom Christians worship designate a very particular God? Can one really pray to a specific God without naming him as such? And would one *want* to pray to a God without specifying who that God is? It is understandable that Derrida elsewhere asks—in this case with explicit reference to Marion—"Having *declared* that it [the call] excludes any determinable content, why does Marion determine 'the pure form of the call'[15] (and therefore of the gift) as call 'in the name of the Father'?" (*GT* 52). In other words, Marion cannot have it both ways.

Is Derrida justified in his criticism? Thomas Carlson argues that at least in one regard he is not.

> [Derrida's challenge] misses the mark to the degree that, within Marion's phenomenology of the *interloqué* or *adonné,* the "source" of the call, or the instance of absolute, unconditional givenness, must—contra Derrida—necessarily remain indeterminate, unknown, and anonymous. The necessity of such indeterminacy—on this point Marion is clear and insistent—stems from the basic definition and structure of the *interloqué*.[16]

On Carlson's read, Marion insists on the "unconditional poverty" of the call out of "phenomenological necessity."[17] To support that point, Carlson quotes Marion as saying:

> This objection rests . . . on the illusory presupposition that it is necessary to name the instance that claims in order to suffer its convocation. Now, following the order of a strict phenomenological description, the reverse happens: I recognize myself as *interloqué* well *before* having consciousness or knowledge not only of my eventual subjectivity, but especially of what leaves me *interloqué*. (*RG* 202)

But this is, it seems to me, precisely what is open to question. On Marion's account there is an ontologically separate, and thus presumably temporally separate, moment of the call—a moment in which my *logos* is suspended (in effect, held in *epochē*). At this point I am unable to name or identify the caller. It is only *after* the call has been heard that consciousness and knowledge (i.e., my own human *logos*) enter the picture.

Yet in the same way that Nietzsche criticizes Plato for postulating the existence of the forms without any justification, Marion can be criticized

---

[15]Derrida is here quoting from *RG* 197.
[16]Thomas A. Carlson, *Indiscretion: Finitude and the Naming of God* (Chicago: University of Chicago Press, 1997), p. 207.
[17]Ibid., pp. 208 and 207, respectively.

for postulating this claim from nowhere and no one. Could there be truly a *phenomenological* grounding for Marion's claim? If phenomenology is based on actual experience, is there an actual experience of this radically anonymous call? Perhaps there is. Perhaps Marion has himself experienced such a call. I'm not sure how I could disagree with his personal experience, though then Marion would have to modify his claim to be a personal claim, or a claim based on the experience of *some* people. I have already attempted to argue that it seems logically impossible for there to be a call without a caller. But maybe this thing that seems logically impossible happens anyway.

Or perhaps we should put the question slightly differently: is Marion here making a strictly phenomenological claim concerning what is the case, or is he making a *faith* claim? Marion wants to maintain that it is the former, rather than the latter, when he says that his project is "merely philosophical and without any theological presupposition or bias" (*GGP* 70). But when he goes on to identify the caller as the Father, it seems to be more the latter. So which comes first? Is Marion primarily a theologian who employs phenomenology to make a theological point? Or is he a phenomenologist who also happens to be a theologian? In other words, is the horizon of Marion's theology driving the project of a "pure phenomenology"? Or is Marion's concern truly to give us a phenomenology of givenness? But isn't even this last project *itself* a horizon or *logos?*

Is There Truly a "Third Way"?

Having questioned whether Marion can really postulate "pure" givenness without a horizon, it is appropriate to ask whether prayer and praise really represent a "third way" of speaking. Marion claims that "the language of praise plays its own game" (*IAD* 193), one that goes beyond the game of affirmation and denial. Now he quite rightly wants to avoid idolatry by pointing out the distance between God and us. Whenever we set up an idol, that distance is compromised.[18] On Marion's read, the logic of affirmation is the bridging of distance.[19] In contrast, if the lan-

---

[18]I don't think one can rightly say that the distance is "destroyed," since God always remains above all idols. Moreover, while one would normally think of affirmation as idolatrous (in that we affirm as God something that is less than or other than God), Marion claims that "negation, if it remains categorical, remains idolatrous" (*IAD* 147).

[19]Marion asks (rhetorically), "Does language not claim to coincide with that which it exhausts as an object?" (*IAD* 183).

guage of theology—praise and prayer—and its *logia* are kept "within the hierarchical play of distance" (*IAD* 183), then it remains iconic. Whereas the goal of scientific discourse is the setting up of a rigorous language in which there is perfect adequation between words and concepts and the thing they represent, so that all distance between word and thing is eliminated, proper theological discourse does not attempt to erase this distance. It is hard to not applaud Marion on the attempt to refrain from idolatry. But I think he can be faulted in at least two respects, from opposite sides.

On the one hand, Derrida rightly claims that *dé-nomination* never really leaves the realm of affirmation and denial. We have seen that negative theology—whether that of Dionysius, Marion or someone else—attempts to speak of God as "hyperessential" and so go beyond metaphysical terms. That is the reason why Marion wishes to speak of a "God without being."[20] But already in the essay *"Différance"* Derrida claims that even in negative theology God remains within the realm of metaphysics. Although God is "refused the predicate of existence" and so seemingly put beyond metaphysics, he is brought back into metaphysics by being given a "superior, inconceivable, and ineffable mode of being."[21] To this claim Marion responds that "negative theology, at bottom, does not aim to reestablish a 'superessentiality,' since it aims neither at predication nor at Being" (*IAD* 230). Note that the debate here turns on the meaning of *hyperousios*. When we say that God is "above being" (or "above essence," since both are possible translations), do we mean "standing outside of the realm of being entirely"? Or do we mean that God's being is an "above being," a superior sort of being? Marion clearly thinks it is the former of these, but Derrida argues that it ends up being the latter.

But why? Derrida speaks of the paradoxical nature of hyperbole. Literally, in Plato's *Republic, hyperbolē* is "the movement of transcendence that carries or transports beyond being or beingness" (*ON* 64). But this movement of "beyond" *(hyper)* always remains connected to that which

---

[20]Derrida points out the similarity between Marion's title *God Without Being* and Levinas's title *Otherwise Than Being or Beyond Essence* (trans. Alphonso Lingis [The Hague: Martinus Nijhoff, 1981]). Both represent attempts, as Derrida puts it, "to avoid the contamination by Being, in order to 'hear God not contaminated by Being'" (HAS 133).

[21]Jacques Derrida, *"Différance,"* in *Margins of Philosophy,* trans. Alan Bass (Chicago: University of Chicago Press, 1982), p. 6.

it attempts to transcend, which makes it paradoxical. However much negative theology attempts to move "beyond" metaphysics, "it is still a matter of saying the entity *[étant]* such as it is" (*ON* 68). The *étant* may be *donné,* but it is still an *étant,* and thus a part of "being." Even if we affirm that theological claims go beyond the direct affirmations of, say, natural science, it seems that they still end up being affirmations of some sort. In other words, the praise and prayer of negative theology may push beyond the realm of predication, but they never leave it entirely.

Is there a difference between prayer and praise in this regard? Derrida argues that there is.

> Even if it is not a predicative affirmation of the current type, the enco-
> mium [i.e., praise] preserves the style and the structure of a predicative
> affirmation. It says something about someone. This is not the case of the
> prayer that apostrophizes, addresses itself to the other and remains, in this
> pure movement, absolutely pre-predicative. (HAS 137)

It is not difficult to see that praise is predicative in nature—since it necessarily ascribes certain qualities to God.[22] It is likewise not difficult to see that once this encomium is linked with prayer, prayer takes on a predicative nature. But Derrida thinks that there is the possibility of a "pre-predicative" prayer. This would certainly not be a Christian prayer, or a prayer of any given religion. It would have to stand outside of a particular religious tradition. In fact it would have to stand outside of *any* tradition—religious, philosophical or otherwise. Derrida speaks of it as a "pure address" to the other, "without any other determination" (HAS 111). But it is difficult to imagine what such a pure address (without any real address) could look like or sound like. Heidegger speaks of a "simple willingness that wills nothing" (*P* 61), but could there *be* such an address—one without determination of any kind? Even if a prayer is to "the unknown God," like that of the Athenians in Acts 17, there would seem to be *some* sort of accompanying predication (e.g., "this God is above us" or "this God is so remote as to be unnamable"). So it is diffi-cult to imagine what a truly "pure" address could possibly be. One may have remarkably little idea of the One to whom a particular supplication is made, but it seems impossible to have no idea *whatsoever.*

In any case, neither praise nor prayer of any actual negative theology

---

[22]Praise can take varying degrees of specificity. But even at its vaguest, such as when we say that "God is great," praise ascribes some sort of quality to God.

(as opposed to some possible sort) ever reaches this point of total purity. To whatever extent negative theologies have a particular religious identity (as Christian or something else), they can be located within a particular tradition and thus a particular *logos*. Derrida describes the move of negative theology as "internal rebellion" that "radically contests the tradition from which it seems to come" (*ON* 67). Even though negative theology takes issue with its tradition, it is indefinable apart from that tradition. Its contending with its tradition establishes it as firmly connected to it. Dionysius may be an unconventional theologian, but he is clearly a *Christian* theologian. It is precisely the convention of Christian theology—of which he is a part—that makes him seem unconventional.[23]

On the other hand, as has been shown, there is *always* a lack of adequation between our concepts and the things they represent. Note the distinction Marion makes. In affirmation and negation there is no distinction between the predicate and the thing of which it is predicated. When we say, "That leaf is green," we ascribe the quality "greenness" to the leaf. The leaf *is* that quality (though it is not that quality alone). But praise is not the ascription of a quality to God per se. Marion argues that prayer and praise are characterized by an "as" (different from the "hermeneutical as," at least according to Marion). We praise God "as" love or "as" good. We do not say that God "is" love or "is" good, for God is above these characteristics. But is it really possible to maintain the radical contrast Marion wishes to draw? According to Marion, "comprehension suggests adequate knowledge as long as one is dealing with things of the world" (*GGP* 37). Whereas in predication there is an adequation between meaning and referent, in praise there is an infinite distance between the two. Whereas predication is determinate, praise is radically indeterminate or even anonymous.[24] Yet it is hard to see that predication is ever as determinate as Marion makes it out to be. I think he is quite mistaken in thinking that language "eliminates distance" (*IAD* 184). At best, language serves to bring things only a bit closer.

---

[23]Of course Dionysius is not really all that unconventional when compared with either the earlier or later Christian tradition. Themes of negative theology are found throughout the entire Christian tradition, even in Calvin and others whom one would not immediately associate with negative theology.

[24]Following Dionysius and others, Marion reminds us that "anonymity and polyonymy go together, as two banks of the same distance" (*IAD* 186).

While comprehension may "suggest" an adequate knowledge of physical things, that in no way guarantees such an adequation is possible. We have seen that Husserl himself thinks that perfect adequation between intention and real objects is a goal of an infinite sort—one that we seek to achieve but never actually do achieve. Even Marion admits that "no being, even supreme, gives itself to be grasped" (*IAD* 140). Thus predication never provides us with true comprehension—grasping—of anything. Recall that Marion himself distinguishes *dé-nomination* from predication by saying that in the former the object intended "exceeds what the concept can receive, expose, and comprehend" (*GGP* 39). Such seems to be exactly the situation of predication. So is there a *qualitative* difference between predication and denomination? Or is that difference merely quantitative? When I say that "the leaf is green," to what degree have I "grasped" that statement? Or when I simply say, "The leaf *is*," to what extent do I really know what I mean?

I have shown that the spiritual and physical are often contrasted so that whereas the physical can be comprehended, the spiritual is above comprehension. Without doubt, the spiritual cannot be grasped—and God least of all. But physical reality is not really "comprehensible" either. I don't really understand (comprehend) what it means to say that "God is three in one" or even that "God exists," but as noted in chapter six, it is not clear that I have a considerably better grasp on such statements as "This leaf is composed of matter." True, I can go to clarify this statement by saying, "Matter is composed of molecules and atoms." Yet that statement only goes so far in clarifying what matter is. Interestingly, Husserl himself insists that physical things transcend the consciousness that intends them. They are not fully immanent to consciousness; they remain transcendent.

Note that Marion himself points out that there is not merely one saturated phenomenon—that is, God—but many. Not only are Descartes's "idea of the infinite" and Kant's "the sublime" examples of such phenomena (*PTT* 213-14),[25] but Marion also includes "death, birth, love, poverty, illness, joy, pleasure and so on," as well as "an historical event, a painting, the self-affection of the flesh, and the experience of the other" (*GGP* 75). Marion has even included the idol in the category of

---

[25]Descartes argues that the very idea of the infinite exceeds our grasp because it is too much for us to comprehend. Likewise, the sublime for Kant cannot be "ordered" or "limited" by our concepts.

saturated phenomena (see *ED* 23-24). All of these are examples of what Marion calls "the 'counter-experience' of bedazzlement, of astonishment or *Bewunderung*" (*GGP* 75).

But according to Aristotle, astonishment or awe *(thaumazein)* is precisely what got philosophy going in the first place, not just in regard to God but to the cosmos in general.[26] In other words, philosophy arises historically because everything in the cosmos is a source of wonder and mystification. Certainly God is the highest source of that wonder, but the rest of creation is also cause for being "puzzled," as Aristotle puts it. Although Marion claims that saturated phenomena are "special" in that they do not submit to an adequate "conceptual definition" and so "we cannot comprehend" them, *all* phenomena are "saturated" phenomena in that they cannot be fully experienced, comprehended or classified. And if such is the case, then the saturated phenomenon becomes not the exception but the norm. To put this another way: phenomenology always is concerned with saturated phenomena, since there is no other kind.

If there is nothing other than "saturated phenomena," it is not clear that there is either the need for or the possibility of a third way beyond affirmation and denial of predication. Predication itself is already like this third way—that is, *it always says more than it knows.*

As far as I can see, then, there is no third way, nor is there a need for a third way. But for the sake of argument, let's assume for a moment that there is. In that event, it seems to me that there are at least two problems with the status of *hymnein.*

First, echoing Aristotle, Marion claims that "praise is neither true nor false."[27] Earlier I noted that he claims that "faith has nothing like a discourse, at least if discourse implies the succession of arguments," and that "faith neither speaks nor states; it believes" (*GWB* 183). But what exactly is the status of this belief that is "neither true nor false," that neither "speaks nor states"? While the praise of the Christian believer carries with it the recognition that its referent cannot be *established* as true or false (for one's own intellect cannot comprehend that referent and so cannot establish it), is there not a sense in which praise postulates that referent and thus implies predication? In other words, belief always

---

[26]Aristotle *Metaphysics* 1.2.982b.

[27]As Aristotle notes, "Prayer is a *logos* but neither true nor false" (quoted by Marion, *IAD* 184). See *On Interpretation* 4.17a.

speaks and states. How could it (or for that matter any other discourse) do otherwise? Marion's answer is that praise is performative: it requests and gives thanks. Praise and prayer are *done,* thinks Marion, but they do not assert. Marion seems right in situating religious belief in the realm of practice rather than theory. Clearly prayer *is* performative, and that performative aspect is central to its being. Yet even though prayer is never *reducible* to predication, it is difficult to see how it does not *partake* of predication. To request something from someone is to acknowledge that one as able to hear and fulfill one's request. So there are at least two predications required for making a request (and I assume there are others). To give thanks is to acknowledge a source from whom blessings flow. Even an idol to an "unknown" god is already a predication (however inexact) of that god's being.

Second, in the same way that praise seems to be linked to predication—however indirectly—the *logos* of the *Logos* seems inseparable from the *logos* of metaphysics. Marion writes:

> The discourse on God, held within anterior distance, presupposes the gift of the *logia:* we do not say, and never will say, anything of God that does not develop, take up—and ground itself in—the *logia.* Here we reach the decisive threshold: the Christian, in Dionysian terms, is decided according to the acceptance or refusal of the Scriptures as the sole foundation that might validate a discourse on the *Logos,* because they issue from it. (*IAD* 181)

Even though the *logia* of the *Logos* represents a radical departure from the logic of the world, does receiving the *logia* of the *Logos* require the simple suspension of all previously held *logia?* That is, do Christ and the Scriptures present to us a new logic that utterly supplants the old? In the first chapter I noted that such is Nietzsche's reading. Or is that *Logos* a supplement, one that displaces and decenters the old but does not simply dispense with it? Indeed can I even recognize this new *Logos* "as" new—or even "as" *logos*—without holding it up to that of the old? In the same way that deconstruction both questions and reaffirms (albeit in a new form), so the *Logos* does not simply destroy all previous *logoi.* The question here is not merely of the relation of *Logos* and *logoi* but of metaphysics and philosophy in general—to which I turn in the epilogue.

Finally, we must ask whether Marion, despite being immensely helpful in thinking about and overcoming idolatry, might lead us into idolatries of his own.

First, in order to escape any idea of predication, Marion is forced to say that "the facts of the language of praise require that one no longer see in it a predication, that one not distinguish the speaker, the statement, and the unthinkable aim" (*IAD* 191). But isn't the inability to distinguish between the speaker and the "unthinkable aim" *precisely* the definition of an idol—according to Marion's own definition? It is when we see only ourselves in something that it becomes an idol. Seeing God—as other—is what we want to achieve. And that requires the ability to distinguish. Seeking to avoid the possibility of idolatry by way of predication, Marion could be read as leading us into a new sort of idolatry. Once we have ruled out the possibility of identifying God by way of predication, might not any idol take the "place" of God?

Second, Marion wants so much to save God from idolatry that God ends up being *invisable*—unseen and unable to be seen. Graham Ward is right when he notes that although Marion claims that "the image [or icon] is snatched from idolatry by totally destroying the screen of its visibility,"[28] "the image (the visible, the phenomenological) is not 'saved' at all but effaced."[29] What are the implications of "saving" the icon/image from visibility? The problem is not merely that the icon is "effaced" (though that is certainly true) but that the icon stands in danger of losing its very character of being an "icon." Even if there is likewise a very real danger of the icon's coming under our mastery when it appears, it *must* appear—else it cannot be an image. A "virtual" image remains just that— one that only gives the appearance of appearing.

If we translate such a lack of appearing christologically, then Christ as the image of God can no longer be the Word who "became flesh and lived among us" (Jn 1:14). For a fleshly God—one who is a "real" object in Husserl's sense—*must* appear. Does even a letter, then, stand between Marion and Marcion, whose Christ cannot "humble himself" and take on the form of a fleshly body? When Tertullian says the following of Marcion, could it likewise be said of Marion?

> All the [attributes and activities] you make requisition of as worthy of God are to be found in the Father, inaccessible to sight and contact, peaceable also, and so to speak, a god philosophers can approve of: but all the things you repudiate as unworthy, are to be accounted to the Son, who

---

[28]Here Ward quotes from Jean-Luc Marion, *La Croisée du visible* (Paris: La Difference, 1991), p. 152.

[29]Graham Ward, "The Theological Project of Jean-Luc Marion," in *Post-secular Philosophy*, ed. Philip Blond (London: Routledge, 1998), p. 232.

was both seen and heard, and held converse, the Father's agent and minister, who commingles in himself man and God, in the miracles God, in the pettiness man.[30]

Although an invisible and inapproachable icon may be saved from being defiled by the flesh, such cannot be the true God-man who is seen. So Marion's God still ends up sounding a bit too close to the god of the philosophers.

In the end, Marion and Marcion both shy from accepting the fundamental christological *aporia,* that Christ is fully God and fully man. Instead of facing the excruciating demands of an orthodox Christology that attempts to navigate between the Scylla of transcendence and the Charybdis of immanence, Marion denies the true iconic nature of Christ and so succumbs to the idolatry of transcendence.

---

[30]Tertullian *Adversus Marcionem,* ed. and trans. Ernest Evans (Oxford: Clarendon, 1972), 2.27.

EPILOGUE

By now it should be clear why idolatry is so difficult to overcome. Idols are often subtle and elusive. Instead of being unchanging entities, they are constantly developing and shifting in identity. Just when we recognize them and take aim, they can take on a different form, meaning we must begin again to expose them. One of the gravest dangers of idolatry is the false belief that one has overcome it. The fact that one has exposed a particular idol hardly means that one is done with idolatry. Perhaps it would be too much to say that one can *never* eliminate idols, yet total abolition is a goal that is difficult to reach. Thus sounding out idols is a necessary task, but it does not end as soon as the idol has perished.

Although Marion designates something quite different by the term "double idolatry," it seems to me that idolatry tends to be double-sided: the sounding out of one idol often leads to another. While Jesus says the following in regard to an unclean spirit, it is likewise applicable to idolatry:

> When the unclean spirit has gone out of a person, it wanders through waterless regions looking for a resting place, but it finds none. Then it says, "I will return to my house from which I came." When it comes, it finds it empty, swept, and put in order. Then it goes and brings along seven other spirits more evil than itself, and they enter and live there; and the last state of that person is worse than the first. (Mt 12:43-45)

Just as the person rescued from an evil spirit risks being descended upon by the old spirit *and* seven new ones, so we run the risk of overturning an idol and finding ourselves guilty of another idolatry, perhaps one that is even worse. Of course idols are our own creations (rather than, as in the case of an evil spirit, having an existence of their own). But once we create idols they do tend to take on a kind of "life," one that is not completely within our control.

Moreover, idols and icons are far more alike—and far more closely interlinked—than we would like them to be. On the one hand, icons can easily and sometimes almost imperceptibly morph into idols. What begins as an icon slowly (or perhaps very quickly) turns into an idol. On the other hand, even idols are usually not devoid of any truth at all. Indeed a particularly challenging aspect of idols is that they are usually "somewhat" orthodox rather than utterly heterodox. This complexity is often what makes it possible to accept them. We note the orthodox features of an idol and fail to see its heterodox features. The line between idol and icon is often a very fine one; the difference between them can be minuscule and very difficult to see. Indeed the idols we are most inclined to accept as icons are those that have a seemingly insignificant difference. Further, the longer we accept idols as orthodox depictions of God, the harder it becomes to see them as the idols they truly are.

Once we realize that it is impossible to "get beyond" idolatry—as if it were something that could simply be "overcome"—how do we proceed? Obviously there is no simple answer to that question. In fact we are in the greatest of dangers when we think there is a simple answer. But battling idolatry requires being continually aware of several things: (1) the fundamental *aporia* of knowing God, (2) the place of philosophy and "metaphysics" in faith, and (3) our role as those who bear witness to a truth that is not ours and that we do not possess.

The *Aporia* of Knowing God

We have seen that Scripture emphasizes a conception of "knowledge" of God that is based on a relationship. To know *(ginōskō)* God is not to have *epistēmē*. It is to have a relationship with God in which he bears witness to us of his being and character. Marion is right to point out that theology grows out of praise and prayer. True, as we saw in the previous chapter, they are closely connected to predication and thus propositions. Prayer and praise go far beyond propositions and so are not restricted to them, but they do not take place apart from propositions. In other words, praise and prayer are never *only* pragmatic in nature.

Still, right theology grows out of right practice. And because theology is "practical" in the sense that it is practiced, *holiness* takes priority over understanding. To the extent one understands at all, one must live a holy life. Since one comes to understand by actually meeting Christ, only the saintly person actually "knows." While Marion is to be commended for emphasizing this point, it is certainly not new in Marion. Scripture makes it abundantly clear. In the introduction I noted that the attestation of knowledge of the truth is our living by the truth (3 Jn 3). According to John, it is not our word or speech that proves that "we are from the truth" but our love. And love is something that is primarily done. Although it is possible to know the truth and not do it, it is not possible to do the truth and not know it. Thus if we wish to think aright about God, we must live aright in relation to him and to our neighbor. Our goal is not merely to know but to walk in the truth and have fellowship with God (1 Jn 1:3).

The "final" result of this practice is that one recognizes that everything one "knows" about God still falls short: we do not own the truth. While we point to the truth, we are not that truth, nor is it something we possess. At most, God provides glimpses of his truth. Yet to say that we have glimpses is to say that we indeed *see*. God has not left us blind. We have a glimpse of the Word made flesh. And as Jesus attests, "If you know me, you will know my Father also" (Jn 14:7). Scripture is clear that we can know God and his truth in a real sense. Yet we know him in the sense of a personal relationship, not in the sense of grasping his *eidos*. There is true sight, but it is not an exhaustive seeing.

We must not forget, though, that human reason in general is in this same situation. In the same way that Descartes ultimately was forced to trust the natural light, so reason is something given to us that cannot in turn be grounded. Gadamer rightly points out that "the idea of an absolute reason is not a possibility," for reason *"is not its own master."*[1] The unmediated, grounded knowledge *(epistēmē)* that Plato envisions is not to be had, at least in this life. So the position in which art and rhetoric find themselves—giving us "pictures" of reality (which can never be taken as "adequate" or equivalent to that reality) as opposed to unalloyed reality itself—is the position in which philosophy and theology find themselves too. But note that even the way I have expressed this idea—that we have "pictures" of reality—is itself a metaphor. I am not suggesting a "picture theory of epistemology" here. I agree with Husserl that the phenomena are themselves actually "given." However, since the phenomena are always partial and mediated, they are in effect "pictures" of reality.

---

[1]Hans-Georg Gadamer, *Truth and Method,* 2nd rev. ed., trans. Joel Weinsheimer and Donald G. Marshall (New York: Crossroad, 1989), p. 276, my italics.

The humble recognition of our true situation as knowers need not be seen as some sort of problem that we ought to overcome. Rather it is the way human reason has been fashioned by an all-wise God. But it is a feature of which we need to be acutely aware and one that should make us ever vigilant. Our knowledge in general and our knowledge of God in particular is always—by its very nature—mediated not simply linguistically but also culturally and historically.[2] Our sight is provisional and imperfect, meaning that it is always open to the possibility of reproof and correction. The resulting *adaequatio* is—technically speaking—profoundly inadequate; yet it can still be practically adequate. Instead of seeing reason as something that we master and also use to master the world and God, we might better take reason to be something in which we participate but which we do not claim as our own.

Here it is helpful to note the distinction Thomas Aquinas draws between *comprehende* and *cognosci*. Both terms translate into English as "to know." But whereas *comprehende* is knowing in the sense of "comprehending" (to know something in its entirety), *cognosci* is a kind of knowing of a lesser sort. Thus Thomas can say, "God considered in himself is altogether one and simple, yet we think *[cognoscit]* of him through a number of concepts because we cannot see him as he is in himself."[3] A similar distinction can be found in the apostle Paul, who contrasts "now I know *[ginōskō]* only in part" with "then I will know fully *[epiginōsomai]*" (1 Cor 13:12). So it is still possible to speak of "knowledge" of God (and of other people and truth), as long as one recognizes that this knowledge is of a partial and mediated sort (not *epistēmē*). Such a distinction between types of knowing, of course, is most pronounced in relation to God, and Scripture constantly reminds us of this fact.

At least ostensibly, Derrida and Marion give opposing reasons for the lack of adequation between God and our knowledge. On Derrida's account, when we think of God or speak his name, there is a lack of presence. That is, God in his full being is not "present" to our minds. Not only is there a lack of *fullness,* but there is also a lack of *immediacy.* In contrast, Marion emphasizes that God's presence is so great that he overwhelms any attempt to conceive him. Thus God is the ultimate "saturated phenomenon," so full of presence that no human concept or

---

[2] Paul Ricoeur makes this point in "Experience and Language in Religious Discourse" in *PTT* 129-30.

[3] Thomas Aquinas *Summa Theologiae* 1a.13.12.

name can do him justice. For Marion, God is also present in an *unmediated* way. Must we choose between these two possibilities—that God remains aloof from our minds, revealing himself only partially and incompletely, and that God's presence is so great that we cannot fully understand it?

We have already considered the paradigmatic example of Moses, but returning to it might be helpful. If there is anyone who can rightly be said to have had a full and unmediated encounter with God, it is he. In Deuteronomy 34:10 we read: "Never since has there arisen a prophet in Israel like Moses, whom the LORD knew face to face." At least at first glance, Moses' knowledge of God appears to be direct or unmediated. The phrase "face to face" would suggest a full or complete knowledge. This interpretation is even more strongly supported by Numbers 12:7-8, where God describes Moses as "my servant" and says that he speaks "face to face" with God and "beholds the form of the LORD." While it is difficult to be completely clear on the full meaning of "the form of the LORD," the Septuagint translates "form" using *eidos (en eidei)*. To behold God's *eidos* is a staggering honor for Moses, for God discloses his glory to Moses. As noted in the introduction, to behold God's *eidos* is not merely to see God's outward form but to see (and comprehend) his true being. If Moses beholds God's inner form, the "what-isness" of God, the implication is that Moses is put on almost an equal footing with God. We might go so far as to say that Moses would in effect gain a kind of mastery of God; for God in his very being has been revealed to Moses, and Moses now knows God as God knows himself. In such a case Moses could be said to have a *true* ideology concerning God. At least that is what the idea of possessing God's *eidos* would imply.

But what does it mean for Moses to "see" God's glory? The most detailed account of God's revealing himself to Moses in found in Exodus 33:12-23. Moses says, "Now if I have found favor in your sight, show me your ways."

God replies, "You have found favor in my sight, and I know you by name."

At this point Moses ups the ante by boldly asking for the epistemological holy grail: "Show me your glory, I pray."

God says two crucial things in response to Moses. First, he says, "I will make all my goodness pass before you, and will proclaim before you the name." Here we seem to have the promise of a complete and unmediated presence before Moses: Moses is seemingly promised God's *eidos*. Not only does God promise to reveal *all* of his goodness (which is tantamount to saying his "glory"), he also says he will reveal his name. In effect, by disclosing his name (Yahweh) to Moses, he is disclosing his very identity or essence.

But then God suddenly adds a caveat. Having just promised to reveal all, he qualifies the promise: "But . . . you cannot see my face; for no one shall see me and live."

As it turns out, Moses does not even truly "see" God's glory, for God places him in a cleft and covers him with his hand. It is only *after* the glory has passed by that Moses is allowed to look. The result is that Moses does not see God's face. Technically, his encounter with God is not literally face to face, even though Moses certainly converses with God in a way that is highly unusual and in which God is truly present.[4]

From this account it seems that God's presence to Moses is neither complete nor unmediated—even though it is *real*. Much (or even most) of God's glory literally passes Moses by—he gets to see only the tail end of it. So one can hardly term this a complete revelation of God's glory to Moses. And even the way God talks to Moses seems highly mediated by a human *logos*. Although God can be said to speak "accurately" concerning himself, the use of terms such as *face* and *back* seem difficult to square with the God whom Jesus describes as "spirit" (Jn 4:24). God indeed shows himself to Moses in a way that had far greater "presence" than what Moses normally experienced— and he had already experienced God to a much greater degree than most of us do, for he had previously spoken with God at various times. Yet this heightened presence is still not a *complete* presence, for God does not show himself fully.

Does the New Testament contain an account of full presence? One might appeal to the transfiguration witnessed by Peter, James and John, in which Jesus "was transfigured before them, and his face shone like the sun, and his clothes became dazzling white" (Mt 17:2). Clearly this was a remarkable moment of revelation. No doubt they saw Jesus in a rather

---

[4]Although Israel is said in Deuteronomy 4:12 to hear God's voice, we are explicitly told that they "saw no form." In Psalm 17:15 David speaks only of *someday* beholding God's face, not of having already done so. So Moses' encounter with God is the strongest recorded in the Old Testament.

new and startling light—in this case, quite literally. But did they see the *eidos* of Jesus, or Jesus as he truly is? Matthew describes the transformation in Jesus' appearance as *metamorphoō*—before their very eyes Jesus undergoes a metamorphosis. Luke uses the phrase *egeneto heteron*, which translates as "became different." Yet neither of these accounts suggests that Peter, James and John see Jesus' *eidos* or true form. It seems reasonable to assume that they saw "more" of who Jesus is at that moment. But that "more" doesn't seem to translate into something as significant as Jesus' *eidos*.

Even the Johannine formula "The Word became flesh and lived among us, and we have seen his glory" (Jn 1:14) needs an important qualification. In taking on flesh, Christ presents himself to us as "one of us." While that presentation is a true phenomenon "which shows itself" (to borrow Heidegger's phrase, *BT* 51), it is not an unmediated full presence. Rather Christ "emptied himself, taking the form of a slave, being born in human likeness" (Phil 2:7). So God *is* "with us," but in a way mediated by human "likeness."

In all these instances in which God reveals himself, his showing of himself is a saturated phenomenon that leaves our powers of comprehension in disarray. Yet from what we have seen in Moses' case, it would seem that God's appearance can be characterized as *both* a presence that is less than a "full" presence *and* a presence that overwhelms us nevertheless. Despite Marion's emphasis on the "saturation" of intuition, in *Etant donné* he speaks of "the inability to decide between excess and scarcity" (*ED* 341). It seems safe to say that Moses was overwhelmed by God's presence, even though it was not a full and unmediated presence. And it does not seem that Peter, James and John experienced Jesus in *all* of his glory, even though they obviously experienced a greater degree of that glory than they normally did. Our experience of God always lacks full presence, but even the little that we do experience is overwhelming. If such is the case, then both Derrida and Marion are right.

We have seen that all theologians who aspire to orthodoxy face a fundamental *aporia*—that we both can and cannot know and speak of God. Marion speaks of the "paradox of paradoxes" that both *kataphasis* and *apophasis* must be affirmed (*ED* 340). Augustine puts it as follows: "If that is ineffable which cannot be spoken, then that is not ineffable which can be called ineffable. This contradiction is to be passed over in silence rather than resolved verbally."[5] On the one hand, Christians affirm the possibility of knowing *about* God and even knowing *him* in a personal way. We are made in God's image; our intellect is capable of understanding God to some extent, because there is some sense of likeness between human and divine minds. Thomas Aquinas points out that the human mind "is not altogether disproportionate to the created mind to know God."[6] We have a sense of God's qualities—his love, justice and mercy, for instance. On the other hand, since "we cannot speak of God at all except in language we use of creatures," and since "we never use words in exactly the same sense of creatures and God," we must say, therefore, that words are used of God and creatures in an analogical way.[7] John Calvin points out this lack of univocity in terms of God's accommodating himself to the limits of the human intellect.

> The Anthropomorphites, also, who imagined a corporeal God from the fact that Scripture often ascribes to him a mouth, ears, eyes, hands, and feet, are easily refuted. For who even of slight intelligence does not understand that, as nurses commonly do with infants, God is wont in a measure to "lisp" in speaking to us? Thus forms of speaking do not so much express clearly what God is like as accommodate the knowledge of him to our slight capacity. To do this he must descend far beneath his loftiness.[8]

Yet even the "analogy" between God and our knowledge is itself aporetic, for it is impossible to spell out exactly the extent to which our knowledge of God is either adequate or inadequate. Why so? To be able to make a strong distinction between adequacy and inadequacy means, in effect, that one can see the inadequacy of one's thought. Yet to see those limits would require that one be able to go beyond them, so that one could see them, so to speak, from the other side. This is precisely

[5]Augustine, *On Christian Doctrine,* trans. D. W. Robertson Jr. (New York: Macmillan, 1958), p. 11.

[6]Thomas Aquinas *Summa Theologiae* 1a.12.1.

[7]Ibid., 1a.13.5.

[8]John Calvin, *Institutes of the Christian Religion,* ed. John T. McNeill, trans. Ford Lewis Battles (Philadelphia: Westminster Press, 1960), 1:121. Battles puts this difficulty as well as any when he says, "We are here, cautioned by Calvin's own self-warning, to seek after a definition of divine accommodation which neither repudiates the anthropomorphisms of Scripture in our quest of pure Spirit, nor so clings to the anthropomorphic mode of thought and worship as ourselves, veiled by flesh, to lose sight of our God." See his "God Was Accommodating Himself to Human Capacity," in *Readings in Calvin's Theology,* ed. Donald McKim (Grand Rapids, Mich.: Baker, 1984), p. 21.

what we acknowledge ourselves as unable to do. One "knows" that one's knowledge and thought are inadequate, but one cannot know this in a strong sense.

Will God ever be *fully* present to us? What does Paul mean when he says, "Now we see in a mirror, dimly, but then we will see face to face. Now I know only in part; then I will know fully, even as I have been fully known" (1 Cor 13:12)? Similarly, what does John mean in claiming that "when he is revealed, we will be like him, for we will see him as he is" (1 Jn 3:2)? Probably the best answer—the truly *orthodox* answer—is to say that we do not really know what it will mean to see God "face to face" or "as he is." Clearly the adequation between our knowledge of God and who God truly is will be of such greater magnitude that our speculation cannot even begin to fathom it. "Face to face" implies a lack of mediation, a kind of immediate presence. To *be* in God's presence is, quite simply, the greatest promise given to believers.

Yet perhaps a cautionary note is in order. Although John says that "we will see him as he is," he prefaces this by saying "we will be like him." It seems reasonable to think that we will be able to "see him as he is" to the same extent that "we will be like him." For our present inability to know God properly stems from the ways in which we are unlike him. There are many ways in which we could be "like" God. Given the context, the "likeness" about which John speaks is a moral likeness in which we become righteous like God and thus see God's righteousness in a way that we cannot now see. Of course there may be other ways in which we become like God, but clearly we will never *become* God. A crucial aspect of the Christian faith (and one that separates it from certain other religions) is that the distinction between God and human beings will never be erased. There are no promises in Scripture that we will become God or even that we will suddenly know all that God knows. So it would seem that the lack of adequation between our knowledge and God's true being, between human *noesis* and divine *noema,* will always remain. Even if our knowledge of God were one day *unmediated* (and even that is open to question), it still would not be *complete.*

Should Faith Overcome Philosophy?

Marion (as well as Levinas) rightly reminds us that religious faith is easily corrupted by philosophy. But whereas Marion thinks that philosophy as metaphysics needs simply to be replaced with philosophy as phenomenology (albeit in a new form), John Milbank insists that philosophy be left completely behind. In making these moves, Marion and Milbank can be read as following Heidegger, who famously characterized "Christian philosophy" as "a squared circle and a misconception," an inappropriate blending of Greek metaphysics and Christian theology.[9] Arguing that theology should be freed from metaphysics or ontology (and thus philosophy) is a typical move of postmodern theologians. But should faith repudiate philosophy? And if so, what would that mean?

In an essay titled "Only Theology Overcomes Metaphysics," Milbank affirms Marion's "usurpation" of phenomenology for theological purposes but criticizes him for not taking this usurpation "far enough." Milbank claims that theology "must entirely evacuate philosophy, which is metaphysics." But of course the lurking question is what we mean by "philosophy" and "metaphysics." Milbank here is working off Marion's own query "Is philosophy equivalent to metaphysics?" (MP 279). Milbank takes the answer to be yes, but only *if* philosophy ends up being reducible to metaphysics and *if* metaphysics is somehow antithetical to theology is it clear that we should follow Milbank.[10]

Is philosophy equivalent to metaphysics? Like Milbank, Heidegger assumes the answer is yes, and he bases that on Aristotle. We have already seen in chapter seven that Aristotle describes metaphysics as "a science which investigates being as being" and seeks "the first principles and highest causes," yet that this science of "being *qua* being" is linked with "divine science" and called "first philosophy."[11] There are several aspects here that deserve closer scrutiny. When Aristotle speaks of "science," the term he uses is *epistēmē*. At least in principle, then, the point of metaphysics is to gain a complete and unmediated knowledge of all things. Moreover, since there are natural, mathematical and divine sciences, the implication is that complete and mediated knowledge can even be had of God. Although the English word *investigation* could connote only the idea of "study," *theōria* should be read in a stronger sense. Earlier I noted that Aristotle interprets philosophy as beginning in *thaumazein*—awe or wonder. But even though science begins with awe,

---

[9]Martin Heidegger, *An Introduction to Metaphysics,* trans. Ralph Manheim (New Haven, Conn.: Yale University Press, 1959), p. 7.

[10]Milbank's more recent interaction with Marion is John Milbank, "The Soul of Reciprocity: Part 2, Reciprocity Granted," *Modern Theology* 17 (2001): 485-507.

[11]Aristotle *Metaphysics* 4.11.1003a and 6.1.1026a, respectively.

Aristotle says that it "must in a sense end in something which is the opposite of our original inquiries."[12] So the point of science is to do away with *thaumazein* by substituting *theōria*. We no longer wonder once we are able to explain phenomena in terms of first principles and highest causes, since to comprehend something's *archē* is to know its source and to possess its *aitia* is to be able to explain it. It is understandable, then, for Heidegger to claim that "Being grounds beings." It is this grounding that is the problem.

Both Marion and Milbank accept the definition of metaphysics found in Aristotle and taken over by Heidegger. But for Marion that rigid definition proves to be helpful. Marion argues that only if we can properly define metaphysics can we escape from it.

> From the moment when "metaphysics" admits a precise concept, historically verifiable and theoretically operative, it follows that it can be subject to criticism within its boundaries, but it can also offer, thanks to these same boundaries, the possible horizon of its transcendence. (MP 283)

There are two claims here. First, while it is true that metaphysics can be criticized only once it has defined itself, Marion thinks that precisely at the moment of defining itself, metaphysics undermines itself. For it claims to give a universal grounding but cannot do so, and so falls apart. Thus Marion claims that "the 'end of metaphysics' is in no way an optional opinion" (MP 283). Second, whereas Derrida and others think we are unable to "escape" from metaphysics in that it has no clear borders, Marion thinks that Heidegger's establishing of its borders enables us to move beyond it. Since we are able to define metaphysics, we can say, "That is metaphysics," and what we are doing is something else.

While Heidegger may rescue God from the ontotheological oppression of God's being made into the highest being, Marion thinks that God is reinscribed in onto-theology by being submitted to the "screen" of being (*GWB* 71). So Marion and Milbank see their moves as following Heidegger yet distancing themselves from him. For Marion, the move is as follows. Instead of defining philosophy as "metaphysics," Marion suggests that we define it as "phenomenology" in which givenness is central. Rather than attempting to ground itself, then, Marion's version of phenomenology is always overwhelmed by the transcendence of saturated phenomena.

---

[12]Ibid., 1.2.983a.

Thus phenomenology goes unambiguously beyond metaphysics to the strict extent that it rids itself of any *a priori* principle, in order to admit the donation which is primary in as far as it is *a posteriori* for the person receiving it. Phenomenology goes beyond metaphysics insofar as it renounces the transcendental project. (MP 286)

Whereas in traditional metaphysics, concepts such as *ousia* (Aristotle) and cause (Aquinas) are "first" principles, determining how beings must appear, Marion sees phenomenology as a radical submission to the givenness of phenomena. So "phenomenology takes up the title 'first philosophy' only by inverting it—'last philosophy.'"[13] Phenomenology becomes "true" philosophy by demurring to the phenomena, so that its "principle of principles" is not a "first principle" but a "last principle."

But whereas Marion is content to work between phenomenology and theology, Milbank wants everything to be taken up into theology. The problem is that, according to Milbank, Marion is "still within a self-sufficient metaphysics, which is identical with secular modernity."[14] Milbank admits that "theology can still have recourse to *theoria* and *logos,* and if the latter constitutes 'metaphysics,' then talk of its overcoming is absurd." What, then, is Milbank really criticizing? By "philosophy" he means something that is characterized by autonomy and "a secularizing immanentism."[15] Yet such a definition of philosophy is open to question. On my account, what Milbank means is more accurately "vain philosophy," as I defined it in the introduction. However much vain philosophy has characterized philosophy, it needs to be clearly distinguished from philosophy in general. Moreover, if philosophy has been a source of *theoria* and *logos* (not exclusively but certainly centrally), then rejecting philosophy is not only unwise but impossible—as Milbank himself admits.

Yet perhaps we need to take issue with the traditional definition of *metaphysics* as found in Aristotle. First, must "first philosophy" be the *science* of "being *qua* being"? Why could it not simply be the *study* of being? Were metaphysics to take that route, it could give up the pretension of providing *epistēmē.* And then philosophy would still have room for *thaumazein.* As Heidegger reminds us, *thaumazein* was "the basic dis-

---

[13]Jean-Luc Marion, "The Other First Philosophy," *Critical Inquiry* 25 (summer 1999): 797.
[14]John Milbank, "Only Theology Overcomes Metaphysics," in *The Word Made Strange: Theology, Language, Culture* (Oxford: Blackwell, 1997), p. 47.
[15]Ibid., p. 50.

position of the primordial thinking of the orient."[16] To recover that disposition would be to recover what was originally essential to philosophy.

Second, even though metaphysics has held out the possibility of "knowing," one can argue that it has never truly delivered. After all, I noted in chapter one that however much Socrates holds out the ideal of *adaequatio,* the promise is never fulfilled. Even though philosophy might seem to be a *technē* capable of giving us certainty, such has not been the reality. If that has been the case, then the "promises" of metaphysics have simply been promises that turn out to be ideologies.

If philosophy must be defined by way of metaphysics and metaphysics truly makes claims of "autonomy" and "immanence," then Milbank is fully right in rejecting them both. But assuming that metaphysics is redefined as I have done so above, it is not clear that either metaphysics or philosophy need be rejected. So long as philosophy does not turn into an *epistēmē* that precludes *thaumazein,* it is not necessarily antithetical to theology.[17] Moreover, it is not clear that a radical separation of metaphysics and theology would solve the problem of theology's being "corrupted" by metaphysics. Keeping theology and metaphysics apart would not necessarily keep theology from turning into onto-theology, since onto-theology could always be reinscribed within theology itself. And keeping them together in no way means that the result must be onto-theology.

But if philosophy is not simply reducible to metaphysics and metaphysics need not be defined as Heidegger does, then how does faith relate to philosophy? As we have seen, Marion's proposal is that the *logos* of philosophy be rejected in favor of the revealed *Logos,* the ultimate saturated phenomenon who always *precedes* any human *logos,* so that human *logos* is subject to *theos.* In place of onto-theo-logy we have theo-onto-logy. But must we choose between an all-controlling onto-theo-logy and a pure theo-onto-logy? Rather than simply accept the reversal of onto-theo-logy into theo-onto-logy, I wish to argue for another way. As admirable as Marion's reasons are for making revelation prior to all other *logoi,* I do not think such a move is possible any more than Descartes's move to "begin again" was possible. In chapter nine we

---

[16]Martin Heidegger, *Basic Questions of Philosophy: Selected "Problems" of "Logic,"* trans. Richard Rojcewicz and André Schuwer (Bloomington: Indiana University Press, 1994), pp. 140-41.
[17]Indeed, philosophy might be better off remaining simply an *elenchus.*

already considered ample reasons why this move is problematic, so I will not repeat them here, except to say that the denial or suppression of all *logoi* prior to the advent of the *Logos* actually robs the *Logos* of its meaning and force. It is precisely because we already understand something that we are able to understand more. Jesus can meaningfully call himself a shepherd only to those who understand sheep. But much more important, to deny the validity of all other *logoi* is to deny what are *also* gifts. While Marion claims that the *adonné* receives *logos* as a gift (*ED* 397), what we call "reason"—or what Descartes calls "the natural light"—is *likewise a gift*. Thus as noted in the introduction, Descartes is unable to ground reason, to provide a rational explanation for it.

So when we contrast reason with faith, we are actually contrasting two *gifts*. The latter is obviously a gift, but the less obvious gift-character of the former must also be acknowledged. Ultimately the only difference between reason and faith is the *extent* to which they can be grounded. Reason can provide a little more of a "ground" for itself than faith can, but neither can truly be grounded. The problem is that reason often takes itself as being able to provide a ground and thus offer the last word. That is when reason goes wrong. If we cling to reason and refuse to see its limits, then we profess wisdom and become fools (Rom 1:22). Blaise Pascal speaks of the need for reason to recognize "that there are an infinite number of things which are beyond it" and says that reason is "merely feeble if it does not go so far as to realize that."[18] In the end, all "knowing" of the truth is by faith. Instead of making the *logos* of Greek ontology primary, as people of faith we affirm the presence and value of even "secular" *logoi* and yet attempt to determine the extent to which (and ways in which) this is desirable.

While Levinas is right in calling for the "breakup of the omnipotence of the logos" (*BPW* 148), one need not give up on philosophy. Although philosophy as we know it has been all too often characterized by a *logos* bent on domination and control, there is no obvious reason that philosophy need take the form of a all-controlling *logos*. On the contrary, if philosophy truly is a love of wisdom and wisdom properly begins in fear (Prov 1:7), then philosophy *cannot* take the form of an "omnipotent" *logos,* or else it ceases to be philosophy. The solution to a philoso-

---

[18]Blaise Pascal, *Pensées,* trans. A. J. Krailsheimer (Harmondsworth, U.K.: Penguin, 1966), no. 188,

phy that claims an improper immanence is not less philosophy but more, so that it might examine *itself.*

But if human *logos* is incapable of mastering the phenomena, then the move beyond metaphysics that Marion prescribes turns out to be impossible, for metaphysics can no longer be circumscribed. Only a metaphysics that is fully under our control either needs to be or can be left behind.[19] Of course there will always be vain philosophy that needs to be overcome. Yet the "solution" is not to avoid philosophy altogether but to "arrest philosophical discourse" (as Levinas puts it) by philosophizing. Here one does not attempt to escape from philosophy; instead one attempts to escape from certain *kinds* of philosophy—any that are rightly characterized as empty and vain.

Bearing Witness

How then ought we to bear witness to God? The answer is: boldness coupled with circumspection. As we have seen, our claims to knowledge of God always run the risk of placing a conceptual schema on God that creates him in our own image. The only way to avoid this—if there really is a way fully to avoid it—is constantly to be mindful that God is beyond human thought, predication and control. As John reminds us, "God is light" and we are to "walk in the light as he himself is in the light" (1 Jn 1:5, 7). But as Paul reminds us, it is an "unapproachable light," meaning that "no one has ever seen or can see" God (1 Tim 6:16).

In Romans 11:33-36 the apostle Paul brings together two themes that have been present throughout this book.

> O the depth of the riches and wisdom and knowledge of God! How unsearchable are his judgments and how inscrutable his ways!
> "For who has known the mind of the Lord?
> Or who has been his counselor?"
> "Or who has given a gift to him,
> to receive a gift in return?"
> For from him and through him and to him are all things. To him be the glory for ever. Amen.

There is something initially surprising about this juxtaposition of themes. Paul first speaks of the depth and inscrutability of God's riches,

---

[19]Here my reading is the opposite of Marion's in Jean-Luc Marion, *On Descartes' Metaphysical Prism,* trans. Jeffrey L. Koskey (Chicago: University of Chicago Press, 1999), pp. 342-45.

wisdom, knowledge, judgments and ways. He asks, in effect, Who knows God's mind? Who has given God advice? But then he subtly changes from the theme of God's wisdom to God's gift-giving. Why? Coming at the end of a section on God's choice of Israel as his holy people, Paul's juxtaposition is understandable. Just as God's choice of the Jews cannot be explained by human reason, so that gift cannot be repaid. There is in both cases a kind of asymmetry—between divine and human reason and between divine giving and human giving.

We have seen that a perennial danger of theology is presuming to speak too much of God, claiming to understand his ways to an improper extent. Paul speaks of God's judgments as being impossible for human reason to examine *(anexeraunēta)*. But if they cannot be examined, then they cannot be judged. God's judgments judge us, not we them. Paul also speaks of God's ways as being beyond our tracing *(anexichniastoi)*. They are like paths that we ultimately cannot follow. Even if we can follow his ways to some extent in a practical sense, we cannot follow them in the sense of complete understanding. They defy human logic. The danger of claiming to be able to examine God's judgments and follow his ways is that in a sense we do not allow God to be God. Without doubt, God will always be God without our help or permission. But when we claim to understand him in a strong sense, we create an image of him that is more like ourselves. If we are mindful of the inscrutable character of God's thought, then we cannot but regard it with awe. I have noted how philosophy and metaphysics can go astray when they lose a fundamental sense of *thaumazein*. But theology is no different. It likewise goes astray when it loses *thaumazein* in the face of God. Heidegger reminds us that wonder displaces us and our usual ways of thinking. When we are "lost in wonder, love, and praise" (to quote Charles Wesley), we are no longer central.

Drawing on the distinction Husserl makes between kinds of signs, Derrida argues that signs always have the character of *Anzeigen* (indication)—they point to something that they themselves are not. One way of putting this is that they testify to that which is other than themselves. They act in effect as prophet, bearing witness to something other than themselves. Prophecy in the Hebrew tradition has always had two senses: besides foretelling the future, it involves "forthtelling" a message with which one has been entrusted. Like a sign, the prophet speaks on behalf of someone else. But the goal of such speaking is that the speaker is forgotten and only the message proclaimed is present.

Levinas reminds us that to bear witness to the Infinite is to be "reduced to the 'here I am'" (*OTB* 146). I no longer claim an identity for myself; instead an identity is bestowed upon me. I am left "without having anything to identify myself with" (*OTB* 149) except that which is given to me. However much my identity as Christ's follower is colored by human *logoi,* it is not reducible to them. With the lowering of myself goes a raising of the One to whom I bear witness. To "point to" God is one way of taking Marion's idea that "predication must yield to praise." As we saw in the previous chapter, there is a sense—and an important sense—of predication that is part of praise. One may rightly add a negation—but there must be an affirmation. To praise God is not to be without any idea of who God is and what God is like. Indeed how could one praise that of which one has no idea? Yet such predication likewise requires a recognition that one's idea of God is inadequate. We must recognize that when one "testifies to the Infinite," as Levinas puts it, "no theme, no present, is capable" (*OTB* 146).

Actually praise results precisely when the limits of predication regarding God are recognized. That recognition leads to a simultaneous revelation: we "see" both how limited we are and how unlimited God is. It is in this moment of revelation that true praise can take place. Note that, properly speaking, praise isn't usually something that we can make happen. Instead praise is something that happens to us. And it doesn't really happen very often. Why not? The answer is that we don't really recognize our own limits most of the time. We may acknowledge them intellectually, but actually experiencing them—having them placed in front of our face—is rare. Thus true worship, in which we have a keen sense of God's worth, takes place relatively infrequently.

If predication rightly ends in praise, then the point of predication is not us. Rather its very rationale is for God. Praise may have many beneficial aspects for us personally, but that is not what it is about.

As John the Baptist lowered himself so as to lift up the One whose way he helped prepare, so we as Christ's followers speak humbly on behalf of God and his truth. We do not proclaim *our* truth, nor do we have the pretense of having mastered the truth we proclaim. For the *Logos* to which we point is not our own; it fundamentally resists being mastered by us.

Rather the *Logos* to which we bear witness sounds *us* out.